C0-ANE-407

MONUMENTAL WRITING

To Sister Corona,
with best wishes,
Douglas
April 1989.

Aspects of Rhetoric in Wordsworth's Poetry

MONUMENTAL WRITING

J. Douglas Kneale

University of Nebraska Press

Lincoln and London

Acknowledgments for the use of previously published material appear on page xii.

Manufactured in the United States of America
The paper in this book meets the minimum requirements of American National Standard for Information Sciences—Permanence of Paper for Printed Library Materials, ANSI Z39.48–1984.

Library of Congress Cataloging-in-Publication Data
Kneale, J. Douglas, 1955–
Monumental writing.
Revision of thesis (Ph. D.)—University of Toronto.
Bibliography: p.
Includes index.
1. Wordsworth, William, 1770–1850—Style.
2. Figures of speech. I. Title.
PR5894.K55 1988 821′.7 87–38069
ISBN 0-8032-2720-5 (alk. paper)

Publication of this book was assisted by a grant from The Andrew W. Mellon Foundation.

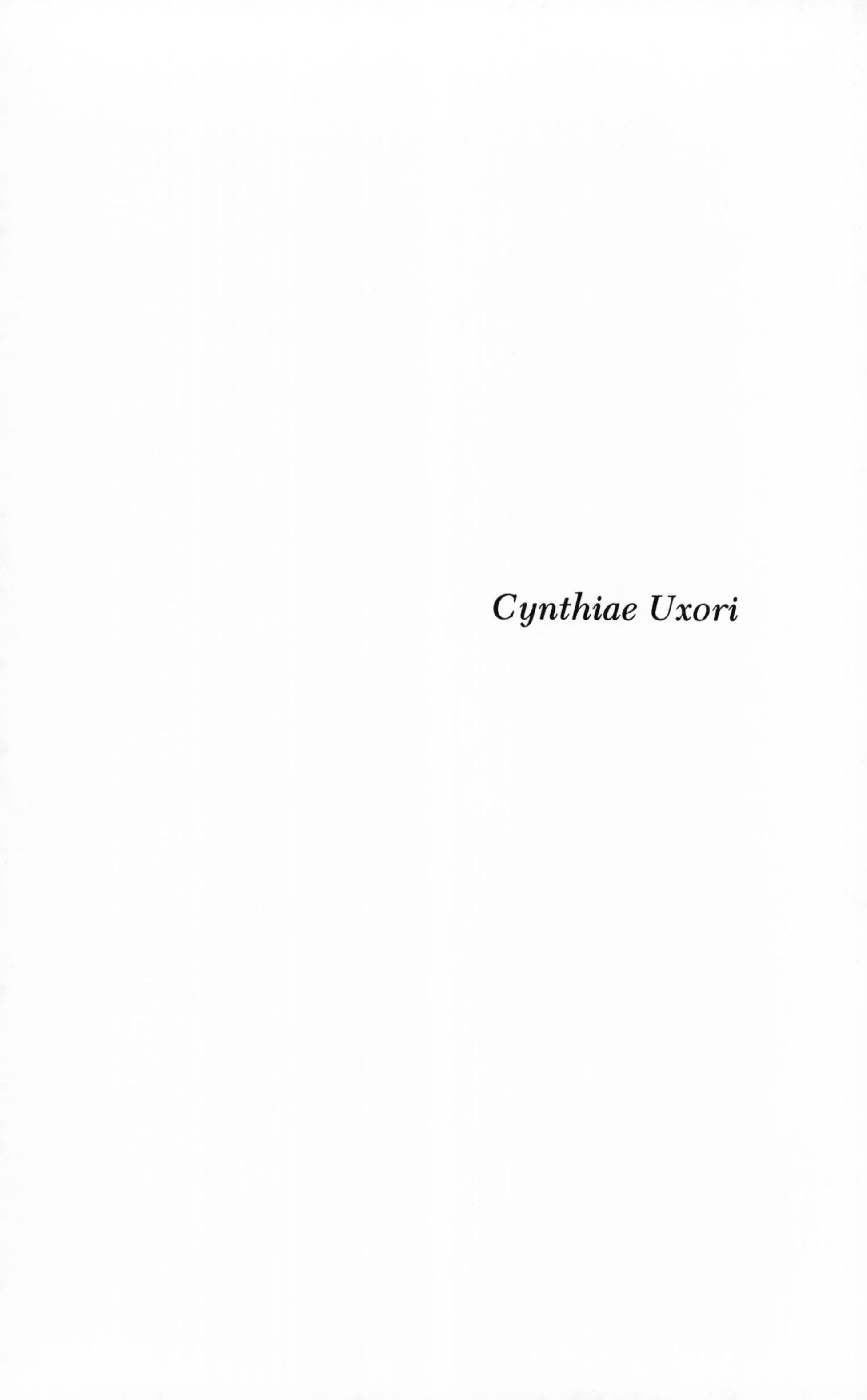

Cynthiae Uxori

CONTENTS

ABBREVIATIONS

de Selincourt	*The Prelude; or, Growth of a Poet's Mind.* By William Wordsworth. Ed. Ernest de Selincourt. 2nd ed. rev. Helen Darbishire. Oxford: Clarendon, 1959.
EY, *MY*, *LY*	*The Letters of William and Dorothy Wordsworth.* The Early Years, The Middle Years, The Later Years. Ed. Ernest de Selincourt. 2nd ed. rev. Chester L. Shaver, Mary Moorman, and Alan G. Hill. Oxford: Clarendon, 1967–1982.
NP	Jonathan Wordsworth, M. H. Abrams, and Stephen Gill, eds. *The Prelude:1799, 1805, 1850.* By William Wordsworth. New York: Norton, 1979.
NS	M. H. Abrams. *Natural Supernaturalism: Tradition and Revolution in Romantic Literature.* New York: Norton, 1971.
Prose	*The Prose Works of William Wordsworth.* Ed. W. J. B. Owen and Jane Worthington Smyser. 3 vols. Oxford: Clarendon, 1974.
PW	*The Poetical Works of William Wordsworth.* Ed. Ernest de Selincourt. Rev. Helen Darbishire. 5 vols. Oxford: Clarendon, 1952–1963.
WP	Geoffrey H. Hartman. *Wordsworth's Poetry 1787–1814.* New Haven: Yale UP, 1964.

ACKNOWLEDGMENTS

This book was written for the most part in 1982–83 as a doctoral dissertation at the University of Toronto. It was revised, quarried, pruned (to almost half its length as the dissertation), and developed (through the addition of Chapter 5) in 1984–86. I wish to thank a number of people who read the manuscript in whole or in part at its various stages, and who offered helpful and supportive commentary: Geoffrey Hartman of Yale University; J. Hillis Miller of the University of California-Irvine; Milton Wilson, Vincent De Luca, and Owen Miller of the University of Toronto; Tilottama Rajan of the University of Wisconsin, Madison; and Ross Woodman of the University of Western Ontario, companion never lost through many a league. To Jonathan Wordsworth, Peter Larkin, Tom McFarland, and other fellow Wordsworthians at the Wordsworth Summer Conference in Grasmere who listened to parts of this book in 1982 and 1984, I offer my thanks for continued dialogue.

I gratefully acknowledge the generous support of the Social Sciences and Humanities Research Council of Canada during the writing of this book. The Council's offer of a postdoctoral fellowship at Yale University in 1984–85 was a great stimulus in the final stages of writing, and the opportunity to consult with Jacques Derrida, Harold Bloom, J. Hillis Miller, and others proved beneficial and instructive. In particular, to Geoffrey and Renée Hartman for invaluable assistance, intellectual engagement and advice, and many social kindnesses, I inscribe fond regards from my wife and myself for making our year in New Haven so enjoyable. I also wish to thank Lena Cowen Orlin of the Folger Shakespeare Library in Washington, D.C., for the offer of a fellowship in 1985, and Hans Aarsleff of

Princeton University for directing a Folger Institute seminar in which I was able to work through some of my ideas concerning Wordsworth's rhetoric.

Part of Chapter 2 originally appeared as "Milton, Wordsworth, and the 'Joint Labourers' of *The Prelude*," *English Studies in Canada* 12, no. 1 (March 1986):37–54; a shorter version of Chapter 3 was originally published as "Wordsworth's Images of Language: Voice and Letter in *The Prelude*," *PMLA* 101 (1986):351–61; and parts of Chapter 6 originally appeared as "The Rhetoric of Imagination in *The Prelude*," *Ariel* 15 (1984):111–27. I thank the editors for permission to reprint articles in revised form here.

I am grateful to the University of Western Ontario for its support of my research and writing. To my colleagues and students, past and present, at the University of Toronto, Bishop's University, Quebec, Yale University, and the University of Western Ontario I express deep appreciation for their interest and engagement. I especially thank my family for their support, and my daughter Helen for much joy, centering all in love. My final acknowledgment, last and best, goes to my wife, to whom I dedicate this book with love, respect, and gratitude sincere.

PREFACE

The aspects of Wordsworth's rhetoric that I discuss in this book are related to a fundamental question of language: What is the place of voice in Wordsworth's poetry? By "voice" I mean not only personal style or rhetorical "figures of speech" but also such aspects as the performative stance of "a man speaking to men," voice and its intertextual echo, the epitaphic voice of nature, and the relation of speech to writing. Because I read voice as "always already" a form of writing—a "monumental writing" (1805 *Prelude* 11.295)[1]—my approach is "grammatological," in Jacques Derrida's terms; that is, it recognizes the priority of "the signifier over the signified" as that of "a Master o'er a Slave" ("Intimations Ode" 120), or of language over meaning. But this hierarchy, the paradigm of all others in Wordsworth's poetry, continually experiences a rhetorical "strength / Of usurpation" (*Prelude* 6.599–600) that centers on a death, and this death is but another name for *difference.*[2]

The term *difference* I take first from Saussure, who uses it in contradistinction to a nomenclature theory of language to signify a linguistic structure in which both signifiers (words) and signifieds (concepts) are defined by their relation or non-coincidence with the other terms in the system (117–18); and second, from Derrida, whose coinage *differance* (with an "a") both subverts Saussure's favoring of voice over letter and replaces his non-coincidental structure of language with a non-hierarchical system of *écriture*—that is, a grammatological field comprising both speech and writing. Difference is a strategic trope in the rhetoric of criticism because it points to a problematic *locus* of language—a place of voice that is also a place of writing.

Several critics have explored Wordsworth's rhetoric, notably Geoffrey H. Hartman in *Wordsworth's Poetry 1787–1814*, David Perkins in *Wordsworth and the Poetry of Sincerity*, Roger Murray in *Wordsworth's Style*, Colin Clarke in *Romantic Paradox*, and Herbert Lindenberger in *On Wordsworth's "Prelude"*. Since the appearance of these studies in the 1960s, however, criticism has undergone considerable rethinking of its philosophical and linguistic assumptions with the rise of Derridean poststructuralism and deconstruction. Derrida's argument, by now so well known that I need hardly rehearse it here, is that a "logocentric" or idealist tradition underlies Western thought, and that this tradition perpetuates the mystification that language holds "the ideal presence of an identical meaning-content,"[3] or that words innocently "contain" or "present" truth.

In contrast to the methodology of the New Criticism, which devoted its energy to close readings of texts to show the harmony of form and content, deconstructive readings, equally sensitive in their attention to linguistic detail, locate those moments in a text when its language becomes what Wordsworth would call a "counter-spirit"—that is, a rhetorical power "unremittingly and noiselessly at work to derange, to subvert, to lay waste, to vitiate, and to dissolve" conventional meaning (*Prose* 2:85). As the deconstructor par excellence, Paul de Man never accepts "the assumed convergence between statement and *lexis*, between what is being said and the mode of its saying," but repeatedly shows how the text "turns back upon itself in a manner that puts the authority of its own affirmations in doubt" (*Allegories* 26–27). This turning, which can be variously described as reflexivity, metalanguage, *mise en abyme*, or self-consciousness, constitutes an "allegory of reading," in de Man's terms—that is, a rhetorical operation that the text performs on itself, rather than a method that a critic applies to a text. The function of the critic is to uncover and in a sense repeat the text's rhetorical maneuvers by means of what J. Hillis Miller calls "the linguistic moment, that is, the moment of criticism which hovers in a prolonged interrogation of language as such. Such a 'moment' recognizes that literature accomplishes whatever it can accomplish by means of language" ("Deconstructing" 29).

Though fundamentally in agreement with poststructuralist critical theory, my own reading of Wordsworth is not what I would describe as uncompromisingly deconstructive—not, at least, in the first two chapters. Nor is it, to borrow Geoffrey Hartman's phrase, "mildly deconstructive" ("'Timely Utterance'" 45). Wordsworth thought that rhetoric was a power and a virtue as well as a spirit of error, that it could "uphold, and feed, and leave in quiet" (*Prose* 2:85) as well as derange, subvert, and deconstruct. What concerns me, however, is less what Wordsworth thought about language than what he did with it, and it would only be committing the intentional fallacy to judge the latter by the former. I am not as interested, therefore, in constructing a theory of Wordsworth's opinions on language—W. J. B. Owen and Frances Ferguson have preceded me there[4]—as I am in pursuing a descriptive criticism of Wordsworth's rhetoric.

By "rhetoric" I mean figural language, indeed language itself, since even the simplest scientific assertion is never far from experimenting with its rhetorical potential. I follow de Man, paraphrasing Nietzsche, in his understanding that the rhetorical trope "is not a derived, marginal, or aberrant form of language but the linguistic paradigm par excellence" (*Allegories* 105). Certainly for Wordsworth the trope of the poet as a *rhetor*, "a man speaking to men" (*Prose* 1:138), is central, as shown by the way in which he frames the sequence of questions leading up to his great definition in the Preface to *Lyrical Ballads*: "What is meant by the word Poet? What is a Poet? To whom does he address himself? And what language is to be expected from him?—He is a man speaking to men . . ." (*Prose* 1:138). Here, in a passage interpolated for the 1802 Preface, Wordsworth conceives of the poet fundamentally in terms of his relation to an audience: "To whom does he address himself?" Certain aspects of Wordsworth's theory classify it, in M. H. Abrams's terms (*Mirror* 14–26), as "expressive" or concerned with the emotions of the poet, but these expressive aspects are balanced by a corresponding "pragmatic" awareness of the audience or reader, most of all, perhaps, when that reader is Coleridge.

As autobiographer, Wordsworth would appear to have two choices in seeking a ground for the self: the object and the subject worlds. Using his own terms, we could designate these two choices as nature and imagination, respectively, but if we did, we would tend to repress the linguistic structure interpenetrating them. The *topos* of the *liber naturae* is ancient, as E. R. Curtius has shown (308, 319–26), and at least since Freud, and even more explicitly since Lacan, we have come to speak of the textualization of consciousness. Once we name these two choices in rhetorical or linguistic terms, once we specify their intertextual participation in some form of discourse, any attempt to find a solid ground for the self becomes radically problematized because that ground shifts from what de Man calls "the ontological stability of the natural object," on the one hand ("Intentional Structure" 69), or from the totalization of the *cogito* on the other, to the conditions of language, "a thing," Wordsworth reminds us in the 1815 Essay Supplementary, "subject to endless fluctuations and arbitrary associations" (*Prose* 3:82). The coherence of the self becomes neither ontological nor epistemological but rhetorical, that is, given tropological form but seeking hermeneutical completion. Where these three concerns of a stable natural object, a self-present consciousness, and language come together is in the *epitaph*, which for Wordsworth is an arche-genre, a "master trope," in Burke's phrase (503), in which a speaking subject intersects with a marmorealized text. This brings us back to the genre of autobiography, since Wordsworth called the epitaph "an epitomized biography" (*Prose* 2:89). Why not *auto*biography? Doubtless there are historical reasons—more epitaphs are written in the third person than in the first—but I feel that a more persuasive answer may be found in the intersubjectivity of the autobiographical text. Who really writes it? Is not autobiography, in its effect, biography in the first person? By writing "about" oneself one is necessarily writing about an Other, though retaining a grammatical vestige, a self-referential illusion, in the first-person pronouns. Perhaps this helps to explain de Man's paradox that every text is, and yet no text can be, autobiographical ("De-Facement" 70). Texts can have only the intentional structure of autobiography. The Wordsworthian epitaph directs us inevitably to questions that are fundamental to critical theory generally as well as to Wordsworth's rhetoric specifically.

My choice of the 1850 *Prelude* as the main text for study perhaps requires defense or explanation, especially when recent Wordsworth scholarship has made available a variety of texts, from the two-part poem of 1799, to the thirteen-book 1805 version, and to the fourteen-book 1850 edition, as well as variants and cancelled passages from all versions.[5] Despite the trend toward examination of these now easily accessible earlier states of *The Prelude*, I prefer to confine my readings, for the most part, to the final text, not because I wish to respect the author's final intentions so much as because I find the 1850 text rhetorically richer, more resonant, and more problematic in its use and questioning of language. In close analyses of some passages, however (the Simplon Pass, for one), I recall the early variations to point up specific aspects of Wordsworth's style, or to suggest certain inevitabilities in the development of the text as a self-governing artifact.

Since *The Prelude* is too large and complex a poem to make a sequential reading of its books practical for rhetorical analysis, I have organized my commentary around a series of high and low vantage points, large-scale structural analysis and small-scale close readings. Each chapter treats a significant aspect of Wordsworth's rhetoric, and wide-ranging as these aspects are, they all acknowledge the pull of language toward a declaration of its inherent rhetoricity. I begin with a reading of the Prospectus to *The Recluse* to demonstrate the range and scope of Wordsworth's figural language and to establish an attitude of reading which I subsequently apply to *The Prelude*. A major concern, though not an exclusive one, is the function of Miltonic and Shakespearean intertexts, or "*h*intertexts," as I occasionally call them (the "h" is for "history"). The question of allusion in Wordsworth properly deserves a study of its own, from both theoretical and practical perspectives, but I consider echo and allusion as part of the larger question of Wordsworth's style. While Wordsworthian criticism since the early 1970s has talked a great deal about "the presence of Milton,"[6] what is still not fully recognized is the "underpresence" (1805 *Prelude* 13.71) of Shakespeare in Wordsworth. Though I discuss some central passages in which Shakespeare seems to out-maneuver Milton intertextually, more work needs to be done to show how Shakespeare and Milton act as contraries in the imagination of Wordsworth, usurping and displacing each other in non-hierarchical difference. It may turn out that the same two powers that fought for the soul of Keats also fought for the soul of Wordsworth.

A second chapter, on Wordsworth's rhetoric of intertextuality in *The Prelude*, pursues the tropes of quotation, reference, allusion, and echo beyond the poem's surface linguistic texture to its larger structural patterning. The massive influence of Milton on Wordsworth finds expression not only through verbal reminiscence but through less obvious effects of structure and movement. Using what I call a "trope of collaboration," I read the Wordsworth-Coleridge partnership as a thematization of intertextual affiliations involving

Milton and his pair of laborers, Adam and Eve. I deliberately define "intertextuality" broadly, keeping it within the realms of both text and discourse, in view of the recent arguments of some critics (e.g., Kristeva, *Semiotikè*; Culler, "Presupposition") to dismiss text-oriented approaches in favor of semiotic, discursive, or cultural models of intertextuality.[7] While such models are helpful in offsetting narrow influence or source studies, my preference here is for the insights that can be generated by a rhetorical reading concerned with questions of form and genre.

Chapter 3 explores the intersection of speech and writing in *The Prelude* as part of the text's "allegory of reading," by which I mean, following de Man, that the so-called "literal" level of the text is always already an allegorized or thematized version of its tropological level. What this implies for Wordsworth's narrative is that at certain moments the text's rhetoricity becomes foregrounded, and the narrative or thematic line repeats its semiological substructure. In *The Prelude*, speech and writing enjoy alternating valorizations: voice appears as an appropriate linguistic ideal for a poet who saw himself as "a man speaking to men," but Wordsworth's desire for a more durable language produces a competing "insistence of the letter," in Lacan's phrase—a "strength / Of usurpation" in which "images of voice" in nature exist with the written characters that nature imprints on the landscape. Out of the intersection of voice and letter again emerges Wordsworth's master trope, the epitaph, in which the (absent) autobiographical self attempts to give itself textual form. Perhaps nowhere do we see so powerful a *mise en abyme*, a moment in which the text reflects on itself, as in Wordsworth's meeting with the blind Beggar in Book 7, which strikingly illustrates the interpenetration of voice, self, and writing. Writing, for Wordsworth, is not the death of voice but the consummation: like the Spirit of the Hour in *Prometheus Unbound* (3.3.67), Wordsworth breathes in "spousal verse" (Prospectus 57) "a voice to be accomplished" in his poetry.

The next chapter attempts to situate Wordsworth's rhetoric of self-encounter in a dramatic context in which the poet is differentially "a man speaking to men" (*Prose* 1:138) and a *spectator ab extra* (Coleridge, *Table Talk* 189, 210–11). Cambridge, London, and France represent distinct "acts" in the continuing drama of the growth of a poet's mind, and each uses a performative rhetoric to show the poet at once engaged with and yet disengaged from his experience. The text continually questions its series of binary oppositions in these episodes (self/other, outside/inside, proximity/distance, early/late) to reveal how each term of the pair interpenetrates the other in a deconstructive "strength / Of usurpation." Wordsworth appears simultaneously as a rhetorical participant in a drama of specularity, and as a spectator of sublime textual theatrics. While Keats's epithet of "the wordsworthian or egotistical sublime" (279) has perhaps clouded our understanding of the dramatic figuration of much of Wordsworth's longer poetry, close attention to his rhetoric and structure reveals a language imbued with traces of the drama, masque, and pageant.

In Chapter 5 I focus on another Wordsworthian "scene of reading" in the first "spot of time," attempting what I call a "semiotic psychoanalysis" or double reading of the letter. How language and mind interact in Wordsworth's poetry is shown in the way that linguistic characters carved in the landscape become imprinted in the mind as "the characters / Of danger or desire" (1.471–72). But gradually this mental writing becomes a "monumental writing" (1805:11.295) whose import is a matter of life and death for the poet. The legibility of the letters in the turf, their *writtenness*, acknowledges an eerie permanence of language, but also raises questions concerning the apparent silencing of voice, the status of Biblical and Shakespearean hintertexts, and the possibility, "psychoanalytic" in method, of reading the unreadable, of brooding over a text that foregrounds its own absence of meaning.

The final chapter addresses the "adequacy of language," in David Perkins's phrase (*Sincerity* 84–107), in books 6 and 12 of *The Prelude*. The Simplon Pass episode presents problems of both language and structure: the "sad incompetence of human speech" (6.593) is at once a complaint against language and a dissatisfaction with poetic form in the representation of the crossing of the Alps. I set Wordsworth's "strength / Of usurpation," regarded usually in terms of a dialectic of imagination and nature, in the context of the Saussurean usurpation of writing over speech; the poet's "incompetence" recalls Noam Chomsky's distinction between competence and performance in language, with linguistic implications for the hermeneutically "deep" structure in the Simplon passage. The "words that are unknown to man" (12.255) in the "spots of time" sequence repeat the competence/performance dilemma, and help to explain the nexus of Shakespearean and Miltonic echoes in the episodes. Since Wordsworth's strategies of approach to "the hiding-places of man's power" (12.279) are, first and last, determined by language, a meditation on language such as Shelley's *Defence of Poetry* can illuminate the problematics of Wordsworth's text. The theoretical prospect that *The Prelude* repeatedly obliges us to consider is that it is a narrative about its own composition but, more precisely, about the problems of that composition. The result is a text that thematizes its figural language of autobiography and epitaph, intertext and *mise en abyme*, voice and letter, metaphor and metonym, creating a monumental allegory of a trope called "Imagination," which is but a meta-name for an awful power of language itself.

—A Voice shall speak, and what will be the Theme?
Home at Grasmere

RHETORICAL STRUCTURE OF THE PROSPECTUS TO *THE RECLUSE*

1

The one hundred seven lines of poetry at the end of the Preface to *The Excursion* are described by Wordsworth "as a kind of *Prospectus* of the design and scope of the whole Poem" *The Recluse*, of which *The Excursion*, as the 1814 title-page and the first line of the Preface state, is but "a portion."[1] As a "prospectus," the verses should literally give an outlook, or overview, the word prospectus being derived from the Latin *prospicere*, to look forward, or, in transferred usage, to look forward to something. But because Wordsworth's Prospectus is also an excerpt, a fragment "taken from the conclusion of the first book of The Recluse" (*Prose* 3:6), it thus holds a dual status: as overview, the Prospectus stands outside its object of regard; and yet as extract it is part of that object—a self-regarding Prospectus whose view of the outside is performed from the inside, in a model of specularity-from-within. The inside/outside positioning of the Prospectus translates into another set of figures based on the synecdochic relation of part to whole. As excerpt, "taken from" a larger piece, the verses are admittedly fragmentary, but they are able, Wordsworth claims, to give an overview "of the whole Poem."

It is a contrary beginning. The style and structure of *The Recluse*, as conceived by Wordsworth, are described in detail in the prose Preface, but the Prospectus mentions no particulars of "design and scope"; and as for its being part of a "conclusion," it displays a strenuously preliminary quality in its words. There is more expectation than overview in the Prospectus, and nothing conclusive in any sense. On the grammatical level such anticipation is created by the future and conditional verb constructions—"I would give utterance" (13); "I shall need" (25); "the discerning intellect of Man . . . shall find" (52, 54); "I . . . would chant" (56, 57); "by words . . . would I arouse" (58, 60)—and on the structural level by the conventional forward-looking invocations to the Muse for her help in the immediate future. The Prospectus is another "glad preamble," to use Wordsworth's description of the opening lines of *The Prelude* (7.4)—a kind of prologue taken from the middle of things that proceed no further than the middle.[2]

The juxtaposition of the Prospectus with *The Excursion* gives an obvious sense of textual self-containment: the Prospectus stands, as Edward E. Bostetter has said, "at the beginning, as the publication of *The Excursion* stands at the end, of Wordsworth's significant activity" (13).[3] And yet whatever historical closure might be suggested by such a collocation of texts is counter-balanced by the allusive gesturing of both the Prospectus and the Preface to those "performances either unfinished, or unpublished" (*Prose* 3:6).[4] Structural containment and closure vie with rhetorical expectation and ambition. The Prospectus as conclusion curiously doubles with the Prospectus as preface: they are both and neither *hors-textes*.[5]

A Rhetoric of Voice

The Prospectus begins with a suitably epic announcement of its theme—"On Man, on Nature, and on Human Life" (1)—but the conventional expectations that this first line creates are undercut in the next by a participle that directs the poem away from *propositio* toward first-person narration, even meditation, with an "oft" making the narrative aspect recurrent, not unique: "Musing in solitude, I oft perceive / Fair trains of imagery before me rise . . ." (2–3). Wordsworth is never far from narrative, either here or in his shorter poems. The first line is not, we discover, a statement of epic subject and heroic theme; those elements are not announced until the fourteenth line, with the surprisingly ambitious catalogue of the real subjects of the poet's song:

> Of Truth, of Grandeur, Beauty, Love, and Hope,
> And Melancholy Fear subdued by Faith;
> Of blessed consolations in distress;
> Of moral strength and intellectual Power;
> Of joy in widest commonalty spread;
> Of the individual Mind that keeps her own
> Inviolate retirement, subject there

> To Conscience only, and the law supreme
> Of that Intelligence which governs all—
> I sing. . . . [6]

"Indeed," wrote Wordsworth to a friend, "I know not anything which will not come within the scope of my plan" (*EY* 212). The list is dense with anaphoric "of" phrases, reminiscent of Milton's modified anaphora in "Of Man's First Disobedience, and the Fruit / Of that Forbidden Tree" (*PL* 1.1–2).[7] "Of Truth, of Grandeur, Beauty, Love, and Hope" is an heroic line, with every noun the brunt of heavy stress, every iamb a *topos*, but it takes its place beside the more personal, reflective statements of the poet's theme. Wordsworth has already announced that he "would give utterance in numerous verse" (13) to certain "emotions," namely, "affecting thoughts / And dear remembrances" (6–7) and "feelings of delight / Pure, or with no unpleasing sadness mixed" (4–5). The giving of "utterance" to these emotions is complex, however, for the poet is unsure whether their affective quality comes from external or internal stimuli—"whether from breath of outward circumstance, / Or from the Soul—an impulse to herself" (11–12). The "breath of outward circumstance" reminds one of the familiar Romantic trope of a "correspondent breeze" (*Prelude* 1.35):[8] the breath is inspired (literally) by the poet and he (figurally) by the breath; it is then uttered or "outered" again in "breathings," as Wordsworth calls them in *The Prelude* (3.190), in a metonymy of composing aloud, by "a man speaking to men" (*Prose* 1:138). The "numerous verse" which the poet hopes to compose is not, as many editors suggest, simply "metrical" verse: as in its source in *Paradise Lost* 5.150, where it is juxtaposed with "various style" (*PL* 5.146), "numerous" retains here—especially here, as Jonathan Wordsworth puts it, in this "moment of Wordsworth's greatest confidence" ("Secession" 355)—the sense of abundant production, the hope for numerous "performances," including *The Recluse* itself.

These progressive restatements of theme have the effect of an extended version of the figure of climax, in which the preliminary announcements, impressive as they are, are superseded by even higher themes. The Prospectus really has two such climaxes: the first declares "the mind of Man" (40) as what Wordsworth calls "My haunt, and the main region of my song" (41); and the second, turning outwards from singular to plural first-person pronouns, and from the mind alone to the mind and its fitting to the "grateful haunts" of the world (72), states: "this is our high argument" (71). The shift from "my song" to "our . . . argument," linked by a corresponding shift from "haunt" to "grateful haunts," is doubly significant—first, for its adaptation of the Miltonic turn in Book 1 of *Paradise Lost* from "my advent'rous Song" to "the highth of this great Argument" (13, 24), in which the genres of lyric song and epic argument are brought into creative proximity; and second, for the expansion from the personal pronoun "my" in speaking of lyric process to the more inclusive form of "our" in dealing with formal argument (compare Milton's "all our woe" [*PL* 1.3]). The Prospectus combines both song and argument, lyric and epic elements, but in a self-contesting way, for one feels that the heroic potential of the Prospectus is continually being turned aside into lyric expressiveness, with the result that the text becomes a lyrical argument in much the same way that *The Prelude* turns out to be a lyrical epic, appropriating both song and argument in a text whose tale is only of itself.

Thus while the Prospectus is supposed to have been "taken from the conclusion of the first book of *The Recluse*," it bears more thematic and structural similarities to an introduction than to a conclusion. Its wavering balance may also be described in formal rhetorical terms.[9] The initial proposition or *principium* "On Man, on Nature, and on Human Life," we saw, radically modifies the conventional epic structure by shifting into personal reminiscence; but a secondary *principium*, beginning "Of Truth, of Grandeur, Beauty, Love, and Hope" and extending over ten lines, reorients the poem and leads it into the invocation:

Urania, I shall need
Thy guidance, or a greater Muse, if such
Descend to earth or dwell in highest heaven!
(25–27)

Instead of a progression into the *exordium* or narrative proper, the fluxes and refluxes of the Prospectus carry the reader back into another *principium* in which the poet announces what he "must" do: "I must tread on shadowy ground, must sink / Deep—and aloft ascending, [must] breathe in worlds / To which the heaven of heavens is but a veil" (28–30). A long descriptive passage follows in which Wordsworth changes his notes to what he "would" do ("would chant" [57], "would . . . arouse" [60]), but he soon reverts to the sense of constraint that compels him to forego his "grateful haunts" and commence his loco-descriptive journey.

The Prospectus is not topographical poetry, though it does survey the world from "lowest Erebus" (36) and the "nether sphere" (93) to "the heaven of heavens" (30). Its tone is an uneasy mixture of conjecture—"if I oft" (72), "if with this" (93), "if such theme" (99)—and compulsion—"must turn" (73), "must hear" (76), "must hang" (77). After the enumeration of these sad tasks and hard which the poet faces, the text slips back into an invocatory mood that continues to the end of the Prospectus. "Come, thou prophetic Spirit," wrote Wordsworth initially (Darlington 104), but perceiving the structural parallel to his earlier invocation to "a greater Muse, if such / Descend to earth," he altered the apostrophe to signal the parallel descent verbally too:

> Descend, prophetic Spirit! that inspir'st
> The human soul of universal earth,
> Dreaming on things to come; and dost possess
> A metropolitan temple in the hearts
> Of mighty poets: upon me bestow
> A gift of genuine insight. . . .
> (83–88)

The Prospectus, then, formally oscillates between *principium* and *invocatio*, or between proposal and apostrophe, between argument and song. The fluctuation between these two "voices" of the Prospectus is pointed up by the diction, which shifts from speaking into singing and back again frequently. The poet begins with "utterance" (13), but completes the first verse paragraph with the exclamation "I sing!" (23). The trope of singing is carried into the line "My haunt, and the main region of my song" (41), but then is successively modified to a "chant" (57) and to "words / Which speak of nothing more than what we are" (58–59). The poet's "voice proclaims" (62) its own immediacy as that of "a man speaking to men"—a hope which, as we shall see, seeks to command an "unmediated vision" (Hartman's title) by creating what Tilottama Rajan has called a "poetics of presence" (17). Voice is complemented by hearing; and thus Wordsworth also "must hear Humanity in fields and groves / Pipe solitary anguish" (76–77), even as in "Tintern Abbey" he hears

> oftentimes
> The still, sad music of humanity,

Nor harsh nor grating, though of ample power
To chasten and subdue.
(90–93)

"May these sounds," Wordsworth says (80), and the noise of the "storm of sorrow . . . / Within the walls of cities" (78–79) "have their authentic comment" (81).

But in what sense will their comment be "authentic"? Authorized, as by the author? The guarantee of an authentic voice, strangely, appears to come from the muse's anticipated "gift of genuine insight" (88) to the poet, who hopes, in his final shift from hearing back into singing, that his "Song / With star-like virtue in its place may shine" (88–89). What it means for a song to shine, in this rich confusion of vocal and visual tropes, is so deeply central to Wordsworth's "mighty world / Of eye, and ear" ("Tintern" 105–06) that it verges on a kind of divine *fiat*, the originary creating voice of Genesis.[10] Voice for Wordsworth here is a divine creative power able to sing and shine at the same time, even as the divine voice is able to say "Let there be Light," and to make that light in the same breath. In other words, "a Voice to Light [gives] Being," as Wordsworth says in his poem "On the Power of Sound" (209), and sheds "benignant influence" (90) on all that it has created. The "shedding" (90) of influence works in two directions: it is, first, the casting off of past influences; and, second, the diffusing of its own newly created influence. Though Harold Bloom doubtless overstates "Wordsworth's deepest obsession" to be "a monstrously strong poet," he is right to point out that Wordsworth's lines here ask "to be an influence, and not to be influenced" (*Anxiety* 126).

But more than that, they implicitly assert an originating status equal in power to the usurpation of Jehovah earlier in the Prospectus. What is worth remembering here, in the context of voice in Wordsworth, is that the whole Prospectus, as it was printed with *The Excursion* in 1814, consists of one entire quotation (see Darlington 101). The quotation marks around the Prospectus serve both to emphasize the *quotedness* or intertextuality of the poem and to remind the reader of its (un)*spokenness*—that is, its consisting "chiefly of meditations in the Author's own person," as the Preface states (*Prose* 3:6). As the 107 lines of the Prospectus stand in manuscript with the rest of *Home at Grasmere*, however, the vocal emphasis is actually a response to the question posed in the line that immediately precedes the passage:

> A Voice shall speak, and what will be the Theme?
> On Man, on Nature, and on Human Life,
> Musing in Solitude. . . .

The theme, as it turns out in our reading of the rhetorical structure of the Prospectus, is none other than what it means for a voice to speak, to sing, to chant, to utter, to shine; and thereby to express a power original and creative enough to be more than just an echo of the divine voice of creation, more than just a noisy moment in the life of the eternal silence. "A Voice shall speak" is a determined utterance; it expresses not simple futurity but verbal necessity for a voice to come into the world and for the silence not to overcome that voice. But what will be the theme or content of a voice that sheds both light and silence in speaking? Wordsworth's reply is equally determined: his "Theme . . . but little heard of among Men" (67) is none other than a

> creation (by no lower name
> Can it be called).
> (69–70)

Allusion and Echo

When M. H. Abrams speaks of "the unparalleled density of the Miltonic reminiscences" in the Prospectus (*NS* 21), he is recording an observation that most commentators have made to some degree, though the "unparalleled" status of the claim has never been statistically proven. The frequency of the "reminiscences" of Milton is certainly high, if not unparalleled, and the manner of reminiscence intricately various. Even to a reader not overly familiar with Milton's poetry, the quotations and references and allusions and echoes, as well as other modes of recall, do seem to indicate the powerful, if enigmatic, "presence of Milton."[11]

The most common explanation of the purpose of the Miltonic allusions is that they serve as implicit points of comparison between Wordsworth and Milton. This notion is behind Abrams's discussion of the Prospectus when, for example, he states that "Wordsworth is setting out to emulate his revered predecessor—and rival—by writing the equivalent for his own age of the great Protestant English epic" (*NS* 22). By alluding to or echoing Milton, then, Wordsworth invites comparison with him, not only in terms of subject, vision, or genre, for example, but also in terms of the very style in which he invokes the earlier poet.

There is some truth to this idea of allusion as an implicit comparison, as long as one remembers that points of contrast and dissimilarity between the two poets are held in juxtaposition with their points of congruence. In the nexus of echoes surrounding Wordsworth's initial invocation one can see how such a process is at work:

I sing:—'fit audience let me find though few!'

So prayed, more gaining than he asked, the Bard—
In holiest mood. Urania, I shall need
Thy guidance, or a greater Muse, if such
Descend to earth or dwell in highest heaven!
(23–27)

The adverb "so," placed emphatically at the opening of a sentence and a new verse paragraph, grammatically signals a comparison—almost an identity—between the prayer of "the Bard" and the song of the narrator, though the structural direction of the comparison—from the present ("I sing") to the past ("So prayed")—acknowledges a temporal as well as rhetorical difference between them. The comparative adjective "greater" obviously implies another comparison—this time between the poets' respective muses—but the possibility that no such "greater Muse" exists inverts the relation into a potential contrast, like the deep contrast hidden in the comparative construction "more gaining than he asked," which cannot avoid the worry that the present poet might gain less. The superlative phrase "in holiest mood," which Wordsworth changed from "holiest of Men" for the 1845 edition of *The Excursion*,[12] deflects the impossible comparison between the speaker and a predecessor pinnacled in holiness by transferring the holiness from the individual to a state. What begins as a metonymic displacement from "Urania" to her "guidance" is reversed by the transcendent movement to "a greater Muse," with its conventional associations: "Thy guidance, or a greater Muse, if such / Descend to earth or dwell in highest heaven" (26–27). Though one might wish to render this first line as "Thy guidance, or [that of] a greater Muse," Wordsworth's rhetorical shiftiness resists, and even discourages, such paraphrase. If Wordsworth seems to be dismissing Urania and replacing her with a greater, his action is but a foreshadowing of how he will, by implication, forsake the "greater Muse" from "highest heaven" by surpassing the "heaven of heavens" and reaching the *locus formidolosus* of his own mind, where he becomes a muse unto himself.

Hence the rhetorically balanced closure of "My haunt . . . my song" (41): the doubly emphatic "my" is to distinguish Wordsworth's "haunt" from those conventional places "where the Muses haunt / Clear Spring, or Shady Grove, or Sunny Hill" in *Paradise Lost* (3.27–28), and to contrast his "song" with the "Celestial Song" (*PL* 7.12) of Milton's Urania. As Wordsworth said in his Virgilian motto to the "Intimations Ode" (1807), *paulo maiora canamus*: Milton may have risen to "the Heav'n of Heav'ns" (*PL* 7.13) by following Urania's "Voice" (*PL* 7.2), but Wordsworth will surpass both heaven and voice by following a song of his own making. "My own voice cheered me," he writes in *The Prelude*, "and, far more, the mind's / Internal echo of the imperfect sound" (1.55–56).[13]

Aside from the similarities and contrasts implicitly offered in the trope of echo, whether internal or external, the device has other functions. W. J. B. Owen, dealing with literary echoes in *The Prelude*, has argued that "the concept of authority" is "the prime reason for the presence of literary allusion" there ("Literary Echoes" 14). Owen does not specify what he means by "authority," but his use of the term is associated with the *topos* of classical authority as bestowing legitimate poetic status on a work. Such an argument, while valid with some texts, raises problems with respect to Wordsworth's Prospectus, where the conventional idea of authority—literary and otherwise—is openly challenged by the poet. If, as David Simpson has argued, the "disestablishment of the text as authority" (25) is one of the Romantics' central preoccupations, then anything within the text, including, in Paul de Man's words, "such intertextual tropes as allusion" ("Epistemology" 13), is liable to the same process of dismantling. Owen seems almost to anticipate this argument in his observation that *The Prelude* represents "a dwindling of authority" (14), but even a diminished form of an appeal to poetic legitimacy remains there.

Yet precisely the reverse of the notion of allusion as an appeal to tradition and literary authority may be true. The presence of echo may not be intended by the author, insofar as it may be intended at all, to confer imaginative dignity or legitimacy, but to expose or to parody the limitations and the errors of the source. In speaking of Wordsworth's "assonant homage to Spenser" in Book 3 of *The Prelude* (281–82), Simpson, in somewhat different but related terms, suggests that emulative allusion may even be "a rite of exorcism, the expunging of a predecessor by means of the mastery of his style" (61). For Harold Bloom, similarly, allusive appeals to authority are too easily turned into repudiations of that authority, into a poetic misprision that constitutes "a sin against continuity, against the only authority that matters" (*Anxiety* 78).

Once we shift our focus from the egos of the poets to their texts, however, once we stop thinking of personalities and start thinking of language, an alternative rhetoric becomes possible. Insofar as words, phrases, images, and figures are shared by two texts—whether these signs are "borrowed," "stolen," or "adapted," to use the conventional terminology—it is permissible to speak of a *collaboration* between texts, a kind of joint effort in which authors and texts find themselves on the same side in a ceaseless mental fight against a common enemy (Time, Error, Mutability) whose greater threat renders trivial the in-fighting among the ranks. In such a trope of collaboration the "turning" or troping involves an intertextual accommodation usually signalled by echo on a lexical or structural level. But a rhetoric of collaboration does not dispel other antithetical questions. Does echo suggest a similarity between two texts or does it throw into relief contrasts in the handling of such aspects as theme or character? Does the presence of a Miltonic voice, or its echo, confer authority upon the alluding text or does it actually work as a destabilizing linguistic element by denying closure to its foster poem and by introducing unavoidable ironies? These questions are as relevant to echo and allusion as they are to the more foregrounded tropes of quotation and reference: they all repeat a tale of two texts. Literary allusiveness operates by evoking and combining texts to produce another text; and "to evoke and to combine," Wordsworth reminds us in the 1815 Preface, "belong as well to the Imagination as to the Fancy" (*Prose* 3:36). Allusion arguably has a rhetorical status equal to that of metaphor, and a structural relationship with the source-text equivalent to synecdoche, the trope in which the part (echo) stands for the whole (source-text).[14]

Allusions are sometimes thought to call attention to the temporality of a text by attempting to bring the full weight of the past to bear on the present, but usually the rhetorical effect is rather an apocalyptic transformation that recreates what Eliot called the "pastness of the past" through the *presentness* of it.[15] Though a trope of echo presupposes a temporal element, and not, as Alan Nadel has argued, "a concept of simultaneity" (639), the historical distance between the original and the later text is frequently so compressed as almost to be elided. But compression and juxtaposition through echo and allusion are not the same as a real presence, though it is understandable that a reader might be fooled by an echo's occasional implicit denial of its borrowedness. Allusion takes out tenancy in a new text while regularly casting backward looks to its former residence; its doubleness is a synecdochic version of a doubleness inherent in poetic discourse itself—Roman Jakobson's ambiguity of the "split reference" in poetry (371), or Northrop Frye's "centrifugal" and "centripetal" functions of words (*Code* 58–61; *Anatomy* 73–82). The often self-declared two-way reference of allusion—to its present and to its original text—resists closure in a structural sense, as it draws the bounds of the alluding text outwards and backwards to something that it does not contain. In this sense the doubleness of echo is not unlike Wordsworth's response to the echoic aspects of his retrospective narrative viewpoint in *The Prelude*. He writes:

so wide appears
The vacancy between me and those days
Which yet have such self-presence in my mind,
That, musing on them, often do I seem
Two consciousnesses, conscious of myself
And of some other Being.
(2.28–33)

The historical "vacancy" which "appears" to be "so wide" between the here-and-now speaker and "those days" of his youth is rhetorically contradicted by the fact that the past has "yet" a presentness to it—a "self-presence," as Wordsworth calls it in tautological emphasis; but paradoxically it is this "self-presence" that generates the sense of alterity and doubleness: "two consciousnesses." In intertextual terms, whatever temporal "vacancy" there may be, for example, between *Paradise Lost* and *The Prelude* is rhetorically bridged by allusion, which at once figures its own "self-presence" in Wordsworth and points to the self-absence, which is "yet" a presence, of Milton.

Since the literary term "echo" is a trope for an acoustical phenomenon (not least a phenomenon of voice), we might do well to consider the function of literal or natural echoes in Wordsworth's poetry as a means of understanding the workings of intertextual echo. John Hollander has written perceptively on this topic in *The Figure of Echo*, blending acoustics and intertextuality to the benefit of both, while on a more literal level John S. Martin has explored the business of natural echoes in Wordsworth, arguing that they reflect the poet's "sensitivity to sound" and indicate the operation of a traditional pathetic fallacy in which nature participates in the poet's feelings. But echoes, Martin says, function in other ways:

> Generally speaking, they are more than reverberations of the primary sound; they betray a measure of independence from it, and signify the presence of a transcendent power whose mood or spirit may radically differ from that of the primary sound's originator. (187–88)

Martin's description may be applied to literary as well as natural echoes: the way that sounds are echoed and reverberated in Wordsworth's natural landscape provides an analogue of the way that literary echoes are bounced between poems. That nature should offer a paradigm of intertextuality comes as no surprise: nature is conventionally a text (the *liber naturae*), and Wordsworth's response to it is quite legitimately a "reading."[16]

The Boy of Winander, to take an exemplary case, may be read as "the primary sound's originator," and the owls as the reverberations of his "skill" (5.380). But the Boy's "hootings" are in fact "mimic hootings" (5.373)—which is to say, already echoes of the sounds he produces—and the owls' responses are thus echoes of echoes, as Wordsworth writes, "redoubled and redoubled, concourse wild / Of jocund din" (5.378–79), in which the poet's tautology ("redoubled and redoubled" implies a four-fold redundancy) conveys the shock and surprise of the experience. With the echoes of both the Boy and the owls bouncing off the landscape, adding to the "din," it becomes clear why he is "baffled" when "a lengthened pause / Of silence" (5.379–80) does not return his sounds but is followed by a different voice, "the voice / Of mountain torrents" (5.383–84).

To read this episode as an allegory of intertextuality might be to force the narrative into the unwilling service of theory, but we can at least point out some possibilities. As with the natural echoes, literary allusions "betray a measure of independence" from their source: they are not simultaneous with it—there is a temporal delay between incidence and echo—they do not reproduce the original sound in full, and what part they do recall is usually distorted to some degree. Where the analogy becomes particularly enlightening is in the function of what Martin calls the "transcendent power" which, like Wordsworth's "alien sound" (1.443), "radically differ[s]" in "mood or spirit" from the source. It is but a short step to Harold Bloom's antithetical ratios in which Wordsworth, as "transcendent power," gives an "alien sound" to his original. As our trope of collaboration suggests, however, this transumption need not be wilfully antithetical, though the accommodation of the source by the echo is always charged with difference and difficulty. The revival and perpetuation of sound through its echo in nature is a recurrent example of verbal allusiveness in literature: intertextual allusions, like the literal landscape sounds that Martin explores, are "echoes of immortality" (192).

If we suggest that images of literal echoes in Wordsworth's poetry are analogues of figural echoes reverberating there, we are constructing an "allegory of reading" in which the text offers the reader a clue as to how it is to be read. By saying this I do not mean that the text offers only one way for itself to be read; clues naturally invite divergent interpretations, and clues, of course, are never proof in themselves. But I do mean that insofar as a text attempts to say something about itself to itself or to another reader, an allegory of reading implies the reflexive nature of all texts, the tendency for language to talk about itself *as language*. It is related, with significant differences, to a statement in the "Essay, Supplementary to the Preface" (1815): what Wordsworth says of the author we would say of the text. "Every author," he writes, insofar as "he is great and at the same time *original*, has had the task of *creating* the taste by which he is to be enjoyed" (*Prose* 3:80); that task, Wordsworth suggests in a letter to which his statement alludes, is also to "teach the art by which he is to be seen" (*MY* 1:150). The "art" of "a man speaking to men" is essentially a rhetorical art, and the way in which his texts are to be seen, or heard, or read becomes an allegory of its own figuration.

A Marriage of Heaven and Hell

The central passage of Miltonic echoes occurs when Wordsworth is at his most apocalyptic:

> For I must tread on shadowy ground, must sink
> Deep—and, aloft ascending, breathe in worlds
> To which the heaven of heavens is but a veil.
> (28–30)

The late *caesura* in the first verse, combined with the line break after "sink," leaves both poet and reader hanging; the line literally falls away from "shadowy ground" to nothingness until the downward motion is reversed in the next line. This is, it could be said, a different art of sinking in poetry, but one that demonstrates an alacrity in sinking no less profound than Falstaff's: "If the bottom were as deep as hell," Falstaff says, "I should down" (*Merry Wives* 3.5.12–13). As it turns out, Wordsworth's bottom here is deeper than "the darkest pit / Of lowest Erebus" (Wordsworth had earlier written "the darkest Pit / Of the profoundest Hell" [Darlington 102]) in terms of its imaginative awfulness. If the pattern of descent and reascent owes something to Milton's invocation to light in Book 3 of *Paradise Lost*, it is clearly structural in its influence. Milton has been

> Taught by the heav'nly Muse to venture down
> The dark descent, and up to reascend,
> Though hard and rare . . .
>   (3.19–21)

but it is the rehearsal of this structural pattern again in the invocation to Book 7 that provides the analogue not only of descent and reascent but of the breathing in worlds beyond the heavens. Milton says to Urania:

> Up led by thee
> Into the Heav'n of Heav'ns I have presum'd,
> An Earthly Guest, and drawn Empyreal Air,
> Thy temp'ring; with like safety guided down
> Return me to my Native Element. . . .
>   (7.12–16)[17]

The collocation of these passages in Wordsworth's imagination gives him the structural and rhetorical model of prophetic discovery, but the astonishing changes that he introduces point out a new territory that he "must tread." Milton's "Heav'n of Heav'ns" recedes into the distance as Wordsworth, in the vertically spatial allegory, ascends through it as through "a veil." Now, it is in the nature of veils to be rent, and what Wordsworth "must" do is remove the film that separates his superior "worlds" from Milton's inferior "heaven of heavens." The curtain must be torn as Wordsworth, not this time in his priestly robes but naked, as in the presence of divinity itself, puts off his soul's garments to stand before his own divinity of imagination, as he does in Book 4 of *The Prelude*:

> Gently did my soul
> Put off her veil, and, self-transmuted, stood
> Naked, as in the presence of her God.
> (4.150–52)

It is permissible to speak in these theological terms because Wordsworth himself does. It was, in fact, the theological diction and the dismissing of Jehovah that exasperated Blake when Henry Crabb Robinson showed him Wordsworth's Prospectus (Robinson 1–27). In the year before his death Blake copied out by hand all 107 lines of the Prospectus, as well as the last paragraph of the prose Preface to *The Excursion* (Blake 655), but after such close attention to Wordsworth's verses it was the old charge of "the Natural Man rising up against the Spiritual Man" (Blake 654), and not the question of the Miltonic presence, that Blake noted in both his marginalia and his conversations with Crabb Robinson. Could Blake have missed the Miltonic allusions? It seems unlikely for one so steeped in the poetry of Milton; but nonetheless, what attracted his attention more were the lines dealing with the imaginative usurpation of Jehovah:

> All strength—all terror, single or in bands,
> That ever was put forth in personal form—
> Jehovah—with his thunder, and the choir
> Of shouting Angels, and the empyreal thrones—
> I pass them unalarmed.
> (31–35)

Blake's intestinal upset over these lines—"a bowel complaint which nearly killed him," as Crabb Robinson describes it (15)—seems to have been aggravated by a mental cramp as well: "Is Mr. Wordsworth a sincere real Christian?" Blake asked. "If so, what does he mean by the worlds to which the heaven of heavens is but a veil and who is he that shall pass Jehovah unalarmed?" (Robinson 15–16).

It is difficult here, as in so many crucial passages of Wordsworth's poetry, to unravel the syntax and the uncertain punctuation to produce meaning. But one thing seems sufficiently clear: the "fear and awe" that Wordsworth experiences on looking into his own mind are distinguished from the "terror" of a Nobodaddy like Jehovah. The "fear" is a religious fear, the "awe" a divine awe. Geoffrey Hartman rhetorically asks: "Is Wordsworth afraid of his own Imagination?" (*WP* 39). The Prospectus' reply is straightforward:

Wordsworth is not "afraid" of his imagination, but he does "fear" it. His sweeping dismissal of "all strength" looks ahead contrastively to his celebration of the "strength / Of usurpation" in Book 6 of *The Prelude*, an experience that bears structural similarities to the usurpation here. Yet the detail that "all strength—all terror" must have been "put forth in personal form" is problematic: in what sense "put forth"? Written, as in a text? And what kind of "personal form"? Autobiography, lyric, or prosopopoeia?

Wordsworth's image of terror in personal form is primarily acoustic: "Jehovah—with his thunder, and the choir / Of shouting Angels, and the empyreal thrones." The Godhead's thunder is what Satan remembers best in Hell; its connotations are precisely strength and terror to him, though Moloch boasts that there is "Infernal thunder" (2.66) as well as divine. Wordsworth's evocation of the "choir / Of shouting Angels" at first recalls the cadences of Milton's "choir / Of squadron'd Angels" (12.366–67), but the oxymoronic effect of a shouting choir gives a parodic twist to the customary Miltonic emphasis on the harmony of heaven and the harmonious representation of it. W. J. B. Owen, however, has pointed out that "Angels shout in *Paradise Lost*, II, 520, and in Milton's 'At a Solemn Musick,' 9" (*Prose* 3:11). What Owen does not mention is that in *Paradise Lost* at this point it is the fallen angels who shout; and in "At a Solemn Musick" the sound is a "saintly shout," not a "deaf'ning shout" by "all the host of Hell" (*PL* 2.520, 519). There are, in fact, two clear instances of the unfallen angels' shouting in *Paradise Lost*, but in each the shout is qualified by the speaker to distinguish it from its demonic version and from the common "shout / Of Battle" in the war in heaven (6.96).[18] What kind of shout is Wordsworth's? Are the angels to which he alludes fallen or unfallen, and their shouts demonic or divine?

The word "choir," it must be remembered, means both a musical chorus and any one of the nine angelic orders. The identity of Wordsworth's angels is ambiguous, both for the suggestion of a heavenly choir and for the darker implication of a demonic rout. But the "empyreal thrones," belonging to a choir of angels third from the top, are easier to identify. The only time that the phrase occurs in *Paradise Lost* is a significant one: it is the address to the angels in hell as Satan accepts, in foreshadowed parody of the Son, to "seek / Deliverance" for them all (2.464–65). "O Progeny of Heav'n," Satan says,

Empyreal Thrones,
With reason hath deep silence and demur
Seiz'd us, though undismayed: long is the way
And hard, that out of Hell leads up to light. . . .
(2.430–33)

Satan, like his author, and more like Wordsworth, "must tread" a path "unattempted yet" (*PL* 1.16) as he crosses Chaos on his forbidden voyage to Paradise. Wordsworth, in the combined roles of Christ rending the veil in the temple, Satan defying the "ten thousand Thunders" (6.836) of God, and the Son harrowing hell with its myriads of fallen angels, sets out on his journey, disdaining heaven and hell and everything between—"the heaven of heavens," "the darkest pit of lowest Erebus," and "Chaos" itself. His quest, like Satan's, is for Paradise:

Paradise, and groves
Elysian, Fortunate Fields—like those of old
Sought in the Atlantic Main—why should they be
A history only of departed things,
Or a mere fiction of what never was?
(47–51)

"History" and "fiction" constitute the two poles of discourse on a continuum of truth—history being "factually" more truthful than fiction—but both modes represent a discourse of absence: history speaks "only of departed things," and "mere fiction," "of what never was." The speaker hopes for an imagination able to create a real poetic presence in contrast to a fictional or historical absence, but even his hopes betray an uncertainty of success, a wishing to suspend or defer the moment of arrival. Hence he writes, "long before the blissful hour arrives" (56), that he "would chant" (57) and "would . . . arouse . . . and win" (60,61)—all verbal constructions which by their conditional futurity create a sense of postponement. Yet this uncertainty follows a conative future construction which, by its transposing the normal first- and third-person auxiliaries for simple future expression, gives a compulsive aspect to the words:

For the discerning intellect of Man,
When wedded to this goodly universe
In love and holy passion, shall find these
A simple produce of the common day.
(52–55)

Simple futurity would require that the "intellect" *will* find the paradises that Wordsworth describes; the emphatic form of "shall find" conveys a sense of assurance, but the conditions set for the discovery are considerable: the "intellect" must be "discerning," "wedded" to the universe, and wedded "in love and holy passion." "When" these things coincide, then it "shall find" both the "history" and the "fiction" of departed or imagined things turned into a presence, like the "living Presence" of "Beauty" (42).

Wordsworth's grammar is significant. The sudden change in number that occurs over the line break—"shall find these / A simple produce"—moves from the plural to the singular: multeity is being compressed into unity, to use Coleridge's terms (*Miscellanies* 17), not only grammatically, by changing "these" to "a," nor merely through juxtaposition ("these / A"), but also through the use of the adjective "simple," which means unity or singularity itself, as distinct from something that is complicated, in the literal sense. The reconciling of multeity into unity, which is Coleridge's definition of beauty (*Miscellanies* 19–20), is also a supreme function of the imagination for Wordsworth; recall his discussion of "consolidating numbers into unity, and dissolving and separating unity into number" in the 1815 Preface (*Prose* 3:33–34). Here, the natural "Beauty" (42) that "waits upon [his] steps" (45), like the nature in *The Prelude* that plays "handmaid to a nobler than herself" (14.260), surpasses "the most fair ideal Forms" (43) that art can reproduce "from earth's materials" (45) in a usurpation that has physical nature triumphing over art even as the "Mind of Man" supersedes the "heaven of heavens." The "simple" or singular aspect of this "produce" finds its supplement in the line's other noun phrase "the common day," in which the word "common," as Roger Murray says in his discussion of "Michael," "should lead us quickly from the thought of something ordinary to the thought of something shared" (19). *Simple* produce, *common* day: unity grows out of multeity, as something unique comes out of something dialectically shared. The day is "common" because it is ordinary, but also because it is shared between the "intellect" and the "goodly universe": mind and nature, when "wedded," discover their unique offspring through the life common to them both. The phrase "common day," which recurs in the "Intimations Ode," retains there its meaning of something shared, but takes on other associations as it is juxtaposed with the "light" (70) of "the vision splendid" (74) which is said to "die away, / And fade into the light of common day" (76–77).

Wordsworth's figure here for the relation of man's intellect to the universe is that of a marriage. But what kind of a marriage is it? Today it is understandably easy to invest Wordsworth's spousal figure with twentieth-century marital notions, but we would do well to remember that his marriage is very much a nineteenth-century union: mind and nature are not equal, even as husband and wife in Wordsworth's view are not equal. Though Wordsworth objected to Milton's description of Eve in Book 4 of *Paradise Lost* as presenting "a low, a very low and a very false estimate of woman's condition" (Grosart 3:457), he nevertheless seems to have perceived marital roles along traditionally demarcated lines. For example, when Michael cares for his son Luke, he performs what Wordsworth calls "female service" (154)—in which the "female" modifier calls attention to Michael's transgression of traditional roles, though both the boundary and the trespass are important. In the wedding of mind and nature there is still a privileging of mind over nature, of subject over object, but this priority is by no means absolute. In the 1805 version of *The Prelude*, Wordsworth can write that certain experiences show that "the mind / Is lord and master" (1805:11.271–72), but by MS D² (1828 or later, according to de Selincourt [445]), he seeks to know only "to what point, and how, / The mind is lord and master" (12.221–22). One is tempted to speculate: did Wordsworth's actual marriage teach him anything about the rhetorical relation of mind to nature? Did Mary have anything to do with the shifting priorities of subject and object? When mind and nature are "wedded," Wordsworth will chant "the spousal verse" (57)—a phrase that he takes from Spenser (Potts 290)—to a "great consummation" (58).

The best commentary on the marriage metaphor in Wordsworth is found in the opening pages of Abrams's *Natural Supernaturalism*, where the trope is located in its Romantic context and traced to its archetypal forms in the Biblical metaphor of the marriage between the Lamb and the New Jerusalem (27–31, 37–46). While the marriage trope has seemed justified to many readers (though not to Blake, who refused to believe in such a metaphysical arrangement,)[19] Wordsworth's rhetoric of marriage and consummation requires close reading to reveal aspects which are no less problematic for an understanding of the poetry than the sexual connotations of the same figure were for Biblical commentators on the Song of Songs and the Book of Revelation (*NS* 42–46). It is surprising that, given such an important trope in Wordsworth's poetry, interpreters have not pursued the connection of marriage and sexuality much beyond the "Nutting" fragment and the "Lucy" poems. Older psychoanalytic readings of the sexuality of the poet himself—including the kind of study that F. W. Bateson has attempted—too often lead us into areas of little relevance to rhetorical analysis; rather, our concern should be: how does the trope function in the text?

The most significant point, perhaps, has already been mentioned: the marriage itself is postponed; the poet speaks "long before the blissful hour arrives" (56), but is there not also the suggestion that the bridegroom could come quickly and the marriage be fulfilled immediately? "When shall the destined hour arrive?" Asia asks Demogorgon halfway through *Prometheus Unbound*; and his reply, an apocalyptic performative, reveals the answer to be the *now* of her asking (2.4.128). With Wordsworth the question is never put; the consummation remains deferred, suspended, devoutly to be wished. The poet chants "in lonely peace" (57) his soliloquy of "words / Which speak of nothing more than what we are" (58–59), as he hopes to "arouse the sensual from their sleep / Of death" (60–61). Abrams says that the source of the phrase "sleep / Of death" is Psalms 13:3 (*NS* 484n24), but the sleep/death analogy is so common that it is difficult if not impossible to point to a single source. It is arguable, however, that Wordsworth's appropriation of the phrase is mediated by Hamlet's use of it in his famous soliloquy in Act 3.1:

'Tis a consummation
Devoutly to be wished. To die, to sleep—
To sleep—perchance to dream: ay, there's the rub,
For in that sleep of death what dreams may come
When we have shuffled off this mortal coil,
Must give us pause.
(63–68)

By tying Wordsworth's "sleep / Of death" to a Biblical source ("Consider and hear me, O Lord my God: lighten mine eyes, lest I sleep the sleep of death" [Ps. 13:3]), Abrams is able to support on a textual level his thesis of Wordsworth's adaptation of "the Christian pattern of the fall, the redemption, and the emergence of a new earth which will constitute a restored paradise" (29). But the close proximity of "consummation" and "sleep / Of death" sets up the other allusive resonances of Hamlet's soliloquy. The word "consummation," of course, has a number of possible meanings that richly complicate interpretation. In the context of a marriage, consummation has specific sexual connotations, but in Hamlet's use of the word, consummation is associated with death as the "end" of "the heartache, and the thousand natural shocks / That flesh is heir to" (3.1.61, 62–63). In "The Tuft of Primroses," where Wordsworth reprises his echo of this speech from *Hamlet*, consummation is similarly linked with death, but in the sense of completion:

> all was gentle death,
> One after one with intervals of peace,
> A consummation, and a harmony
> Sweet, perfect, to be wished for. . . .
> (154–57)

Here, life is "perfect," that is, accomplished, in death; death is the completion of life. But elsewhere, consummation is fulfillment in a different sense, as in Wordsworth's climactic statement of "the discipline / And consummation of a Poet's mind" at the end of *The Prelude* (14.303–04). In Abrams's reading, the consummation of the world, which is to say, the Apocalypse itself, is prefigured in Wordsworth's "great consummation" in the Prospectus. Could it be that there is a sexual analogy behind the exquisite "fitting and fitted" (Blake 656) arrangement of the mind and nature? Wordsworth's marriage is indeed apocalyptic to the extent that it ushers in "clear sight / Of a new world" (*Prelude* 13.369–70), and it is proleptically epitaphic insofar as the consummation figures a death, a sexual "dying" or even the end of life. His "spousal verse" will in part allay the "natural shocks" of "Humanity in fields and groves / Pip[ing] solitary anguish" (76–77) by giving "blessed consolations in distress" (16) and winning "the vacant and the vain / To noble raptures" (61–62). The absence which history and fiction stand for is meant to be turned into a presence, but the effort is fraught with tentativeness and deferral. The wedding is postponed, "surely yet to come" (*Prelude* 14.443). Like Adam waiting for Eve, with her "sweet reluctant amorous delay" (*PL* 4.311), the consummation is "about to be" (*Prelude* 6.608).

Shakespeare and Milton

After reaching the second structural climax ("this is our high argument" [71]), Wordsworth descends to "turn elsewhere" (73) to those objects and characters that he will "see" (74) and "hear" (76) in his song/journey. He considers that if he must

> travel near the tribes
> And fellowships of men, and see ill sights
> Of madding passions mutually inflamed;
> Must hear Humanity in fields and groves
> Pipe solitary anguish; or must hang
> Brooding above the fierce confederate storm
> Of sorrow, barricadoed evermore
> Within the walls of cities—may these sounds
> Have their authentic comment; that even these
> Hearing, I be not downcast or forlorn!
> (73–82)

Blake again took exception, claiming that these lines did not demonstrate an exquisite fitting "to Mind but to the Vile Body only & to its Laws of Good & Evil & its Enmities against Mind" (656). What Blake does not comment on, curiously, is another nexus of Miltonic allusions and echoes. "Brooding above the fierce confederate storm" surely harks back to the opening of *Paradise Lost* and to the Creation, where the Holy Spirit "Dove-like satst brooding on the vast Abyss / And mad'st it pregnant" (1.21–22); and looks ahead to the conclusion of *The Prelude*, where Wordsworth, in a late revision, describes his vision of a natural "emblem of a mind / That feeds upon infinity, that broods / Over the dark abyss" (14.70–72).[20] The image of brooding was a favorite of Wordsworth's; the action occurs both literally and figurally in a number of his poems and in his discussion of Imagination and Fancy in the 1815 Preface, where he also discusses the word "hang" as a metaphor (*Prose* 3:31)—as, for example, in the above phrase, to "hang / Brooding," in which Wordsworth places "hang" at the end of the line, and without any stabilizing punctuation.

Milton's use of "brooding," despite the compressed simile "dove-like," arguably challenges a figural interpretation, as God, in Milton's view, literally and efficiently makes Chaos "pregnant";[21] Wordsworth's trope recalls the realized fecundity of the Miltonic creation, but again surpasses it: his "creation (by no lower name / Can it be called)" (69–70) is the "simple produce" of the union or reciprocal crossing of mind and nature—a union which Wordsworth rhetorically imitates through a chiasmus: "Mind" (63) . . . "external

World" (65) . . . "external World" (68) . . . "Mind" (68). That in this chiasmus the external world is rhetorically contained by the mind, and that both world and mind are expressed tropologically are highly significant. The Miltonic "brooding on the vast Abyss" results in a breeding, from Chaos' having been made pregnant, but Wordsworth swerves from giving Chaos equal procreative powers. "Not Chaos, not / The darkest pit of lowest Erebus," he says (35–36), "can breed such fear and awe" as can "the Mind of Man." The other sense of brooding as meditation reminds the reader of the poet's "musing in solitude" (2) at the beginning of the Prospectus, and his anticipated double emphasis on "the thing / Contemplated" (94–95) and "the Mind and Man / Contemplating" (95–96). What the poet says he will brood on are the sounds "of sorrow, barricadoed evermore / Within the walls of cities" (79–80). The image of being trapped "within the walls of cities" recurs at the beginning of *The Prelude*, and will be discussed in detail in Chapter 2. "Barricadoed," as most editors point out, echoes *Paradise Lost* 8.241, where Raphael describes the gates of hell as "fast shut . . . and barricado'd strong." But the full context of the passage in Milton shows Raphael relating to Adam specifically what he *heard* on his surveillance mission to the doors of hell on the day of Adam's creation:

> But long ere our approaching heard within
> Noise, other than the sound of Dance or Song,
> Torment, and loud lament, and furious rage.
> (8.242–44)

Like Raphael, Wordsworth has "ears that can hear the agonies / And murmurings of hell" ("Away, away, it is the air" 11–12). "May these sounds / Have their authentic comment," he writes with allusive inclusion, "that even these / Hearing, I be not downcast or forlorn!" Wordsworth can boast to pass "unalarmed" (35) heaven, chaos, and hell, but the "solitary anguish" of "Humanity"—which he by allusion compares to the tortures of the damned—threatens to leave him "downcast" and "forlorn." Milton's model of the forlorn poet in Book 7 of *Paradise Lost* expresses a similar fear that his flight above "Pegasean wing" (4) might lead him to such forbidding and forbidden heights that the ensuing drop would be far worse than simply awakening on the cold hill's side. Milton writes:

> Return me to my Native Element:
> Lest from this flying Steed unrein'd (as once
> Bellerophon, though from a lower clime)

Dismounted, on th'Aleian plain I fall
Erroneous there to wander and forlorn.
(7.16–20)

"Forlorn!" writes Keats, "the very word is like a bell / To toll me back from thee to my sole self!" ("Ode to a Nightingale" 71–72). Milton's fear of flying is repeated in Wordsworth's fear of falling, that is, of being "downcast or forlorn."

Consequently, in his closing apostrophe to the "prophetic Spirit" (83), Wordsworth seeks to allay his fears of failure in his quest and to "secure" (90) his "Song" (88) "from all malevolent effect . . . / Throughout the nether sphere" (91–93). This is a strong example of what David Perkins has called Wordsworth's "quest for permanence"—a conventional statement of hope for his poem to escape the evils of mutability. Instead of turning to Milton, however, Wordsworth attempts to dispel his fear of being subject to the "malevolent effect" of the "nether sphere" by troping it in a Shakespearean echo. He writes:

Descend, prophetic Spirit! that inspir'st
The human Soul of universal earth,
Dreaming on things to come . . .
(83–85)

and his note in the 1849–50 edition of *Poetical Works* (see *Prose* 3:12) points the reader to Shakespeare's Sonnet 107:

Not mine own fears, nor the prophetic soul
Of the wide world, dreaming on things to come,
Can yet the lease of my true love control,
Supposed as forfeit to a confined doom.

Shakespeare's speaker conventionally hopes for his "true love" to outlast death, but the paradox that emerges toward the conclusion of the sonnet overthrows the convention by confirming the immortality of the poet while implying the death of love. "I'll live in this poor rime," the speaker says, "and thou [true love] in this shalt find thy monument." The "monument," a trope central to Wordsworth, as I shall show in the following chapters, signifies "a history of departed things," while the speaking voice of the poet, and its graphic representation, boast an immortal presence. The Shakespearean phrases that Wordsworth appropriates emphasize the prophetic element ("dreaming on things to come") while masking the inadequacy of prophecy in altering experience (none of these things "can yet the lease . . . control"). He invokes the muse in order

that my Song
With star-like virtue in its place may shine,
Shedding benignant influence, and secure,
Itself, from all malevolent effect
Of those mutations that extend their sway
Throughout the nether sphere!
(88–93)

The intermingling of Shakespeare and Milton here is striking. "Nether sphere," Paul de Man writes in another context, "has an unmistakably Miltonic ring" to it ("Symbolic Landscape" 26), though in fact Milton never uses the phrase. Wordsworth's figure "shedding benignant influence," however, revises Milton's "shedding sweet influence" (*PL* 7.375), a phrase used to describe the constellation of the Pleiades; but the poet's wish for his "Song" to "shine" "in its place" recalls Shakespeare. From 1845 on, the motto to Wordsworth's collected poems was a sonnet ("If thou indeed derive thy light from Heaven") whose third and fourteenth lines exhort: "Shine, Poet! in thy place, and be content." Ben Jonson's dedication to Shakespeare in the 1623 Folio Edition provides a remarkable hintertext, combining stars, poets, shining, and even influence:

Shine forth, thou Starre of Poets, and with rage,
Or influence, chide, or cheere the drooping Stage. . . . [22]

It is intriguing to observe how Milton's presence here is displaced by the underpresence of Shakespeare. Jonson's dedication, if it is the source of Wordsworth's motto, may also be the hintertext for these verses from the Prospectus. Wordsworth's song issues forth to shining light in a spectacular image of illuminated voice.

The Prospectus moves to its conclusion through a final series of exhortations to the muse, who is apostrophized as a "dread Power! / Whose gracious favor is the primal source / Of all illumination" (100–02). The play of chiaroscuro effects is subtle, but there is a progressive movement from the "shadowy ground" (28) of Wordsworth's exploration, with its associated challenges of "veils" and "darkest pits" and even "blinder vacancy" (37), to the "gift of genuine insight" (88) from the muse and its "star-like" ability to "shine" into the mind (89). But the journey metaphor, perhaps the preeminent trope of Wordsworth's poetry, is reintroduced in the closing lines addressed to the "dread Power": "so shall thy unfailing love / Guide, and support, and cheer me to the end!" (106–07). In all manuscripts, "to the end" are the last words of the Prospectus: whatever other revisions he made, Wordsworth knew from the start his rhetorical end. The double sense of closure created by placing the word "end" at the end, however, is deferred by the phrasing "to the end," which offers a direction and intention guided and supported by a "primal source" (101), rather than a sense of already having arrived at a *telos*. At the same time, though, the source naturally points to the end, even as the "feeding source" of imagination in Book 14 of *The Prelude* (193) anticipates its end in "human Being, Eternity, and God" (205).

The Prospectus exhibits many characteristics of Wordsworth's blank verse style. Its rhetorical structure is as sustainedly prophetic as anything Wordsworth wrote, and yet the note of tentativeness, the deferring of consummation, the *topos* of personal inadequacy, and the sheer awesomeness of the entire project seem to mix uneasily with the heroic assurance of usurpation, the confidence and ambition in prescribing the "design and scope" of his plan, and the repeated claim for a new "high argument." Formally, the Prospectus functions in a number of ways not easily harmonized—as part of the Preface to *The Excursion* (1814), and yet the conclusion of that Preface; as part of the first book of *The Recluse*, and yet the conclusion of that first book; and as a preview of a poem never written as planned.

The multiple formal associations of the Prospectus lead one to think of the more complex associations of intertextuality and its self-avowedly central role in these verses. Because of its ambitious subject, the Prospectus is at some pains to position itself in literary history, and the way in which it does that is not by avoiding its precursors but by appropriating them, by assimilating their language and structure to a new context. The clue to such assimilation, frequently, is found in verbal traces, but there are equally significant instances of intertextual liaison on a structural level, as we saw, for example, in Wordsworth's motif of descent and reascent, which reenacts the Miltonic structural pattern. My reading of the Prospectus has raised questions about Wordsworth's rhetoric that must now be pursued. In the next chapter I shall show how echo and allusion work in *The Prelude* on both linguistic and structural levels, and how Wordsworth thematizes a trope of collaboration there.

—*Shakespeare, or Milton, labourers divine!*
The Prelude

THE RHETORIC OF INTERTEXTUALITY: THE "JOINT LABOURERS" OF *THE PRELUDE*

2

In the last chapter we observed how Wordsworth's rhetoric operates on the levels of trope, structure, and intertext. This last level is perhaps the most problematic, as it requires the reader to maintain a double focus on the text and on something outside the text, another text which also points to something outside itself, and so on. This aspect of Wordsworth's language, neither wholly "centripetal" nor "centrifugal," [1] points to a rhetorical space partway between an objectively referential context and a "literary" or interrelating context in which, as Michael Riffaterre has argued, "the representation of reality is a verbal construct in which meaning is achieved by reference from words to words, not to things" ("Yew-Trees" 230). A particular text's meaning may be achieved by internal reference from words to words within its own system of codes, but intertextually, meaning is won by reference from (this text's) words to (that text's) words. This is not to say, as Harold Bloom does, that "the meaning of a poem can only be another poem" (*Anxiety* 94, 70), but that meaning is constituted by the *troping* of another poem, by the intertextual troping of allusion and echo.

It is important to make these distinctions so that one can understand how intertexuality, which is rhetorical, differs from the study of influence, which properly belongs to a history of ideas. I have said elsewhere that the difference between influence and intertextuality—and this is not limited to verbal texts—is that intertextuality is the expression of influence, and thus presents itself as a suitable object of rhetorical analysis. Since it is language with which I am primarily concerned here, I leave the question of literary influence to psycho-biographers and crisis theorists like Bloom in order to direct my attention to the specific ways in which Wordsworth's poetry appropriates the texts of his precursors, especially those of John Milton. A close examination of the workings of such tropes as quotation, reference, allusion, and echo is necessary because despite the considerable amount of interest, both recent and long-standing, in "the presence of Milton"[2] in Wordsworth's poetry, readers continue to discover new aspects of intertextuality in their poetic relationship.[3] When one first seeks to define the Miltonic "presence," stylistic similarities and verbal echoes are what immediately resonate in the reader's mind. But there are richer entanglements, as Keats said—intertextual affiliations which, while incorporating allusion and echo, go beyond lexical similarities to aspects of structure. It may be appropriate here to repeat B. Rajan's warning to those readers who would measure the degree of influence by the number of verbal allusions in a text (ix). Let us instead consider a case that does not involve mere verbal imitation but that brings into play certain structural features of another text.

Should one sense, for example, a recognition of Milton in the apocalyptic close of the later *Descriptive Sketches*? A significant revision that Wordsworth made in 1836 (*PW* 1:324–25) tempers the apocalyptic zeal of 1793 with a maturer vision of human experience. Instead of

> Lo! from the innocuous flames, a lovely birth!
> With its own Virtues springs another earth . . .
> (782–83)

Wordsworth writes,

> Lo, from the flames a great and glorious birth;
> As if a new-made heaven were hailing a new earth!
> (644–45)

—in which the "as if" construction adequately expresses the poet's new-found tentativeness. But Wordsworth then adds:

> —All cannot be: the promise is too fair
> For creatures doomed to breathe terrestrial air. . . .
> (646–47)

Now this addition, at first glance, is indeed Miltonic in its moderating the naive desire of the earlier version, in its sadder and wiser vision of man's proper role on earth, and in its ironic handling of apocalyptic conventions. But is it in fact Miltonically prompted, and if so, what is its rhetorical model? It is quite possible that when Wordsworth revised his poem he was thinking of the "Nativity Ode," and specifically the passage in which Milton too pulls back from a simple-minded enthusiasm for the millennium just around the corner:

> Yea, Truth and Justice then
> Will down return to men,
> Th'enamel'd *Arras* of the Rainbow wearing,
> And Mercy set between,
> Thron'd in Celestial sheen,
> With radiant feet the tissued clouds down steering,
> And Heav'n as at some festival,
> Will open wide the Gates of her high Palace Hall.
>
> But wisest Fate says no,
> This must not yet be so. . . .
> (141–50)

These last two lines do not sound much like Wordsworth's—there is no verbal mimicry—yet there is a formal half-similarity in that both examples are couplets, one pentameter and the other trimeter; and would it be too fanciful to think that Wordsworth's new alexandrine "As if a new-made heaven were hailing a new earth," which immediately precedes the couplet, was motivated by Milton's alexandrine in the precisely corresponding position? One cannot be sure; but the handling of the argument in both poems is exactly similar at this point, and Wordsworth's other echoes of the "Nativity Ode" in *Descriptive Sketches* (71, 344) would tend to support such a reconstruction of his rhetorical operations.

I have offered this first example of structural allusion tentatively, as a limit, as an instance of intertextuality at a far remove from verbal similarity or the conventions of genre. Two particular examples of Wordsworth's rhetoric of allusion in *The Prelude*—one near the beginning and the other near the end of the poem—serve to focus a rhetorical description of the intertextual affiliations between Wordsworth and Milton, and, collaterally, between Wordsworth and Coleridge, and, collectively, among these three figures' status as "joint labourers" (14.441). After describing the structural function of the Miltonic echoes as they relate to the theme of Adam/Eve and Wordsworth/Coleridge as analogous "joint labourers," and showing how collaboration in its literal and historical sense ("*co-labor-ation*" or "joint labouring") acts as the backdrop to Wordsworth's rhetorical dramatization of Coleridge's role in *The Prelude*, I shall expand the trope of "joint labourers" to theorize more generally on its intertextual implications for Romantic poetry. Each variation on the theme of "joint labourers" complements the others in a matrix of echo and collaboration that includes Adam and Eve, Wordsworth and Coleridge, Wordsworth and Milton, reader and text.

I

Let us begin by reconsidering from a structural perspective the familiar echo of *Paradise Lost* in the fourteenth line of Wordsworth's *Prelude*: "The earth is all before me."[4] The same echo recurs in what Wordsworth might call its "ruralized" (1.89) form at the end of Book 1, after he has discovered both his theme and its answerable style: "The road lies plain before me" (1.640). The contraction from all the earth to a road which, like the theme for which it is the metaphor, is "single and of determined bounds" (1.641), is precisely what revives the speaker ("my mind / Hath been revived" [1.636–37]) as it gives him the opportunity to find his own language, and to focus on his proper subject ("the story of my life" [1.639]), rather than treat an "ampler and more varied argument" (1.643)—in the manner of Milton—in which he "might be discomfited and lost" (1.644). The rhetorical translation of "the earth is all before me" into "the road lies plain before me" shows, perhaps more convincingly than any other echoic progression in *The Prelude*, Wordsworth establishing his own voice over the sound of Milton's.

Milton's original version of Adam and Eve about to leave Paradise creates an important structural footing for *The Prelude*:

> The World was all before them, where to choose
> Thir place of rest, and Providence thir guide:
> They hand in hand with wand'ring steps and slow,
> Through *Eden* took thir solitary way.
> (*PL* 12.646–49)

The speaker of *The Prelude* is alone, while there are two characters making their exit in Milton's poem. The difference in number has its significance, since Wordsworth's task of tracing the growth of his own imagination requires that he be single and, unlike Adam, without an help meet for him:

> Here must thou be, O Man!
> Power to thyself; no Helper hast thou here;
> Here keepest thou in singleness thy state:
> No other can divide with thee this work. . . .
> (14.209–12)

"Let us divide our labours," Eve says to Adam (*PL* 9.214); but the labors that Wordsworth means here cannot admit of division. The "singleness" of the poet's task reflects a singularity in the human imagination itself: "Points have we all of us within our souls / Where all stand single" (3.188–89). In contrast to the synecdochic "joint hands" of Adam and Eve (9.244), Wordsworth argues that "no secondary hand can intervene" (14.213) in the work of individuation.

But although the poet begins his "solitary way" like "a home-bound labourer" in Book 1 (101), he ends it in Book 14 in a company of "joint labourers" (441). Like Adam and Eve, though rather more anxiously, as the questioning syntax suggests, Wordsworth is seeking a "place of rest" too:

> What dwelling shall receive me? in what vale
> Shall be my harbour? underneath what grove
> Shall I take up my home? and what clear stream
> Shall with its murmur lull me into rest?
> (1.10–13)

The "clear stream" turns out in the end to be the "stream" (14.194) of "Imagination" (14.189), and its "murmur" the "natal murmur" (14.196) that Wordsworth first hears in its objective correlative of the River Derwent, and later in the Wye. But during the poet's wandering course, whose commencement here has distinct overtones of the errors of Aeneas, the stream is at times far less than "clear," and quite unable to "lull [the poet] into rest" as it is itself "bewildered and engulphed" (14.199).

Wordsworth's search for a place of rest has reminded readers (e.g., Onorato 18) of Odysseus' wanderings, but rhetorically his four-fold questioning is closer to Dryden's translation of the parallel questions of Aeneas in Book 3 of *The Aeneid*: "Where shall we fix? where shall our labours end? / Whom shall we follow, and what fate attend?" (67). The fact that in Virgil's original version Aeneas asks only three questions ("*quem sequimur*? *quove ire iubes*? *ubi ponere sedes*?"), which Wordsworth correspondingly translated in 1823–24 as "What shall we seek? whom follow? where abide?" (*Poems* 2:577), suggests that if there is an influence of *The Aeneid* here in Wordsworth's commencement, it is an influence mediated more by Dryden's rhetoric than by Virgil's.

Again like Adam and Eve, Wordsworth has Providence as his guide, although he is tentative about its form: "And should the chosen guide / Be nothing better than a wandering cloud, / I cannot miss my way" (1.16–18)—in which we hear an echo of the "wand'ring steps and slow" of Milton's travelers. The cloud that appears as a rather uncertain, though not misguiding, navigator is a transformation of the providential "pillar of cloud" in Exodus 13:21 that guides the Hebrews out of Egypt.[5] When seen in this context, the poet's beginning is less an expulsion, as with Adam and Eve, than a deliverance, as with the Hebrews—not a paradise lost, but an escape "from the vast city" (1.7), from "a house / Of bondage" (1805:1.6–7). As allegory addressed to the intellectual powers, the expulsion from Eden and the exodus from Egypt are not antithetical: Adam and Eve are not simply leaving one paradise while the Hebrews are moving toward another; rather, in both cases the travelers, led by God, are seeking the paradise that they will create in the wilderness through their own seeking—for the Hebrews, the land flowing with milk and honey (Exodus 13:5 *et passim*), and for Adam and Eve, the "paradise within . . . happier far" (12.587).

The beginning of *The Prelude* appropriates both of these journeys, as well as a failed quest. Contained within the allusion to the Hebrews' exodus is another echo, this time of Milton, that provides a variation of the Adam and Eve analogy to follow. In describing himself in the 1805 version as "a captive . . . coming from a house / Of bondage" (1.6–7), from "a prison where he hath been long immured" (1.8), Wordsworth is recalling Samson and his first entrance in *Samson Agonistes*. Both Wordsworth's speaker and Samson are imaged as captives newly released from prison, but they also share a more remarkable characteristic in the rhetorical presentation of their states of mind. Milton's argument tells us that Samson bemoans his dejected condition, his frustrated ambition and disappointed hopes of accomplishing his mission in life. His questions to himself, and also his father's doubts, as John Woolford first pointed out, are curious reminders of Wordsworth's self-questioning in Book 1. Samson cries:

> O wherefore was my birth from Heaven foretold
> Twice by an Angel . . .
> Why was my breeding order'd and prescrib'd

> As of a person separate to God,
> Design'd for great exploits . . . ?
> (23–24, 30–32)

Milton follows the same rhetorical pattern of "O wherefore . . . Why" in Manoa's lament for his son: "O wherefore did God grant me my request . . . Why are his gifts desirable . . . ?" (356, 358). And then, in a significant source passage for Wordsworth, Manoa continues: "For this did th'Angel twice descend? for this / Ordain'd thy nurture holy . . . ?" (361–62). Wordsworth cannot lay claim to a divinely annunciated birth, but there is no doubt of his belief that his breeding too was "order'd and prescrib'd / As of a person separate to God," for he is "a renovated spirit singled out, / . . . for holy services" (1.53–54).

"Was it for this," writes Wordsworth of his own sense of frustrated vocation,

> That one, the fairest of all rivers, loved
> To blend his murmurs with my nurse's song . . . ?
> For this, didst thou,
> O Derwent! winding among grassy holms
> Where I was looking on, a babe in arms,
> Make ceaseless music that composed my thoughts
> To more than infant softness. . . .
> (1.269–71, 274–78)

In both cases, however, the speakers are revived, partly by the sheer memory of their divinely ordered and prescribed childhoods, and partly by a healthful breeze: for Samson, the "breath of Heav'n fresh-blowing, pure and sweet" (10); for Wordsworth, the "sweet breath of heaven" (1.33) that bestows the initial "blessing" (1.1) on him. Even in these first lines Wordsworth can discern the likeness of a high responsibility in his poetic calling. "Whate'er his mission, the soft breeze can come / To none more grateful than to me," he says (1.5–6). Should we read the line as "whate'er *his* mission . . ."?—for Wordsworth has one too, and thus the "soft breeze" assumes a double function by providing an analogue of the poet's vocation and then by consecrating, "blessing," that vocation.

In the opening lines of *The Prelude* there is a sense of energy contained as much as energy released; a sense, curiously enough, of libidinal power unable to sublimate itself. I always hear an inexplicable echo of *Antony and Cleopatra* in Wordsworth's description of the breeze that fans his cheek, "like smiling Cupids,"

With divers-coloured fans, whose wind did seem
To glow the delicate cheeks which they did cool,
And what they undid did.
(2.2.203–06)

There is also a doing and undoing in Book 1 with the internal and external breezes that "seem" to contradict each other, half-conscious of the joy which each is able to intimate. The "gentle breeze" (1.1) inspires "a correspondent breeze" (1.35) that becomes "a tempest, a redundant energy, / Vexing its own creation" (1.37–38), which is to say, its own process of being created as well as the things it creates.[6] But both the vexing and the inspiring are interpreted by the poet as beneficent, as they are "promises" (1.41) of a power able to intuit its own potentiality, thereby instilling "a cheerful confidence in things to come" (1.58), the milder version of a desire for "something evermore about to be" (6.608).

II

The opening of *The Prelude* is rhetorically rich and hermeneutically problematic. For historical and biographical critics the dating of the opening lines and the identification of "yon city's walls" (1805:1.7), the "one sweet Vale" (1805: 1.82), and the "pleasant loitering journey, through two days / Continued" (1805:1.114–15) have been puzzling. What "city" does Wordsworth mean? The beginning of Book 7, with its apparent reference to these lines, has caused further uncertainty: does the "glad preamble" (7.4) to which Wordsworth alludes point in fact to the opening of Book 1, or does it, as Margoliouth has suggested (130–31), refer to the Prospectus, which is indeed, as we saw, a sort of preamble to itself? The note to Book 7 in the first edition of *The Prelude* (1850) complicates the matter, as it gives the referent of the city that Wordsworth leaves behind in Book 1 as "The City of Goslar, in Lower Saxony" (373).

The search for a referential context to explain Wordsworth's language may be, for some readers, a necessary complement or even corrective of rhetorical analysis, but here one feels that such an approach runs counter to the mode of discourse that *The Prelude* is attempting to construct. The problem is not merely that a positive identification of a literal city is irrelevant, but that it is impossible because of the way in which the poem's rhetoric has deliberately covered its tracks. Yet many readers have made the attempt. John Alban Finch, for example, who begins his search for the city so hopefully, acknowledges in the end that the mysterious city, vale, and journey are "the result of an imaginative fusion of different experiences" (12). This is undoubtedly the best conclusion that scholarship can offer, although it does not represent an advance beyond Thomas Hutchinson's same conclusion at the beginning of the twentieth century. "I am quite convinced," Hutchinson wrote to the editor Nowell Smith in 1908, "that Wordsworth [in the "preamble"] gives us an idealised account of his past history."[7] "Whether one likes it or not," Finch claims, "there is no alternative to Hutchinson's 'idealised account of . . . past history'" (9). Finch recognizes some intertextual qualities of Wordsworth's language in his brief consideration of Miltonic and Coleridgean allusions; only after his discussion of the allusive, not to say elusive, aspect of Wordsworth's literary city does he conclude that the poem celebrates "something more inclusive and significant than literal escape"—that is, "escape from a deadening way of life into a free and creative existence" (10–11). Here Finch is, I think, more right than he and other critics have realized, but we need to confirm his impression by rooting it in the language of Wordsworth's text, in the way that the following reading demonstrates.

The first word of *The Prelude* signals a trope, a turning to a breeze that sets the poem in motion. The 1850 edition removes three successive addresses to the wind—"O welcome messenger! O welcome friend! / A captive greets thee" (1805: 1.5–6)—with the result that the invocatory, apostrophic aspect of "O" is partially hidden:

> O there is blessing in this gentle breeze,
> A visitant that while he fans my cheek
> Doth seem half-conscious of the joy he brings
> From the green fields, and from yon azure sky.
> Whate'er his mission, the soft breeze can come
> To none more grateful than to me; escaped
> From the vast city, where I long had pined
> A discontented sojourner: now free,
> Free as a bird to settle where I will.
> (1.1–9)

The poem begins in the present tense, in the here-and-now of speaking, with a "there is" formula that recalls, as Geoffrey Hartman has suggested, the conventional ballad opening ("Words, Wish, Worth" 210). The immediacy of the present tense ("is . . . fans . . .

Doth seem . . . brings") recedes as a perfect participle ("escaped") and a pluperfect construction ("had pined") shift the temporal structure of the text into the past. The inflection from a repeated emphasis on the present tense to the past tense is conventionally the grammar of contrast, the means of characterizing a presence partly in terms of an absence. Wordsworth completes the temporal pattern by shifting from the pluperfect into a present or immediate context ("now free"), into an infinitive ("to settle"), and finally into a future or at least determined end ("I will" [will settle/wish to settle]): "now free . . . to settle where I will." What Wordsworth has done in these first nine lines is to reproduce the temporal structure of the "greater Romantic lyric," in Abrams's phrase, which involves an "out-in-out process" ("Structure and Style" 202) that finds its temporal correlative in the present-past-present-future structure of such Romantic poems as "Frost at Midnight," "Tintern Abbey," and *The Prelude* as a whole. It is, in the context of these opening verses, especially significant that Wordsworth should begin as he does, with a simple "O there is" formula that leads into the celebration of freedom and anticipation for the future, while the language enacts the corresponding movement toward verbal infinity and futurity. This temporal progression from the present to the past and to the future—which is to say more generally, from immediacy to distance—has its spatial analogue. The poet calls the reader's attention to "*this* gentle breeze" (emphasis added), which by the use of the definite demonstrative again suggests immediacy and presence as opposed to the distancing aspect of "*yon* azure sky" (emphasis added). The effect of the opening rhetoric is thus essentially dramatic, as it gives the reader the picture of a speaker, a broadly defined scene with a foreground ("this"), and a background ("yon"), and an action taking place. The vestigial apostrophe "O" animates the breeze through the related trope of prosopopoeia, which not even the unauthorized changes in the first edition of 1850—from the pronouns "he" and "his" to "it" and "its"—could completely undo.

I said earlier that the opening lines of *The Prelude* celebrate a new-found freedom, but it is an ambiguous freedom that is curiously short lived. Wordsworth proclaims that he has

> escaped
> From the vast city, where I long had pined
> A discontented sojourner: now free,
> Free as a bird to settle where I will.

> What dwelling shall receive me? in what vale
> Shall be my harbour? underneath what grove
> Shall I take up my home? and what clear stream
> Shall with its murmur lull me into rest?
> (1.6–13)

"Now free," Wordsworth writes, "Free as a bird." The banality of the simile is surprising, especially when we compare the earlier version ("Now I am free, enfranchised and at large" [1805:1.9]), though its connection with the wind, sky, and cloud imagery is clear. The anadiplosis of "free, / Free" does suggest a confidence, a joy in the sense of release, but then the reader learns that the speaker seems free only "to settle." Having just "escaped," the poet wishes "to settle" back again into confinement: he seeks a "dwelling" to "receive" him; he imagines a home "in" or "underneath" nature; and he dreams of a "stream" that will "lull [him] into rest." Whereas Adam and Eve actively "choose / Thir place of rest" (12.646–47), Wordsworth wishes to be transported there by a power like one of nature's. It is an ambivalent celebration of freedom which seeks anxiously to curtail that freedom, though such an agoraphobic response, as Victor Brombert has pointed out, has a distinct literary tradition behind it (63). The *interrogatio* of "what dwelling?" "what vale?" "what grove?" and "what clear stream?" combined with four conative future verbs ("shall . . . shall . . . shall . . . shall"), three of them in a triple anaphoric scheme, amounts to a nervous insistence reminiscent of the hysteria suggested by the similar questionings in Blake's "The Tyger." The speaker does consider the fearfulness of freedom, but seems to reject it:

> With a heart
> Joyous, nor scared at its own liberty,
> I look about; and should the chosen guide
> Be nothing better than a wandering cloud,
> I cannot miss my way. I breathe again!
> (1.14–18)

"Joyous, nor scared": what exactly is the force of the negative conjunction? Does it imply a symmetry—nor joyous nor scared—or does it have the force of "and not"? "Nor joyous nor scared" seems such an implausible alternative, yet syntactically it fits, inevitably suggesting the speaker's subtextual fear of liberty. But why raise the possibility of being "scared" (a surprising word) only to dismiss it? The exclamation "I breathe again," which Quintilian calls a figure of "simulation" designed to intensify emotion, confirms the "joyous" quality. Quintilian's proof text is Cicero's *Pro Milone*, in which the rhetorical structure of his figure is remarkably similar to Wordsworth's: *Liberatus sum: respiravi*: "I am free, I breathe again."[8] The reason that Wordsworth says he breathes *again*, perhaps, is not only because his sojourn in the vast city was spiritually suffocating, but because the inital breathing of the poem, what Geoffrey Hartman calls the "breathing apostrophic O" of the first line ("Words, Wish, Worth" 210), also forms a temporally prior point of reference. The "again" can be read as a successive as well as appositive breathing to the exhalation of the first verse.

Victor Brombert's treatment of the metaphor of the "happy prison," alluded to above, helps to describe the thematic function of Wordsworth's first entrance in the poem. "In its larger mythic dimension," Brombert writes,

> carceral imagery implies the presence of a threshold, the possibility of a passage, an initiation—a passage from the inside to the beyond, from isolation to communion, from punishment and suffering to redemption, from sadness to . . . profound and mysterious joy. . . . (67)

Wordsworth's escape from "the vast city" thus represents the crossing of a threshold, an act that recalls Hartman's conceit of "boundary images" in *The Prelude*, though in a different context.[9] While Hartman conceives of "border" images as drawing a line between the natural and the supernatural, here the line is placed between the natural and the unnatural, the natural being his release into the world of breezes, "green fields," and wandering clouds, and the unnatural being that part which is "shaken off":

> That burden of my own unnatural self,
> The heavy weight of many a weary day
> Not mine, and such as were not made for me.
> (1.20–23)

The echoes of "Tintern Abbey" (37–41) here are noteworthy, but not as intriguing, perhaps, as the Shakespearean reminiscences. "Unnatural" has an unarguable Shakespearean ring to it—not least because of its frequency in *King Lear*, as the *Harvard Concordance* makes clear; the word never occurs in Milton's poetry (see Ingram and Swaim), but Wordsworth uses it here to demarcate his rhetorical transition from one state to another.

For Wordsworth, the crossing of a threshold and the corresponding movement, in John T. Ogden's words, "from expectation through frustration to fulfillment" ("Imaginative Experience" 292) are related structurally to the "spots of time"—consider the "spot" in Book 8 in which Wordsworth, having entered the "vast dominion" (8.543) of London for the first time, says: "The threshold now is overpast" (8.549)—except that in the opening scene of *The Prelude* the other usual criteria for "spots of time" (e.g., a specific place, the role of memory, the locating of the experience in childhood) are elided, and the experience coincides, as both the present tense and the retrospective comment at 1.46–47 are meant to suggest, with its verbal mimesis. The thought that Wordsworth should begin *The Prelude* with an oblique or elided "spot of time" should not be surprising, since historically that is how *The Prelude* in its earliest form existed, as a collection of memorials and affecting incidents linked to dramatize the workings of imagination (see *NP* 512–15). But if we regard the first scene of the poem as a "spot of time" being enacted, then the effect is that right from the start the text is concerned with its own rhetoricity, with its status as a verbal construct, and not as a paraphrase of experience: that is an exciting thought. It helps shed light on the "Imagination!" passage in Book 6, which has been interpreted as declaring a temporal disjunction from its surrounding narrative in a way not unlike this first scene's shift from a "present joy" in the first forty-five lines to retrospective narrative thereafter. At those points where Wordsworth most seems to be paraphrasing his own life, re-presenting his experiences, or remembering his past, his rhetoric works noiselessly to subvert any privileged referentiality and to foreground its status as language.

Before leaving this sustained interrogation of the rhetorical structure of the *The Prelude*'s opening scene, I want to return to the identity of the city from which Wordsworth is escaping. The city, I have said, has no referential status—that is, it does not exist outside language—but it does have an impressive intertextual pedigree. The relevant lines in the 1850 edition are:

escaped
From the vast city, where I long had pined
A discontented sojourner. . . .
(1.6–8)

There is perhaps no better way to decode these verses than simply to juxtapose their source, the way it was juxtaposed in Wordsworth's imagination:

> Escap't the Stygian Pool, though long detain'd
> In that obscure sojourn. . . .

The lines are from *Paradise Lost* 3.14–15, where Milton apostrophizes the "holy Light" (3.1) of heaven in contrast to the "utter and middle darkness" (3.16) of hell and chaos. After an "obscure sojourn" as narrator of the first two books in hell, where he had been "long detain'd," Milton has "escap't." Wordsworth, as "a discontented sojourner," has also "escaped" the place where he "long had pined." It is as if the "vast city" for Wordsworth is identified with hell, even as the "storm / Of sorrow, barricadoed evermore / Within the walls of cities" in the Prospectus is identified with hell.[10] The pattern is the same: a walled city, full of sorrow and pining, from which the speaker has "escaped." What is rhetorically significant is the way that Wordsworth "literalizes" the Miltonic trope of "sojourn" from a textual figure for writing about hell to an experiential figure for living in hell. But it is still a figure, structured by language rather than experience. The 1805 version, while containing the details of the pattern, lacks the crucial Miltonic echo to give the city its rhetorical identity:

> A captive greets thee, coming from a house
> Of bondage, from yon city's walls set free,
> A prison where he hath been long immured.
> (1805:1.6–8)[11]

The allusions to the Hebrews and to Samson are interesting, as we have seen, but what is more important is that by MS D these allusions are partly effaced by the introduction of the new Miltonic echo. "Bondage," "walls," "prison," "immured"—all these references are displaced in the 1850 edition: "captive" becomes "sojourner"; "set free" becomes "escaped"; "long immured" turns into "long had pined." The new sense is that of greater freedom, both within and without the city. The passive voices of "set free" and "hath been . . . immured" change into the active constructions "escaped" and "had pined." On the surface level the city is no longer explicitly a prison; on the intertextual level, however, it is indeed, but not just any prison: it is hell. There is a reciprocal movement in Wordsworth's revisions: the hellishness of the city, latent in 1805, becomes rhetorically dominant in 1850, while the imagery of immurement, explicit in 1805, is suppressed to a degree in 1850. The fundamental characteristics of the city, however, do not change: Wordsworth leaves behind a place of discontentment and pining, an experience of confinement and demonic limitation, and looks ahead to his new "liberty" directed by Providence, a liberty that leads the poet all the way from his "glad preamble" to "human Being, Eternity, and God" (14.205).

III

The strong echoes of Milton near the beginning of *The Prelude* are balanced by another cluster of allusions almost as far from the end of the poem as the above are from its opening. In his apocalyptic vision of human history in *Paradise Lost* Michael comforts Adam, as God had directed him to do, with the knowledge of a Savior's future redemption. The notion of a Savior who is to be of woman's seed puzzles Adam at first (10.1031–35), but Michael's description of the Incarnation later in Book 12 helps to explain. "Now clear I understand," says Adam, "why our great expectation should be call'd / The seed of woman" (12.376, 378–79). Michael tells Adam to

> go, waken Eve . . .
> Let her with thee partake what thou hast heard,
> Chiefly what may concern her Faith to know,
> The great deliverance by her Seed to come. . . .
> (12.594, 598–600)

Now Wordsworth, in a different but no less apocalyptic prophecy at the end of *The Prelude*, concludes with his final apostrophe to Coleridge, in which he speaks of the lamentable possibility of man's imaginative backsliding, but also of the prospect of redemption through the imagination. Though the rest of the world fall back into idolatry, servitude, ignominy, and shame, Wordsworth writes,

> we shall still
> Find solace in the knowledge which we have,
> Blest with true happiness if we may be
> United helpers forward of a day
> Of firmer trust, joint labourers in a work
> (Should Providence such grace to us vouchsafe)
> Of their redemption, surely yet to come.
> (1805:13.435–41)

A late revision to MS D changes this passage (de Selincourt 506)—and specifically the last line—in order to support the Miltonic analogue with a close verbal echo:

joint labourers in the work
(Should Providence such grace to us vouchsafe)
Of their deliverance, surely yet to come.
(14.441–43)

Milton's version is not far off: "The great deliverance by her Seed to come."

This suggestive resonance, with its daring glance backwards to Book 1 and, beyond that, the end of *Paradise Lost*, invites one to consider the implications that transcend linguistic gestures and impinge on Wordsworth's metaphysical argument. Even if Wordsworth did not change "redemption" to "deliverance" in order to foreground the allusion to *Paradise Lost*, the change is nevertheless rhetorically richer. "Deliverance" recalls Wordsworth's deliverance "from the vast city" at the beginning of the poem, the word "deliver" being derived from the Latin *deliberare*, to set free. "Now free," Wordsworth exclaims, "Free as a bird" (1.8–9). Other Miltonisms are present, not least in the line "Should Providence such grace to us vouchsafe," in which the etymology of "vouchsafe" reinforces the poet's acknowledgment of grace extended to him and to his "joint labourer." The verb vouchsafe comes from two separate roots, vouch from *vox* (voice) or *vocare* (to call); and safe from *salvus*, which in turn is derived from *salus* (health or wholeness), probably related to *solus* (alone). Wholeness is akin to aloneness, which is to say, to all-oneness, the state of unity or identity. "Points have we all of us within our souls / Where all stand single," Wordsworth writes (3.188–89). "Possessions have I that are solely mine, / Something within which yet is shared by none" is *Home at Grasmere*'s version (686–87). To be vouchsafed grace is to be called into singleness, like "a renovated spirit singled out . . . for holy services" (1.53–54). "Such favour I unworthy am voutsaf't," Eve says as she and Adam prepare to leave Paradise, "By mee the Promis'd Seed shall all restore" (12.622–23). Wordsworth, thinking of these final lines of Eve's speech, and of the restoration which, not frivolously, his own "fair seed-time" (1.301) shall in part effect, offers another version in *Home at Grasmere*:

The boon is absolute; surpassing grace
To me hath been vouchsafed; among the bowers
Of blissful Eden this was neither given
Nor could be given, possession of the good
Which had been sighed for, ancient thought fulfilled

> And dear Imaginations realized,
> Up to their highest measure, yea and more.
> (103–09)

This passage recalls *The Prelude*, Book 8, where Adam is seen "yet in Paradise / Though fallen from bliss" (659–60)—a situation which for Wordsworth dramatized an internal/external duality operating in both his poem and Milton's. For Milton there is the garden which Adam and Eve must leave, and there is the garden "within" which is potentially "happier far" (12.587). A similar doubleness exists in Wordsworth's poem: there is nature external to man—"the earth / On which he dwells" (14.449–50)—and there is the internal paradise of "the mind of man" (14.448). With Wordsworth as with Milton, the internal paradise is potentially superior to the external one—"more divine" (14.454) or "happier far"; but it is crucial to emphasize the conditions only under which the internal garden can surpass the external garden. For Milton, the "paradise within" (12.587) is achievable only if Adam can "add / Deeds to [his] knowledge answerable" (12.581–82)—if he can

> add Faith,
> Add Virtue, Patience, Temperance, add Love,
> By name to come call'd Charity, the soul
> Of all the rest. . . .
> (12.582–85)

"Then," continues Michael—and only then—"thou shalt possess / A paradise within thee, happier far" (12.586–87).

Wordsworth is no less specific in defining the superiority of the internal paradise of man, and the conditions which must be met before the mind of man can assert its ascendance. Such contingency is made clear not only at the conclusion of *The Prelude* but, for example, in the introductory passage to the "spots of time" sequence, in which Wordsworth writes that certain moments of insight "give / Profoundest knowledge to what point, and how, / The mind is lord and master—outward sense / The obedient servant of her will" (12.220–23). The key phrase is "to what point, and how": the superiority of mind is not absolute. The 1805 version at first glance appears more assured, as it says "that the mind / *Is* lord and master, and that outward sense / *Is* but the obedient servant of her will" (1805:11.271–73; emphasis added); but this anaphoric insistence, we should note, is balanced by the fact that it is "deepest feeling" (1805:11.271) and not "profoundest knowledge" that tells us so. That is to say, the more assured tone of 1805, moderated by the voice of feeling, becomes in 1850 the voice of knowledge moderated by its own experience.

In the closing lines of Book 14, Wordsworth makes it clear that the earth—"this frame of things" (450): his plain diction understates the claim—is divine; the mind of man is "more divine" (14.454). And it is more divine in both degree and kind—in "quality and fabric" (14.454). But when Wordsworth speaks of the mind of man as "a thousand times more beautiful than the earth" (14.451), the status of his claim shifts from an absolute "is" to the progressive sense expressed in the verb "becomes": "the mind of man becomes / A thousand times more beautiful than the earth / On which he dwells" (14.448–50). The achieving of the mind's highest index of power and beauty is for Wordsworth a process, a becoming, not something simply given. It is contingent on his adducing evidence of an imagination puissant enough to validate the factor of a thousand between the beauty of earth and the beauty of mind. The process of becoming in *The Prelude* is largely educative—hence the emphasis on what nature has taught the poet, and what he is able to impart to others: "what we have loved, / Others will love, and we will teach them how" (14.446–47). The trope of process, of becoming rather than being, is appropriate to the theme of the growth of imagination, but it also has a formal propriety in the concept of a canonically "preparatory poem," as *The Prelude* nominally claims to be (*Poems* 2:36).

What the reader has, then, is a poem that begins with the deliverance from bondage of a poet who constructs analogues of himself in breezes that have divine missions, in the exodus of the Hebrews, in the wanderings of Aeneas, in Milton's sublime narrator, in Adam and Eve, and Samson; and who strikes off on a three-day journey following the guidance of Providence until he comes to his "chosen Vale" (1.93) where he is united with his sister and his wife (14.256–75). The story of Wordsworth's own life, as it is rhetorically presented, assumes the mythos of a walking tour, a kind of "stepping westward" toward a "heavenly destiny" ("Stepping Westward" 12), like the youth in the "Intimations Ode" who "daily farther from the east / Must travel" (71–72). The conventional westward movement is consistent with the allegory of walking that Wordsworth develops throughout his poetry. His poems are, correspondingly, the "memorials" of the "tour" (to use his own poetic classification)[12] that the poet must take as he retraces his growth of imagination. Wordsworth does a great deal of walking in *The Prelude*, beginning with a "pre-amble" and continuing through the two climactic mountain-climbing episodes of Snowdon and the Alps. The allegory of walking presides over Wordsworth's *oeuvre* from the beginning almost to the end: the first substantial poem that he published was *An Evening Walk* (1793), and the poem by which he was best known during his lifetime was *The Excursion* (1814). *The Prelude*, composed between these two dates, embraces the titular metaphor of both poems, subsuming the itinerant movement of *Descriptive Sketches* and *An Evening Walk* while reaching forward to the dramatic form and philosophical texture of *The Excursion*.

The back-and-forth imagistic movement of *The Prelude*, its simultaneous progressive and retrospective temporality—emblemized in the boy rowing the boat, who combines forward motion with retrograde vision—is intersected with an up-and-down allegory of ascent and descent structurally intrinsic to romance. "Day after day," Wordsworth writes in Book 6, "up early and down late, / From hill to vale we dropped, from vale to hill / Mounted" (494–96). A transformed quest-romance[13] is writ large in *The Prelude*, not only in the speaker's walking tour through the poem, but in his characterization of his auditor and co-worker S. T. Coleridge, whose experience as a failed quester is in part restored through his association with Wordsworth. The romance has its alternatives. Though *The Prelude* in its overall movement affirms a growth from singleness to community, it does not do so at the expense of those points "within our souls / Where all stand single" (3.188–89).

IV

If the kind of verbal and structural relation between Wordsworth and Milton that I have been describing can be called "collaborative" on an intertextual level, there is another collaboration, literal and historical, that deserves consideration. It is the relation of Wordsworth to Coleridge, and although we cannot embark on a study of their complex intertextuality—that would require a separate volume—we can read their historical association as recorded in *The Prelude* as a thematized complement of the Wordsworth-Milton question. Where attention needs to be directed, however, is not to the historical literalness of their relationship—numerous biographical studies have already done that[14]—but to its rhetorical treatment in the poem. Whatever Coleridge's actual relation to Wordsworth may have been (scholarship cannot reconstruct their association completely), the concern here is with Wordsworth's poetic account of it: the characterization of Coleridge, a role that Coleridge himself in part sustains in his response "To William Wordsworth," takes imaginative liberties with a figure whose referential identity is continually subordinated to the inevitabilities of the text's own rhetoricity.

Coleridge's status as a "joint labourer" with Wordsworth is established earlier than his designation as such in the last book of *The Prelude*. His collaborative role in the production of *Lyrical Ballads* alone would qualify him for such a title, and it is doubtless for this reason that Wordsworth, before articulating his prophetic plan at the conclusion of the poem, returns briefly to their original experience as "joint labourers" when they "first / Together wantoned in wild Poesy" (14.417–18). Wordsworth addresses his "beloved Friend" (14.392) to recall "that summer" (14.395) when

> Upon smooth Quantock's airy ridge we roved
> Unchecked, or loitered 'mid her sylvan combs,
> Thou in bewitching words, with happy heart,
> Didst chant the vision of that Ancient Man,
> The bright-eyed Mariner, and rueful woes
> Didst utter of the Lady Christabel . . .
> (14.396–401)

while for his own part Wordsworth quietly classes himself as being "associate with such labour" (14.402)—a self-description that places Coleridge as the principal actor, and Wordsworth as a secondary who is only "associate." The history of the *Lyrical Ballads*' publication, and the ratio of Coleridge's contributions to Wordsworth's suggest, in fact, the reverse.[15]

If Wordsworth in 1805 hoped to use an idealized version of their collaboration on the *Lyrical Ballads* of 1798 as the model of future endeavors, he was constructing a fiction that ignored the reality of their diverging paths. In fact, the extent of their activity as "joint labourers" even in the above passage is ironically limited: the "rueful woes" of Christabel, for example, never did appear in *Lyrical Ballads*; and as for the "bright-eyed" Ancient Mariner, Wordsworth's ambivalent criticism of the poem in his note of 1800 (Brett and Jones 276–77), not to mention his abortive collaboration on the work, makes his prophetic hopes not a little ironic. By 1805 the possibility of Wordsworth's and Coleridge's ever again being "joint labourers" in an ideal way was gone, and what remained for Coleridge as for Wordsworth was just the "memory of that happiness" (14.410). "When thou dost to that summer turn thy thoughts" (14.408), Wordsworth continues to Coleridge,

> To thee, in memory of that happiness,
> It will be known, by thee at least, my Friend!
> Felt, that the history of a Poet's mind
> Is labour not unworthy of regard:
> To thee the work shall justify itself.
> (14.410–14)

Unlike Milton's argument of *Paradise Lost*, to which Wordsworth is here alluding, which involves a mediating poet to "justify the ways of God to men" (*PL* 1.26), *The Prelude* incarnates a self-justifying argument: a product of imagination justifies its production, and the faculty that produced it. Yet even in this "labour not unworthy of regard" Coleridge has dwindled from collaborator, as epitomized in the *Lyrical Ballads* allusion, to respondent, the single version of Milton's plural "men" to whom "Eternal Providence" is asserted (*PL* 1.25). Wordsworth's ways, like God's, are justified to Coleridge because he understands the structural pattern behind the creation. It may have been "a thing unprecedented in Literary history that a man should talk so much about himself" (*EY* 586), but it was not unjustified, at least, to Coleridge, who imagined to what greater work this poem was to be "prefixed" (Griggs 2:1104).

Coleridge thus assumed the role of respondent: if he could not regain the blissful seat of collaborator or "joint labourer," he would at least fulfill his titular function of addressee in the "Poem (Title Not Yet Fixed Upon) by William Wordsworth Addressed to S. T. Coleridge" (de Selincourt 1); if he could not share the role of poet-prophet, he would at least become the audience: it would be Wordsworth for God only, Coleridge for God in him. Yet is it too radical to see in Wordsworth's closing apostrophes to Coleridge this element of irony? Why the choice of the "Ancient Mariner," a poem controversial in its publication in 1798, and "Christabel," controversial in its being dropped from publication in 1800?[16] And what special reasons might Wordsworth have had in mentioning, for his part, only "The Idiot Boy" and "The Thorn"?

Jonathan Wordsworth's suggestion that "Coleridge would enjoy the humour and self-mockery" (*NP* 480) of the allusions to his friend's poems may be true, but it is possible that Wordsworth had a more serious purpose in mind. He might have wished to point up certain common elements in each pair of poems—the "rueful woes" (14.400) of Christabel and the "misery" (14.407) of Martha Ray; or the Idiot Boy's "perils of his moonlight ride" (14.405) and the Ancient Mariner's even stranger journey. But equally he might have wished to stress the differences between these pairs, especially the two different approaches which he and Coleridge took in their collaboration on the *Lyrical Ballads*. In his discussion of this very matter years later in Chapter 14 of the *Biographia Literaria*, Coleridge writes how in 1797

> the thought suggested itself . . . that a series of poems might be composed of two sorts. In the one, the incidents and agents were to be, in part at least, supernatural. . . . For the second class, subjects were to be chosen from ordinary life; the characters and incidents were to be such as will be found in every village. . . . (168)

Coleridge elaborates on this generic distinction and on the corresponding division of labor:

> . . . it was agreed that my endeavours should be directed to persons and characters supernatural, or at least romantic. . . . Mr. Wordsworth, on the other hand, was to propose to himself as his object to give the charm of novelty to things of every day. . . . (168–69)

Coleridge's description corroborates Wordsworth's allusion to their collaboration. The four poems that Wordsworth mentions divide themselves into these two categories. The "incidents and agents" in the "Ancient Mariner" and "Christabel" are, "in part at least, supernatural," and the "persons and characters . . . at least romantic"; "the characters and incidents" in "The Idiot Boy" are "such as [might] be found in every village"; and the "object" of "The Thorn," from this point of view, is "to give the charm of novelty to things of every day"—or, as Wordsworth said in the Isabella Fenwick note to the poem, to make the thorn permanently as impressive as a passing storm had made it to him (Brett and Jones 290).

As far as his characterization in *The Prelude* is concerned, Coleridge is more than just the once and future "joint labourer"; he is also a joint traveler who is included in Wordsworth's numerous first-person plural constructions. The opening of Book 9 provides a representative example:

> Even as a river . . .
> Turns, and will measure back his course, far back,
> Seeking the very regions which he crossed
> In his first outset; so have we, my Friend!
> Turned and returned with intricate delay.
> Or as a traveller . . .
> . . . is tempted to review
> The region left behind him . . .
> So have we lingered. Now we start afresh
> With courage, and new hope risen on our toil.
> (9.1–17)

Of the three or four epic similes contained in *The Prelude*,[17] two are juxtaposed here ("Even as a river"; "Or as a traveller"), and the repetition of "so have we . . . / So have we" concludes the extended analogy each time. Even though Wordsworth at points emphasizes his solitary course which no one can share—"Here must thou be, O Man! / Power to thyself; no Helper hast thou here" (14.209–10)—and despite the allusions to Coleridge's physical absence—"wandered now in search of health" (6.240) to Malta and Sicily, or "seeking oft the haunts of men" (2.468) in London—the figure of Coleridge is always present to the imagination of the poet: "But thou art with us, with us in the past, / The present, with us in the times to come" (6.242–43).

Coleridge's journey differs from Wordsworth's, yet it discontinuously crosses and recrosses the poet's narrative, leading to a common terminus: "But we," Wordsworth writes, "by different roads, at length have gained / The self-same bourne" (2.453–54). The crucial difference between the two roads lies in their respective points of origin: Wordsworth's begins with the "natal murmur" (14.196) inside the mother, which becomes externalized in the River Derwent, but Coleridge's begins, as Wordsworth notes on a number of occasions, "in the great city" (2.452), "in the depths / Of the huge city" (6.266–67), in "the heart / Of London" (6.278–79). Yet despite the alleged disadvantages of a city childhood, and the images of Coleridge placed "in the depths" of urban confinement, he is not utterly beyond the pale of redemption through nature; he can still, "by internal light" (6.271) see his "native stream, / Far distant, thus beheld from year to year / Of a long exile" (6.272–74); he has, moreover, served "in Nature's temple" (2.463) as "the most assiduous of her ministers" (2.464).

Coleridge begins in the city, then, but he can still remember a prior beginning in nature. The first extended apostrophe to him alludes to this origin and its implied destination. "I, too, have been a wanderer," writes Wordsworth in Book 6,

> but alas!
> How different the fate of different men.
> Though mutually unknown, yea nursed and reared
> As if in several elements, we were framed
> To bend at last to the same discipline,
> Predestined, if two beings ever were,
> To seek the same delights, and have one health,
> One happiness.
> (6.252–59)

It is relevant here to note Reeve Parker's analysis of the allusions to "Lycidas" in this and the later apostrophes to Coleridge (Parker 222–38), and to add that while Milton's "uncouth swain" ("Lycidas" 186) and Lycidas "were nurst upon the self-same hill" (23), Wordsworth and Coleridge were "nursed and reared / As if in several elements." Interestingly, Wordsworth and the "Maid of Buttermere" in Book 7 of the 1805 *Prelude* are described as being much closer to the model of Lycidas and the "uncouth swain":

> For we were nursed, as almost might be said,
> On the same mountains; children at one time
> Must haply often on the self-same day
> Have from our several dwellings gone abroad
> To gather daffodils on Coker's stream.
> (1805:7.341–45)

When Wordsworth revised MS D in 1832 or 1839 he added the "Lycidas" allusion to the passage from Book 6 dealing with Coleridge; the same allusion in the "Maid of Buttermere" passage still stands in MS E, though with this marginal note: "Revise this page and the next"—that is, lines 334–40 and 341–70 of 1805 (see de Selincourt 188–89, 238–39, xxii-xxiii). Although one cannot say for certain with the present evidence, the suggestion is that the introduction of the Coleridge-Lycidas echo displaced the Buttermere-Lycidas allusion, much as the "Stygian Pool" echo in the opening of Book 1 displaced the allusions to Samson and the Hebrews. As well, the foregrounding of the expression "as almost might be said," which calls attention to the intertextual status of the comparison, is dropped when Wordsworth inserts the echo in the Coleridge passage, as if, having acknowledged the borrowing once, he were free to use it again without acknowledgment. The propriety of the "Lycidas" allusions to Coleridge becomes clearer in larger structural terms: while Milton's poem moves from present separation through a remembered unity to a regenerate sense of harmony symbolized in the "sweet Societies" (179) in heaven, Wordsworth's and Coleridge's twin journeys move from a former separation toward an inevitable, if deferred, intersection: "one health, / One happiness."

Such union was not to be at Cambridge, as Wordsworth left the University eight months before Coleridge arrived. Having taken his "retrospect / Of . . . collegiate life" (6.286–87), Wordsworth laments Coleridge's "stormy course" (6.281) at Jesus College—his "ten thousand hopes, / For ever withered," as the 1805 version reads (295–96). Recounting Coleridge's biography, Wordsworth compares himself as narrator to

> a man, who, when his house is built,
> A frame locked up in wood and stone, doth still,
> As impotent fancy prompts, by his fireside,
> Rebuild it to his liking.
> (6.291–94)

This passage is yet another declaration of the poem's rhetoricity, its self-proclaimed non-referential nature. The poet's dismantling and rebuilding of Coleridge's life, like "a frame locked up," remains a function of the "impotent fancy" which can use only "fixities and definites" (*Biographia* 167). The fancy is thus "impotent" in an objective or referential sense because it does not actually alter the object, the substantial thing made of "wood and stone." The rebuilding, however, goes on despite it. Wordsworth plays "with times / And accidents as children do with cards" (6.289–90)—shuffling them, arranging them in patterns, building them into houses. Language's potential for fictiveness, for playing with the "accidents" of life, is realized in the following lines that impose a different set of accidents on Coleridge. His mind is

> Debarred from Nature's living images,
> Compelled to be a life unto herself . . .
> (6.302–03)

—in which the parallel, repeated iambic stress of "Debarred" and "Compelled" tragically pronounces Coleridge's sentence. But Wordsworth's fancy then images what might have been:

had we met,
Even at that early time, needs must I trust
In the belief, that my maturer age,
My calmer habits, and more steady voice,
Would with an influence benign have soothed,
Or chased away, the airy wretchedness
That battened on thy youth.
(6.308–14)

Here we are close, not to what Geoffrey Hartman in another context has called a "genre of surmise" (*WP* 8–12), but rather a genre of remorse, or at least of "vain regrets" (6.316) prompted by an "impotent fancy." Wordsworth's rhetoric oscillates between recalling apocalyptic hopes for Coleridge and then emphasizing that they are forever gone; he begins climactically with praise of Coleridge's "learning, gorgeous eloquence, / And all the strength and plumage of [his] youth" (6.295–96), and then finishes with a lament over the self-frustrating and lonely aspects of a mind starved of human acceptance, "and unrelentingly possessed by thirst / Of greatness, love, and beauty" (6.304–05). But Coleridge is not left in such straits. Wordsworth inevitably images him first in dejection; but even as the Lord throws down therefore that He may raise, each apostrophe ends with Coleridge's restoration, his being set upright again—a process that takes for its model Wordsworth's own regeneration through the "spots of time," which "lift us up when fallen" (12.218). Here in Book 6 the typical pattern of fall and restoration is completed with a consoling, if not entirely redemptive, gesture from Wordsworth: "But thou hast trod / A march of glory, which doth put to shame / These vain regrets" (6.314–16).

But Coleridge, as the negative double of Wordsworth himself, remains limited in his role as a failed quester who is proleptically restored. The pattern is repeated in Book 11, in which Coleridge is again cast into exile, symbolized by his visit to Sicily, but is offered "a ladder for [his] spirit to reascend / To health and joy and pure contentedness" (11.397–98). He is imagined to stand, finally, "on Etna's summit" (11.454). The climbing of a mountain, recalling Wordsworth's expedition across the Alps in Book 6 and all its apocalyptic associations, prepares the way for an ambiguous passage that follows:

Oh! wrap him in your shades, ye giant woods,
On Etna's side; and thou, O flowery field

Of Enna! is there not some nook of thine,
From the first playtime of the infant world
Kept sacred to restorative delight,
When from afar invoked by anxious love?
(11.418–23)

Surely what Wordsworth intends here is an image of Coleridge in the benevolent embrace of nature, rather like Wordsworth's own love-making in *Home at Grasmere*: "Embrace me then, ye Hills, and close me in" (110). Yet despite the ostensibly generous wish for Coleridge's restoration, the business of being wrapped in Etna's "shades" has a distinctly darker side, closer to death and mummification than to life and restoration. What textual support is there for this reading?

The references to Etna go back some forty lines to Wordsworth's lament for Sicily. Apostrophizing Coleridge, Wordsworth writes how his poem is

A story destined for thy ear, who now,
Among the fallen of nations, dost abide
Where Etna, over hill and valley, casts
His shadow, stretching toward Syracuse,
The city of Timoleon! Righteous Heaven!
How are the mighty prostrated!
(11.375–80)

Wordsworth's experience in France during the Revolution is compared to Coleridge's experience in Sicily and, as the "gratulant" (14.387) mythos requires, Wordsworth and France come out ahead of Coleridge and Sicily. "If I suffered grief / For ill-requited France," Wordsworth says to Coleridge, "a far more sober cause / Thine eyes must see" now in Sicily (11.383–84; 387–88). Coleridge "do[th] abide / Where Etna . . . casts / His shadow"; this "shadow" over him later turns into the "shades" of the "giant woods" around him, but he is finally characterized as both physically and intellectually transcending these enclosing shadows and shades:

thou wilt stand
On Etna's summit, above earth and sea,
Triumphant, winning from the invaded heavens
Thoughts without bound. . . .
(11.453–56)

Reeve Parker has argued that the analogy underlying this sustained apostrophe to Coleridge is again to be found in "Lycidas," in the fate of a promising poet drowned but eventually resurrected (221–38). In these terms, Coleridge's experience in the poem repeats Wordsworth's own experience—indeed, the rhetorical structure of *The Prelude* as a whole—which we have been tracing through the trope of collaboration. But the "analogue of the drowned poet," Parker argues (228), is also adapted by Wordsworth on the model of some of Coleridge's meditative poems, specifically "This Lime-Tree Bower, My Prison," and "Frost at Midnight." Wordsworth takes up the temporal structure of these poems (the present-past-future shifts that he appropriates at the beginning of *The Prelude*) and "quietly superimpos[es] their shape and gestures on his adaptation of Miltonic elegy" (223). The result is that Coleridge "heard *The Prelude* as an elegy for himself, an elegy he had helped shape" (221).

Such an argument raises interesting intertextual questions. What Parker calls a process of "superimposing" is in fact achieved by a technique of allusion, by Wordsworth's invoking specific texts as well as particular structural patterns and conventions of genre. The trope of "superimposing" introduces problematic spatial and temporal hierarchies—how can Parker be certain that the conversation poem is mapped onto the elegy and not the other way around?—which in turn lead to an evaluative hierarchy: the passage is "'un-Wordsworthian' in style and digressive from the poem's central concerns" (227). "Agile as imitation and resourceful in analogy," Parker concludes, this passage "nevertheless does not go beyond deft literary pastiche" (227). The more important question here, however, is not which genre comes first, the elegy or the conversation poem, nor whether Wordsworth's apostrophe is 'un-Wordsworthian,' but how elegy and apostrophe are accommodated in a text that is hardly "pastiche."

I have already suggested that the structural placement of this extended address to Coleridge is significant for its relation to Wordsworth's resolution of his own traumatic involvement in France (books 9 to 11). The pattern that Wordsworth has just completed—triumphantly too—is transferred by him to Coleridge, whose success is somewhat uncertain, and not only because it is anticipatory and not retrospective. Even in the 1850 edition, when the narrative point of view of Coleridge's visit to Sicily is retrospective, the tentativeness remains. But if we return to the image of being wrapped in Etna's shades, another pattern emerges. The elegiac tone of the apostrophe to Coleridge is confirmed by the unarguable echoes of "Lycidas":

> To me the grief confined, that thou art gone
> From this last spot of earth . . .
> A lonely wanderer art gone, by pain
> Compelled and sickness, at this latter day,
> This sorrowful reverse for all mankind.
> (11.399–404)

In 1805 the last line reads: "This heavy time of change for all mankind" (10.986). The source in "Lycidas" is familiar enough:

> But O the heavy change, now thou art gone,
> Now thou art gone, and never must return!
> (37–38)

Immediately one is tempted to point out that while Lycidas is "gone" because he is dead, Coleridge is gone because he is "a lonely wanderer." Yet a leave-taking is a little like death, Donne has taught us, and Wordsworth seems to recur to the death-like aspects of Coleridge's absence. The lines following the imperative to the "giant woods" to "wrap" the "lonely wanderer"—much as Wordsworth was "enwrapped" as a "lonely traveller" in the Alps (6.595–96)—pose a question which could be interpreted either literally or figurally:

> thou, O flowery field
> Of Enna! is there not some nook of thine,
> From the first playtime of the infant world
> Kept sacred to restorative delight
> When from afar invoked by anxious love?
> (11.419–23)

The reference to the "flowery field / Of Enna" recalls Milton from Book 4 of *Paradise Lost:*

> Not that fair field
> Of Enna, where Proserpin gath'ring flow'rs
> Herself a fairer Flow'r by gloomy Dis
> Was gather'd, which cost Ceres all that pain
> To seek her through the world. . . .
> . . . might with this Paradise
> Of Eden strive.
> (4.268–75)

The rape of Proserpina by "gloomy Dis" is perhaps an eccentric allusion, yet it is consistent with Wordsworth's descent-and-reascent motif; Proserpina gathering flowers is herself gathered by Dis and carried below to his shades of death. Thus Wordsworth's question "is there not some nook . . . Kept sacred to restorative delight?" can be stripped of any "rhetorical" intention by being interpreted literally: no, there is no nook kept sacred, as Ceres herself discovered on her quest in "all that pain / To seek her [daughter] through the world."

Yet there might, after all, just be one "nook" for "restorative delight": Grasmere, the poet's "chosen Vale." Read now as erotesis, as rhetorical question rather than literal interrogative, Wordsworth's inquiry asserts what it seems to ask: the field of Enna in myth cannot "strive" with Eden, nor can the actual Enna in Sicily compare with the actual Grasmere. The sacred nook is not to be found on the "flowery field / Of Enna"; if it exists at all, it can only be "invoked" by an "anxious love" that comes "from afar." The reference to distance that Wordsworth introduced for 1850 emphasizes the contrast between speaker and addressee, between the "calm fireside" (11.450) in Grasmere and the "pain / . . . and sickness" (11.402–03) in Sicily. Imaged in solitude and sickness, Coleridge is nevertheless offered a means of grace to restore himself. The offer takes the characteristic Wordsworthian form of a *benedictus*:

> Thine be such converse strong and sanative,
> A ladder for thy spirit to reascend
> To health and joy and pure contentedness;
> To me the grief confined, that thou art gone
> From this last spot of earth. . . .
> (11.396–400)

The phrase "this last spot of earth," to which one may compare *Home at Grasmere*'s "fairest spot of earth" (73), recalls Adam's description in *Paradise Lost*, Book 8, of "this Earth a spot" (17) or "this punctual spot" of Eden (23):[18] again the implication is that Paradise has shrunk to the poet's chosen vale, from which Coleridge is exiled. "Dejection: An Ode" anticipates such myth-making in its characterization of Coleridge with his "viper thoughts" (94) as the Satanic *spectator ab extra* of the Edenic circle of William, Dorothy, and Mary.

If Wordsworth's lament for Coleridge as "a lonely wanderer" contains associations of death in the assonant allusions to Etna and Enna, then the echoes of "Lycidas" tend to support such a reading. But there are other references that conjure up similar associations.

The thought of Sicily brings a dark train of imagery to the poet's mind, including Empedocles, Archimedes, Theocritus, Comates: the first committed suicide by jumping into the volcano of Etna; the second was murdered in Syracuse as he was preoccupied with his abstruse research; and Theocritus writes about the strange imprisonment of Comates in a chest. Apostrophizing Theocritus, Wordsworth says that

> not unmoved,
> When thinking on my own beloved friend,
> I hear thee tell how bees with honey fed
> Divine Comates. . . .
> (11.441–44)

Thinking on these suicides and victims, and "thinking on [his] own beloved friend," Wordsworth writes, "thus I soothe / The pensive moments by this calm fireside" (11.449–50). This comes as a surprising admission, no less equivocal than the accumulation of allusive imagery dealing with death and imprisonment. Yet one must surely agree with Parker that "Wordsworth's intent was not, of course, to bury Coleridge" (221). Nevertheless, Coleridge himself seems to have made this darkly ironic interpretation, responding to the elegiac tone of these passages in his poem "To William Wordsworth," in which he draws his self-characterization on the model of Milton's drowned poet. Wordsworth's reading of *The Prelude*, Coleridge says, revived him "even as Life returns upon the drowned" (63); all the "throng of pains" that the poem rekindles are

> but flowers
> Strewed on my corse, and borne upon my bier
> In the same coffin, for the self-same grave!
> (73–75)

The pattern of fall and restoration is transposed into a movement of death and resurrection, intertextually invoking from "Lycidas" the "wat'ry bier" (12) and the "self-same hill" (23) that is now become a "grave." Coleridge, dead, buried, and wrapped in Etna's shades, is nevertheless given his apotheosis:

> Our prayers have been accepted; thou wilt stand
> On Etna's summit, above earth and sea,
> Triumphant . . .
> (11.453–55)

—not as "a captive pining for his home" (11.470), Wordsworth continues, as Proserpina was a captive, or as Comates was a captive, but as a "glad votary" (11.469) beside some pastoral spring. Coleridge is metonymically associated as a "votary" with the antique temples of Sicily, which "in their ruins yet / Survive for inspiration" (11.462–63). Coleridge, surviving yet as inspiration for *The Recluse*, is given the fragments of a redemptive mythos to shore against his personal ruins.[19]

This second extended apostrophe to Coleridge appears after Wordsworth has been "tracing faithfully / The workings of [his] youthful mind" (1805:10.942–43)—which is revised in MS A, in order to strengthen the Miltonic affiliation of the text, to "the perturbations of a youthful mind" (1850:11.372). The echo is of *The Reason of Church Government*, Second Book, in which Milton prescribes his theory of poetry—specifically, that the cathartic function of poetry, as distinct from its ethical and celebratory functions, is "to allay the perturbations of the mind and set the affections in right tune" (Milton 669).[20] Wordsworth's perturbations, which he hopes to allay through his poetry, refer, not least, to his frustrating experience in the French Revolution, his separation from Annette, the war between England and France, the Reign of Terror, his personal uncertainty of vocation, and finally the perversion of what he calls, echoing his play *The Borderers* (line 1496), an "independent intellect" (11.244)—that is, the neurotically aggravated dissociation of a sensibility independent of or cut off from the human affections which should be recomposed and set "in right tune" through the spontaneous overflow of powerful feelings recollected in initial tranquillity.

The rhythm of perturbation and regeneration begins in the first book, in which Wordsworth is frustrated in his search for a poetic voice:

> How strange that all
> The terrors, pains, and early miseries,
> Regrets, vexations, lassitudes interfused
> Within my mind, should e'er have borne a part,
> And that a needful part, in making up
> The calm existence that is mine when I
> Am worthy of myself!
> (1.344–50)

Typically, the passage begins in "terrors, pains, and . . . miseries" and ends in a "calm existence," while being suspended in a rhetorical scheme that questions and surprises itself: "How strange . . . !"

This same rhythm in part governs the larger rhetorical structure of *The Prelude*, although it becomes attenuated in the books on France, coming almost to a halt in Book 11. "This was the crisis of that strong disease," Wordsworth writes of his own psychic vexation, "this the soul's last and lowest ebb" (11.306–07). But out of the depths of this descent come two ascents, two restorations: Coleridge's apotheosis on Etna, as we have seen, and Wordsworth's growth toward a regenerate humanism, to which we now turn.[21]

The pattern of experience described in the books on France can be read as *The Prelude*'s tragic downward movement, corresponding in its crucial structural placement and thematic relevance to Milton's tragic notes in Book 9 and following in *Paradise Lost*. But *The Prelude* does not end with "the soul's last and lowest ebb" in Book 11 (307); Book 12 follows, with its regenerated version of the opening of Book 1 (Wordsworth reprises his address to the breeze at 12.9–12), and the symbolic return to beginnings. The comic upturn of the last three books treats the process of restoration explicitly, as Milton had treated it implicitly, with the speaker's imagination (as the title of Book 12 puts it) "impaired and restored." There is another tragic movement in the poem, however, that Wordsworth attempts to reverse with lucky words. The tragic isolation of Coleridge, with his mind "compelled to be a life unto herself" (6.603), is countered by Wordsworth's numerous apostrophes in which he seeks to include him in a human community. Coleridge's self-description in an early version of "Dejection" as "a wither'd branch upon a blossoming Tree" (Heath 484) suggests, in the vehicle of the metaphor, a naturalistic tragedy, but in fact his failure to find in nature the anchor of his purest thoughts fits into a larger human context of experience. If we attempt to locate what Harold Bloom first called the "hidden tragedy" of *The Prelude* (*Visionary Company* 155), not in a dialectic of Imagination and Nature but, as Ross Woodman has suggested, in Coleridge's "failure to bind" his imagination to nature ("Imagination as Theme" 413), then we begin to see how Wordsworth's restorative function contributes to the poem's comic movement. But the tragic element is not a deficient experience in nature, a mere "failure to bind" the mind to rocks and stones and trees. The real tragedy of *The Prelude* is Coleridge's tragedy, and it ultimately resides in his failure to participate harmoniously in a human community in which he is truly, and not just nominally, a "joint labourer."

The structural pattern of the poem's historical and rhetorical collaboration forms a massively balanced whole. *The Prelude* opens with a release from hell and closes with a vision of two paradises. It begins with a double image of Adam and Eve poised to leave Paradise, with the world all before them; and with Wordsworth, similarly poised in his effort to "fix the wavering balance of [his] mind" (1.622) and begin his "work / Of glory" (1.78–79). It ends with Adam and Eve as they resume their journey toward man's deliverance; and with Wordsworth as he and his "joint labourers" set about their analogous task. What happens in between these simultaneous, frozen images of the "halted travelers," to adapt Geoffrey Hartman's thesis (see *WP* 1), is Wordsworth's "rigorous inquisition" (1.148) of his own imaginative powers, the vital gifts necessary to sustain and consecrate the journey-poem, whose course lies through both solitary landscapes and human communities, and whose destination is the "self-same bourne" (2.454) as that which its auditor-traveler has struggled to reach: a paradise within, "of quality and fabric more divine" (14.454).

V

So far, the concern in this chapter has been to elucidate the rhetorical function of intertextual echoes and allusions on stylistic, thematic, and structural grounds. Wordsworth's figurative glances at Milton at the beginning and the end of *The Prelude* have been shown to act as strong structural supports of the poem's developing mythos, while his numerous other allusions and apostrophes to Shakespeare, to Coleridge, and to himself and his own poetry provide a rhetorical context in which this structure stands defined. But the question of structural intertextuality needs to be examined more closely here, and its implications for the figurative pattern of *The Prelude* as a whole now deserve attention.

It would not be new to suggest that the structural pattern of *The Prelude* adapts that of *Paradise Lost*, or even some aspects of *Paradise Regained*. Abbie Findlay Potts made such a suggestion in 1953 in her study of *The Prelude*'s literary form (305–37); and more recently B. Rajan has sketched the outlines of an argument for "the structural presence of *Paradise Lost* in *The Prelude*" (ix). A systematic examination of correspondences from book to book, or from episode to episode, has never been undertaken, and it is outside our scope to attempt it here. We may, however, note again in passing the frequent observation that *The Prelude* seems to pick up where *Paradise Lost* leaves off in its progressive movement toward a regenerated paradise whose foundations are "within," that is, imaginative rather than actual.[22] Despite M. H. Abrams's claim that *Home at Grasmere*, and not *The Prelude*, is the proper sequel to *Paradise Lost* (*NS* 115–16), the allusive gesturings of Wordsworth's "glad preamble" make it difficult for a reader not to "dovetail," in Edith Sewell's words, Wordsworth's epic into Milton's (342). Similarly, readers have noted how Book 9 of *The Prelude* self-consciously changes its notes to tragic "as if," Geoffrey Hartman writes, "*The Prelude* again were synchronized with *Paradise Lost*" (*WP* 243; see also Potts 323; B. Rajan ix).

Book 7 provides another example. Wordsworth begins the book with a retrospective glance toward his "glad preamble" and a preview of the "tamer argument, / That lies before us, needful to be told" (7.50–51). His two-way prospect recalls Milton's corresponding view in the opening paragraph of Book 7 of *Paradise Lost*, where he surveys his progress through the first six books and declares: "Half yet remains unsung, but narrower bound / Within the visible Diurnal Sphere" (7.21–22). The thematic correspondence between Wordsworth's "tamer argument" and the "narrower bound" argument of Milton is noteworthy, but more interesting in structural terms is how these narrative pauses create a strategic fulcrum between two halves of a "self-balanc't" (*PL* 7.242) whole. *The Prelude*'s balance is more precarious because of its shifting organization from thirteen to fourteen books, but its rhetoric nevertheless invites intertextual juxtaposition with *Paradise Lost*. In addition, the two texts have affiliations here through their similar tropes suggesting the dangers of a poetics of voice—Milton fears to go "hoarse or mute" (7.25), while Wordsworth's song has been "not audible" (7.11)—and their images of ascent and descent, from heaven to earth, and from the Alps to London.

These examples demonstrate that at crucial points in Wordsworth's text the language of Milton's epic is invoked to call attention to the way in which the two structures parallel or coincide with each other. If language points to structure, structure points to theme, and though it is possible, as we saw with verbal echoes, for a structural allusion to invoke another text's organization in order to derange or subvert that organization, Wordsworth's structural allusions to *Paradise Lost* also receive collaborative support from their corresponding structural patterns. A structural allusion need not be the same as a structural parallel; displacements and inversions can be used for rhetorical as well as thematic effects. But what can be learned about intertextuality from observing how the structural pattern of a text changes?

Here again Milton comes to mind, as *Paradise Lost* was significantly altered in structural emphasis by being changed from ten books in 1667 to twelve books in 1674. *The Prelude* (leaving aside the two- and five-book versions), underwent a structural shift from thirteen books in 1805 to fourteen by 1850. In both cases the alteration meant primarily a shift of emphasis, not a rearrangement or substantial expansion of material. The 1850 *Prelude* omits the story of the lost shepherd boy in Book 8 (approximately 89 lines) and the romance of Vaudracour and Julia in Book 9 (some 379 lines, published separately in 1820), and adds the lines on the Convent of Chartreuse (6.420–88) and the genius of Burke (7.512–43), but aside from these revisions there are no significant structural alterations.

The most convincing treatment of Milton's reworking of *Paradise Lost* from ten books into twelve, and the one best suited for rhetorical application to the situation of *The Prelude*, is Arthur E. Barker's essay "Structural Pattern in *Paradise Lost*," in which Barker argues that each of Milton's important poems "assumes as one of its points of departure a tradition of interpretation and a convention of form" (143). The formal convention of *Paradise Lost* is two-fold, dramatic and epic, and what Milton did by dividing books 7 and 10 into into books 7 and 8 and books 11 and 12, Barker states, was to bring his poem into alignment with Virgilian epic form as well as to transform it from a simple five-act structure with the climax at Satan's triumph over Adam and Eve to a new five-act structure that shifted the attention from tragedy to divine comedy: "The purpose of the redivision," Barker writes, was "to reduce the structural emphasis on the Fall of man and to increase the emphasis on his restoration" (151).

What is the analogous situation with *The Prelude*? Within the ten-book *Paradise Lost* there was at least the recognizable form of the drama, with each act composed of two books, but a thirteen-book poem is only a baggy monster, just a bit too big for classical epic and with too few arithmetical possibilities for alternate figural patterns. The twelve-book Virgilian pattern, Barker shows, has three possible arrangements: three movements of four books apiece, six groups of two books apiece, and two movements of six books each (143, 151). Clearly a thirteen-book structure has no such geometric potential, but then what advantage does a fourteen-book poem have in this regard? Two movements of seven books each, and seven pairs of books: not particularly versatile possibilities. Why fourteen books?

It is known that Wordsworth, like Milton, had an inclination toward architectonic metaphors: *The Prelude*, he said, was like the "ante-chapel" to "the body of a gothic church" (*Prose* 3:5); in his letters he refers to it as "a sort of portico to the Recluse, part of the building" (*EY* 594). In *The Prelude* itself Wordsworth speaks "of that interminable building reared / By observation of affinities / In objects where no brotherhood exists / To passive minds" (2.383–86). We have already seen Wordsworth's architectonic troping of Coleridge's life in Book 6.289–94, and we might note, among many other examples, the astonishing description of the visionary city at the end of the second book of *The Excursion*. Specific architectural tropes also shade into larger, more general considerations. The structural pattern of Wordsworth's entire *oeuvre* contains, as Ernest de Selincourt once ironically pointed out, "a Prelude to the main theme and an Excursion from it" (*PW* 5:368). The pattern, despite the irony given it by historical circumstances, involves a series of progressively developed movements: the first is a preliminary advance (*The Prelude*) toward a defined center (Grasmere, the "Centre . . . Made for itself, and happy in itself" [*Home at Grasmere* 148]); the second is the arrival at that center and the taking up of residence there (*Home at Grasmere*); and the third is a corresponding swing away from the center in a new direction (*The Excursion*). A fourth movement, always implied but never attained, involves a return to a regenerated center by a regenerated traveler who sees and knows the place for the first time.

If Wordsworth was able to impose this kind of balanced structure on the curve of his career and to claim, as he did in the 1814 Preface, that each work had its appropriate place within the presiding edifice, like cells and oratories within a Gothic church (*Prose* 3:5–6), then it may be reasonable to assume that his concern for overall form is matched by an equal degree of attention to the shape of individual texts, and that, therefore, his final choice of fourteen books for *The Prelude*, like Milton's twelve for *Paradise Lost*, is meaningful.

What, then, is the meaning of the fourteen-book structure of *The Prelude*? One answer, first suggested by Donald H. Reiman, is that it resembles the structure of a fourteen-line Italian sonnet.[23] According to this pattern, Reiman states, books 1 through 8 constitute the octave; books 9 through 14 constitute the sestet, with books 9, 10, and 11 as one tercet, and books 12, 13, and 14 as another. *The Prelude* invites us to consider its formal organization specifically in terms of the Petrarchan double movement of eight and six books each, or, rather, three movements of eight, three, and three books apiece: Book 8 is entitled "Retrospect," and is a fitting conclusion to the octave of the poem; books 9 to 11 are on France, and act as a distinct narrative unit; books 12 to 14 pull out of the experience of the French Revolution and focus on the restoration of imagination.

Although Reiman describes his idea of the "macro-sonnet" structure of *The Prelude* as "somewhat unorthodox" ("Beauty" 148), other hermeneutical heretics share his view. In his study of "embedded" sonnets in *The Prelude*, Clifford Siskin supports his case for Wordsworth's attempt "to integrate parts into wholes" by pointing to "a sonnet embedded in a Sonnet" (151). Lee M. Johnson has also focused on sonnet structures within the blank-verse form of *The Prelude* (28). Certainly *The Prelude* as sonnet is an intriguing notion, not only because of the way it explains in arithmetically plausible terms the disposition of fourteen books, but because of what it implies about the poem's other formal aspects. Conventionally (though for neither Wordsworth nor Milton) the sonnet is a young poet's verse form: the demands of its highly structured, highly controlled yet liberating form make it a suitable training ground for artists learning their craft. But the first time that the entire *Prelude* is divided into fourteen books occurs in MS D (de Selincourt xxiii; *NP* 391, 522), which suggests that the division took place in 1832, when Wordsworth was hardly either young or learning his craft. Was the change from thirteen to fourteen books an afterthought on Wordsworth's part, a whimsical tinkering with external form, or did Wordsworth come to see certain inevitabilities in his great work which were obscured by its asymmetrical thirteen-book form? These are essentially the questions that Arthur

Barker had to ask of Milton's analogous tinkering in 1674: "What cause . . . ?" (144).

It seems logical to speculate with Jeffrey Baker that Wordsworth never would have allowed the 1805 *Prelude* to pass the press (84), though his reasons for refusing might have had as much to do with structure as with style. The division of Book 10 (1805) into books 10 and 11 in 1832 appears strangely mechanical, as it imposes a new and arbitrary organization on a work substantially completed more than a quarter of a century earlier. From this point of view, Wordsworth's structural revision is hardly significant, nothing more than numerical coincidence between a fourteen-line sonnet and a fourteen-book epic.

Yet there is some manuscript evidence to suggest that a fourteen-book poem is what Wordsworth might have had in mind right from the moment he decided to expand his five-book *Prelude* of 1804.[24] MS Z contains a copy of what in the 1805 version are books 11 and 12, but the significant difference is that these books are already numbered 12 and 13. Ernest de Selincourt thought that the numerical designations had a particular interest:

> The headings *Book 12th* and *Book 13th* suggest that originally Book X of A was divided into two as it was in 1850, and that the division found in D and E was a reversion to the older plan. (xxxii)

J. C. Maxwell closely echoes de Selincourt in his assessment of the book numberings:

> The use of the headings 'Book Twelfth' and 'Book Thirteenth' in accordance with the 1850, not the 1805, division, suggest[s] that the 1850 division of Book X was a reversion to the original plan. (21)

Jonathan Wordsworth reaches a similar conclusion:

> The division of *1805*, X, into *1850*, X and XI, occurs in *MS D* of 1832, but on the evidence of *MS Z* (April–May 1805) seems to be a return to the original pattern of December 1805. (*NP* 391)

If we accept the implications of MS Z, then it is tempting to say that Wordsworth might have perceived or intended the sonnet structure of *The Prelude* as early as December 1804 or early 1805, which would place his realization not long after the period in which he first (with the exception of an early attempt) discovered and experimented with the sonnet form. Dorothy gives a revealing account of Wordsworth's first attempt at writing sonnets: "Friday 21st May [1802]. A very warm gentle morning—a little rain. Wm wrote two sonnets on Buonaparte after I had read Milton's sonnets to him" (*Journals* 127). Wordsworth's own account, while mistaking the date, elaborates the details:

> In the cottage, Town-End, Grasmere, one afternoon in 1801 [sic], my sister read to me the sonnets of Milton. I had long been well acquainted with them, but I was particularly struck on that occasion with the dignified simplicity and majestic harmony that runs through most of them—in character so totally different from the Italian, and still more so from Shakespeare's fine sonnets. I took fire, if I may be allowed to say so, and produced three sonnets the same afternoon, the first I ever wrote except an irregular one at school. (*PW* 3:417)

To suggest a relation between the form of the Miltonic sonnet and the structure of *The Prelude* would be to experience intertextuality in a daring way. Yet other Wordsworthian texts advertise a similar structural reflexiveness: his "Sonnets Upon the Punishment of Death" (*Poems* 2:822–28) comprise thirteen sonnets in series—one for each step in the gallows—and a final sonnet of apology to make fourteen sonnets, or one macro-sonnet.[25] Whatever thematic organization might be created within the series, there is always the supervening formal structure of fourteen poems with fourteen lines apiece.

Wordsworth is also on record for distinguishing the style and structure of the Miltonic sonnet from the Petrarchan or Italian form. In 1833, writing to Alexander Dyce to give him some advice on an anthology he was proposing to publish, Wordsworth demonstrates his sensitivity as a close reader:

> It should seem that the Sonnet, like every other legitimate composition, ought to have a beginning, a middle, and an end—in other words, to consist of three parts, like the three propositions of a syllogism, if such an illustration may be used. But the frame of metre adopted by the Italians does not accord with this view, and, as adhered to by them, it seems to be, if not arbitrary, best fitted to a division of the sense into two parts, of eight and six lines each. Milton, however, has not submitted to this. In the better half of his sonnets the sense does not close with the rhyme at the eighth line, but overflows into the second portion of the metre. Now it has

> struck me, that this is not done merely to gratify the ear by variety and freedom of sound, but also to aid in giving that pervading sense of intense Unity in which the excellence of the Sonnet has always seemed to me to consist. Instead of looking at this composition as a piece of architecture, making a whole out of three parts, I have been much in the habit of preferring the image of an orbicular body—a sphere—or a dew-drop. All this will appear a little fanciful; and I am well aware that a Sonnet will often be found excellent, where the beginning, the middle, and the end are distinctly marked, and also where it is distinctly separated into *two* parts, to which, as I before observed, the strict Italian model, as they write it, is favorable. (*LY* 1:604–05)

Wordsworth admires the overflow of "sense" from octave to sestet, a characteristic of "the better half" of Milton's sonnets, as giving formal unity to the organization of a poem—like a dew-drop—and yet he recognizes that unity can be achieved whether the structure is ternary or binary. *The Prelude* as dew-drop exhibits a special coherence, a unity that is both binary (eight books plus six books) and syllogistic (imagination called forth, imagination lost, imagination regained). Though Wordsworth is often thought of as using primarily the Miltonic form, the one sonnet which it is certain he did compose soon after hearing Milton's sonnets read to him ("I Grieved for Buonaparté") has a separate octave and sestet, without syntactical overflow; and some of Wordsworth's best-known examples have a similar division ("It Is a Beauteous Evening"; "Composed Upon Westminster Bridge"; "London, 1802"). Clearly, when the octave-sestet structure is projected into epic dimensions, it is not possible to achieve *enjambement* in the same way as in a single sonnet. Yet the retrospective summary of Book 8 of *The Prelude*, with its implicit comparison of the "rustic fair" (8.11) of Grasmere to the "blank confusion" (7.722) of Bartholomew Fair in the preceding book, fulfills an analogous task, gathering up the narrative, reiterating its emerging theme, while looking ahead to the books on France through the developing response of the poet first to nature and now to humanity. It is another equivalent of the Miltonic signpost that "half yet remains unsung" (*PL* 7.21), a narrative eddying into "retrospect" that prepares the poet for yet another sallying out into the mainstream of the poem's argument. The concentration of Miltonic echoes at the end of Book 8, some foregrounded, others muted,[26] adds weight to this structural resting-place, and implies the advance into the sestet whose potentially tragic aspect has been anticipated by the allusion to Adam in Book 11 of *Paradise Lost*, "yet in Paradise / Though fallen from bliss" (8.659–60).

How is the notion of *The Prelude* as sonnet related to the question of genre? If, as Arthur Barker has concluded, *Paradise Lost* was revised both to emphasize its affinity with classical epic and to reveal its proper dramatic structure—in effect, to harmonize epic and dramatic conventions—then *The Prelude*'s division into fourteen books would appear to be seeking an analogous marriage of epic and lyric genres, an ennobling interchange of heroic desire and lyric control: the poem seeks to be a "lyrical epic," similar to a "lyrical ballad" or to Shelley's "lyrical drama" of *Prometheus Unbound*. *The Prelude* as sonnet perhaps implies such a harmony, though one needs to be aware of the potential contradiction involved in the yoking together of polarized forms. If the poem adapts certain conventions of lyric tone as the epic conversation poem to Coleridge, then it also assumes a modified lyric form as a macro-sonnet that shapes or misshapes its epic content even as the classical form of *Paradise Lost* controls and modulates its own drama.

These considerations are certainly more exciting from an intertextualist perspective than any attempt to forge links between coincidental episodes in *Paradise Lost* and *The Prelude*. It is true, despite M. H. Abrams's plea, that Wordsworth's poem, rhetorically at least, begins as Milton's ends, and that Wordsworth's experience in France does correspond in some sense to the Fall. The conclusion of *The Prelude* cries out to be recognized in terms of the conclusion of *Paradise Lost*. The ascent of Snowdon not only recalls, but parallels, Adam's ascent to the "top / Of Speculation" with Michael (*PL* 12.588–89). The shifting emphasis in the poet's development from nature to humanity to the imagination can be seen as a revision of the Miltonic shift of emphasis from Satan to the Son and to Man. Michael's revelation to Adam of the course of human history coincides structurally with Wordsworth's consciousness of the shaping spirit of his own history; and the concluding imperative to Adam to "add / Deeds to [his] knowledge answerable" (*PL* 12.581–82) gives force to Wordsworth's climactic expression of "the discipline / And consummation of a Poet's mind" (14.303–04), in which the consummation is nothing without the discipline.

But if we wish to push beyond these obvious enough correspondences and to explore the Miltonic underpresence in other ways, the fourteen-book sonnet structure of *The Prelude* offers a different perspective on the theme of Romantic intertextual collaboration. The sonnet structure is an example of "genius, power, / Creation and divinity itself" (3.173–74) accommodated to lyric form. The form contains the epic material, but it also allows it to unfold in a controlled yet inevitable way, giving a "literary" shape to the rude elements of a poet's "history." For all its being "somewhat unorthodox," critics should scorn not the sonnet structure of *The Prelude*, for it might be said that with this key Wordsworth unlocked the growth of a poet's mind.

VI

It is surprising that intertextual theory has not developed a specific term for the trope of collaboration. It seems a significant aspect of Romantic poetics, and is, as we have seen, a presiding metaphor over *The Prelude*. To limit the application of the phrase "joint labourers" to Wordsworth and Coleridge, however, is to miss a broader perspective that the text invites us to consider theoretically now. That perspective includes Milton, but as more than just a shadowy "presence."

In what sense can Milton be considered a "joint labourer" with Wordsworth? One sense we have already demonstrated: rhetorically. Milton is an intertextual collaborator with Wordsworth in the sense that his texts inform and structure, as well as ornament, Wordsworth's texts, sometimes helping, sometimes hindering, as collaborators often do. Coleridge presents the thematized version of intertextual collaboration in his role as a human, dramatic example of Wordsworth's "joint labourers."

But there is another sense, equally rhetorical but expressed in visionary terms, that is hinted at in Book 5 in the sketch of "Shakespeare, or Milton, labourers divine!" (165), and elaborated in Book 12 (1805) in Wordsworth's account of how he long

> Had harboured reverentially a thought
> That Poets, even as Prophets, each with each
> Connected in a mighty scheme of truth,
> Have each for his peculiar dower, a sense
> By which he is enabled to perceive
> Something unseen before. . . .
> (1805:12.300–05)

Poets are joined "each with each" in a figural structure or "scheme" of truth, just as Wordsworth had wished his days to be bound "each to each" in a personal and natural form of the same thing ("My Heart Leaps Up" 9). When the poet weds the muse—that is, when his "discerning intellect" is "wedded to this goodly universe / In love and holy passion" (Prospectus 52, 53–54)—what he receives in dower (or what "wedding Nature to [him] gives in dower," as Coleridge puts it in "Dejection" [68]) is the poetic insight that allies him to the other poets and prophets in that "mighty scheme." Though Wordsworth conventionally fancies himself as "the meanest of this band" (1805:12.306), he nevertheless hopes that he has been "vouchsafed / An influx" of its privilege and its power (1805:12.307–08), influx being linguistically and thematically cognate with influence.

Shelley provides a good gloss on what all these collaborators—Shakespeare, Milton, Wordsworth, Coleridge—are about: they are poets who have contributed "episodes to that great poem, which all poets, like the co-operating thoughts of one great mind, have built up since the beginning of the world" (493). For Shelley, "all poets" are co-operators or collaborators in this creation insofar as they each represent a stage in the "mighty scheme of truth," a moment in the process of constructing a work which, like Wordsworth's *Recluse*, is continuously being composed and is never completed. Wordsworth's self-chosen models of Chaucer, Shakespeare, Spenser, and Milton (Grosart 3:459–60) suggest a defining of the line of advance, with Milton—"my great Predecessor," as Wordsworth called him (*MY* 2:146—being the point of departure for the next chapter, or episode, of the great mono-poem. It is possible to dwell on the adversative position of Wordsworth vis-à-vis Milton, and to explore the burdens, anxieties, and even embarrassments of that confrontation,[27] but it is also possible to consider that the collaborative relationship might not, after all, be as much a hindrance as all that, especially if we see each poet as actively engaging himself in what he perceives to be a common endeavor. Both poets are "labourers divine" in the inspired work of imagination, and they are "joint labourers" in that their work proceeds from a perceived common center of vision toward a deliverance that is "surely yet to come." The deliverance, like the completion of the *Oeuvre* of literary history, is indefinitely sustained and deferred, the poem continuously created and continually revised. Wordsworth wished to create and perceive paradise in a moment of "present joy" (1.47), but even in his most hopeful composition he can only "chant, in lonely peace" (Prospectus 56), another "glad preamble" to the "blissful hour" of "this great consummation" (Prospectus 57, 58). "Our destiny," he proclaims in *The Prelude*,

> Is with infinitude, and only there;
> With hope it is, hope that can never die,
> Effort, and expectation, and desire,
> And something evermore about to be.
> (6.604–08)

That "something" in which Wordsworth's "destiny" resided was not simply *The Recluse*, the Apocalypse, or the defeat of a ghostly father; it lay closer, curiously, to Blake's notion of building Jerusalem, a sacred act of imagination in which Wordsworth could have said of Milton, as he did say of Coleridge, that he was

> In many things my brother, chiefly here
> In this our deep devotion.
> (2.465–66)

—But a voice
Is wanting, the deep truth is imageless
Shelley, Prometheus Unbound

—But the spoken word is so intimately bound
to its written image that the latter
manages to usurp the main role
Saussure, Course in General Linguistics

IMAGES OF LANGUAGE: VOICE AND LETTER IN *THE PRELUDE*

3

While the question of language in Wordsworth's poetry once tended to focus on poetic diction and the relation of poetry to prose, the emphasis today seems to be less on Wordsworth's repudiation of any "essential difference between the language of prose and metrical composition" (*Prose* 1:135) than on the description of an essential difference" within all language. The issue is no longer simply a stylistic distinction between two forms of written discourse, or even a hypothetical ordering of standard and deviant languages, but an understanding of the difference within and between spoken and written discourses, a difference that divides voice from itself even as it sets the written word against the word. Wordsworth's poetry exhibits a double consciousness of its status as language in its images of speech and writing, which, far from being discrete or hierarchical, tend to enjoy an "interchangeable supremacy" (*Prelude* 14.84), both being inhabited by the same linguistic difference.[1]

I

—Stamped by the ancient tongue
On rock and ruin darkening as we go
"In the Sound of Mull"

These two main forms of language, speech and writing—or their condensed and metonymic images of voice and letter—exist in Wordsworth's poetry with alternating priority. Wordsworth is often, and perhaps chiefly, associated with oral poetry. At one point he defines the poet as "a man speaking to men" (*Prose* 1:138), and it is natural for a reader to follow this oratorical figure at first and to think of the poet as rhetor, as a speaker or performer, even as one who speaks in the language "really used by men" (*Prose* 1:123). This apparent privileging of voice carries over into Wordsworth's habits of oral composition and dictation—as we see, for example, in the fourth book of *The Prelude* (100–30), in his note to "Tintern Abbey" (*Poems* 1:954), in Rawnsley's descriptions of the poet's oral composings (17–18), and in what Wordsworth called his "aversion from writing" (*EY* 407), particularly "the unpleasant feelings which [he] connected with the act of holding a Pen" (*EY* 453). There is considerable evidence for Wordsworth's status as a predominantly phonocentric poet.

But the definition of the poet as "a man speaking to men" contains a participle whose position on a continuum between literality and figurality is shifting. *Speaking* implies voice, audience, and hence the idea of a rhetor. Yet there is also, to adapt Jacques Lacan, an "insistence of the letter" in Wordsworth's poetry, on the engraved or inscribed or imprinted word. Nature impresses or imprints on all forms, Wordsworth says, "the characters / Of danger or desire" (*Prelude* 1.471–72). The poet in "To Joanna" (*Poems* 1:445–47) engraves the "rude characters" of a name into solid rock (82). The boy in the first "spot of time" sees a murderer's name carved in the turf. Even today, at Hawkshead Grammar School, tourists can see Wordsworth's name carved in his desk; and they can visit the Rock of Names outside the Grasmere Museum, where they can read his initials. But Wordsworth's poetry displays larger concerns with the written word than these incidental acts of writing would suggest. While *The Prelude* may be regarded as an epic conversation poem—the poem addressed to Coleridge—the oral emphasis is in part balanced by an entire book devoted, nominally, to "Books," to as literal and "sensuous" an "incarnation" (the metaphors are the poet's [*Prose* 3:65]) as Wordsworth might have conceived for the imagination. J. Hillis Miller, in speaking of Wordsworth's inscriptions and epitaphs, rightly points out that Wordsworth, "far from always believing that poetry exists primarily as spoken language, sometimes felt that a poem only comes into existence in a satisfactory form when it has not only been written down but inscribed permanently on the perdurable substance of a rock" ("Stone and Shell" 129). Wordsworth's poetry does in fact exhibit an insistence on the letter, on writing or, as he says, on "the WORD, that shall not pass away" ("On the Power of Sound" 224).

The relation of speech to writing is a central question in two of the major developments in twentieth-century linguistics, the Saussurean and the Chomskyan. Saussure, we know, has formulated a theory of language that favors the spoken word over the written. As a linguist, Saussure is interested in the features of a language as it is spoken; writing exists, he says, "for the sole purpose of representing" the spoken form (23). But Saussure at points doubts the stability of such a hierarchy and acknowledges a "tyranny of writing" (31): "the spoken word is so intimately bound to its written image that the latter manages to usurp the main role" (24). Now, metaphors of usurpation and tyranny figure prominently in *The Prelude*, not only in Book 12, where Wordsworth describes the tyrannical or "despotic" power of the bodily eye over the imaginative eye (129), but also in Book 6, where, having recounted his crossing of the Alps, Wordsworth is confronted by a "strength / Of usurpation" (599–600) that he calls "Imagination" (592). It would be worthwhile to see whether this usurpation, which Wordsworth describes phenomenologically as the ascendance of an "invisible world" (6.602) over the visible "light of sense" (6.600), can be illuminated by the Saussurean usurpation of writing over speech. In the final form of *The Prelude* the apocalyptic passage on "Imagination" directly follows, and arguably results from, Wordsworth's encounter with a speaking peasant; and yet the passage has been frequently read—at least since 1929, when Fraser first suggested the interpretation—as Wordsworth's response not to a voice but to his own act of composition, to the moment of his writing some fourteen years after hearing and translating a voice that revealed the invisible world. Also of assistance here is Chomsky's distinction between linguistic "competence" (the underlying system of generative syntactical processes) and linguistic "performance" (the concrete use of language)—a distinction roughly analogous, but not exactly similar, to Saussure's distinction between *langue* and *parole*.[2] Wordsworth, "through sad incompetence of human speech" (6.593), gives the name *Imagination* to the "awful Power" that rises "from the mind's abyss" (6.594). That he cites "incompetence of speech," rather than simply the inept performance of the poet, aligns his affected modesty with Chomsky's theory: the naming of the power lies beyond the ability of language itself; it exceeds what Wordsworth calls "the reach of words" (3.187), even as that reach must exceed the eloquent grasp of its author.

The two figures of voice and letter that alternate within Wordsworth's poetry reflect the similar linguistic doubleness the poet perceives in nature: the *liber naturae*, or book of nature, and the *vox naturae*, or voice of nature. The concept, traditional in Wordsworthian criticism, of the reciprocity of mind and nature has, it would appear, its linguistic version: Wordsworth transfers these two forms of human language to nature and then receives them again, as though nature were linguistically prior, as though to understand Wordsworth's rhetoric one must first understand the rhetoric of nature.

What are the tropes of nature? The question is perhaps naive, suggesting as it does a mystified belief in some Adamic language in which the words of human beings are also the things of nature. Enlightened minds no longer think that nature speaks or writes its own language, though they can conceive of a grammar of nature, and one that is not always written in mathematical and geometrical terms, as Galileo thought it was (Curtius 324). Having bestowed the powers of speech and writing on nature, the poet is free to receive that language again, to hear nature's voice and to read its written texts. The growth of a poet's mind is thus also the development of a hermeneutic, an ability to interpret the mind's linguistic projections as a continuous allegory—specifically, an allegory in which the poet keeps discovering his own figurations as language keeps doubling back on itself. The allegory of *The Prelude* is thus related to what Paul de Man has called "a scene of reading" (*Allegories* 162), or perhaps a scene of listening—that is, an account of the literal and figural limits to nature's "calling forth and strengthening the Imagination" ("Influence of Natural Objects" [*Poems* 1:364]) or the boy's learning "to stand and read . . . read and disobey" the text of nature (*Home at Grasmere* 712–13). Let us first consider speech, the more pervasive of these two figures, and then turn our attention to writing. By cataloging a few significant "images of voice," as Wordsworth calls them in his poem "On the Power of Sound" (34), we may establish the peculiarly Wordsworthian quality of voice and then modestly consider one or two scenes of writing in Book 7.

II

—Even from the tomb the voice of Nature cries

Gray, "Elegy Written in a Country Churchyard"

In *The Prelude* we often hear that "Nature" speaks, but we rarely hear what she says. Only once, in Book 6, does Wordsworth give the reader an account of what he heard Nature utter, and even then it is a tentative account. Here is the singular passage:

—"Stay, stay your sacrilegious hands!"—The voice
Was Nature's, uttered from her Alpine throne;
I heard it then, and seem to hear it now—
"Your impious work forbear: perish what may,
Let this one temple last, be this one spot
Of earth devoted to eternity!"
She ceased to speak. . . .
(6.430–36)

What are the tropes of Nature in this Alpine passage? Significantly, her speech is a combination of apostrophe and imperative—a "vain injunction," as Wordsworth described it in a cancelled passage in MS A (de Selincourt 198). Nature speaks in a series of imperative verbs: "Stay, stay"; "forbear"; "Let . . . last"; "[Let] . . . be." The injunctive mood of address links Nature's rhetoric with such epitaphic commands as "Pause, Traveller!"; "Nay, Traveller, rest"; and "Stop here, or gently pass!"[3] Nature sounds curiously like an epitaph, apostrophizing the viewer-listener through an admonishing rhetoric; of all her moods, the imperative seems her favorite. A number of commentators, including Ernest Bernhardt-Kabisch, Geoffrey Hartman, Paul Fry, and Frances Ferguson, have noted epitaphic qualities in Wordsworth's poetry,[4] but I am more immediately concerned with the place of voice in this interpenetration of landscape and text. The rhetorical overlap between the voice of Nature and the "monumental writing" of epitaphs (1805:11.295) suggests connections at thematic levels: Nature personified apostrophizes and commands; the epitaph, Wordsworth points out in his first essay on the subject, frequently employs the "tender fiction" in which the deceased person "admonishes with the voice of one experienced in the vanity of those affections which are confined to earthly objects" (*Prose* 2:60). The bridge that connects the voice of Nature to the voice of epitaphs is what Paul de Man has identified as "the fiction of the voice-from-beyond-the-grave" (*Rhetoric* 77); or what Wordsworth himself calls a "shadowy interposition" (*Prose* 2:60), in which an inscription is troped as voice and the deceased becomes "a man speaking to men." The voice of Nature is not quite the voice of the dead, but there are thematic and rhetorical connections between the two; hence the predominantly elegiac tone of the Alpine injunction: "Perish what may, / Let this . . . last!"

This unique speech illustrates the identification of Nature's voice with an epitaphic voice. *The Prelude* reverberates with similar figures of speaking from the very outset: in the "glad preamble" of Book 1, the poet longs for the soothing "murmur" (1.13) of a "clear stream" (1.12) to allay his perturbations; later in the same book, in the problematic "Was it for this" passage, he speaks of the River Derwent, who "loved / To blend his murmurs with my nurse's song" (1.270–71), sending "a voice / That flowed along my dreams" (1.273–74). A giant vocal chiasmus blends the beginning and the end of *The Prelude*: early in the poem a mature river makes "ceaseless music" (1.277) to "a babe in arms" (1.276), and at the close a mature poet listens "faintly" (14.195) to the "natal murmur" (14.196) of his own "stream" of imagination (14.194). In Book 1 the "nurse's song" appears to have a linguistic and temporal priority over the river's murmurs; the poet says that the river's song blends with the nurse's, and not hers with his. It is a strange blending, however, radically metonymic and substitutive; the chain of associations runs from "murmurs" through "song," "voice," "music," "softness," "calm," and "breathes." We begin with a river's murmurs that first blend with and then usurp the human voice, and we end with "the calm / That Nature breathes." The crucial passage concludes:

For this, didst thou,
O Derwent! winding among grassy holms
Where I was looking on, a babe in arms,
Make ceaseless music that composed my thoughts
To more than infant softness, giving me
Amid the fretful dwellings of mankind
A foretaste, a dim earnest, of the calm
That Nature breathes among the hills and groves.
(1.274–81)

The nurse and her song have been completely elided. They are, like the Wanderer in *The Excursion*, "o'erpowered / By Nature" (1.282–83). Whereas initially it is the nurse's lullaby that is meant to soothe the babe, the River Derwent usurps the voice of the nurse and, through metonymic displacement, gives the infant "a foretaste, a dim earnest" of its strength of usurpation as well as the calm that it can breathe. The babe, by "looking on" the river, hears music that flows along his dreams—an experience to which we may compare "Tintern Abbey": "For I have learned / To look on nature, not as in the hour / Of thoughtless youth; but hearing oftentimes / The still, sad music of humanity" (88–91). The chiasmus of seeing-hearing, common in Wordsworth, invokes here yet another sense: "a fore-taste."

Figures involving voices in nature are more frequent in the earlier books of *The Prelude*, where the poet describes his child-hood and youth. As the poem proceeds, the vocal tropes tend to disappear, rarely occurring in books 9 to 11, but they increase correspondingly with the return to childhood episodes in books 12 to 14.[5] This statistical pattern suggests a close relation to the role of the eye: as the "visionary gleam" ("Intimations" 56) that Wordsworth experiences in childhood fades, so does his auditory capability, though he claims that neither eye nor ear entirely loses its imaginative power. "Though inland far we be," he writes in the "Intimations Ode," the soul can still "see the Children sport upon the shore, / And hear the mighty waters rolling evermore" (163, 167–68). The voice of nature, like the music of the spheres, may once have been heard with the bodily ear but can now best be apprehended through the imagination—that is, as Blake might say, by listening through the ear and not with it. Describing how as a youth he "did converse" with all forms and creatures of nature (2.393), Wordsworth elaborates the paradox:

> One song they sang, and it was audible,
> Most audible, then, when the fleshly ear,
> O'ercome by humblest prelude of that strain,
> Forgot her functions, and slept undisturbed.
> (2.415–18)

Again there is a kind of usurpation: the "fleshly ear" is "o'ercome" by the song of nature; the sound of sense goes out, but with a softness that reveals an almost inaudible world. Keats makes a similar assertion in his "Ode on a Grecian Urn":

> Heard melodies are sweet, but those unheard
> Are sweeter; therefore, ye soft pipes, play on;
> Not to the sensual ear, but, more endear'd,
> Pipe to the spirit ditties of no tone. . . .
> (11–14)[6]

Keats' "sensual ear" is like Wordsworth's "fleshly ear": when it sleeps "undisturbed," it receives "unheard" melodies. But Wordsworth makes it clear that Nature's melodies are never completely "unheard," as the modified anadiplosis of "audible, / Most audible" suggests; it is a matter of degree, and not kind, of hearing. Or it is a matter of chronology: Nature's song was "most audible," he says, "then"—that is, in his "seventeenth year" (2.386)—but is still audible now. The "then" can be read in either a temporal or a conjunctive sense—as either "at that time" or "accordingly."[7]

Wordsworth's vocal tropes often awaken "dead" figures to a new life. Listen to the voice in the nest-plundering episode in Book 1:

> oh, at that time
> While on the perilous ridge I hung alone,
> With what strange utterance did the loud dry wind
> Blow through my ear!
> (1.335–38)

It is difficult not to want to ask literally, "What utterance indeed?" Nature is shouting something at the boy, but the reader, perhaps like the boy himself, never gets the message. The loudness of the utterance resembles the poet's eerie description of "Esthwaite's splitting fields of ice" (1.539), in which

> The pent-up air, struggling to free itself,
> Gave out to meadow grounds and hills a loud
> Protracted yelling, like the noise of wolves
> Howling in troops along the Bothnic Main.
> (1.540–43)

In MS B Wordsworth also describes the sound of the ice as "growling"—"not unlike the sound that issues / From out the deep chest of a lonely Bull" (de Selincourt 34). The air is personified with human attributes, then partially turned back into a simile of nature ("like . . . wolves"; "not unlike . . . a lonely Bull"). The eeriness of the moment for the poet is rhetorical as much as experiential; in highly figural language he invests the air with animate qualities (prosopopoeia), gives it the figural actions of "struggling" and "yelling" (metaphor), and then compares it to the sound of animals (simile). The rhetorical effect is to hear the "pent-up air" howling in tropes along the Bothnic Main.

Nature's voice is often calm, quiet, still, small, or utterly silent for Wordsworth. He begins his walking tour through *The Prelude* with a meditation amid the "perfect stillness" of a grove (1.70), and as he proceeds he speaks of the silence of nature almost as a foretaste of "the eternal Silence" named in the "Intimations Ode" (159)—not just "the silence that is in the starry sky" ("Brougham Castle" 163) but also the "silent neighbourhood of graves" (5.403). The "turf" (1.325), the water (1.374, 386, 448), even the hills are silent (12.168).[8] Usually, however, the extraordinary quiet is juxtaposed with a sound that deepens the calm even as it breaks it. The boy steals the boat to "the voice / Of mountain-echoes" (1.362–63) but rows through "the silent water" (1.386). The "more than inland peace" of Furness Abbey (2.108), like the "more than infant softness" of the babe in arms (1.278), is broken by the thundering, "uncouth race" of horses (2.117), by the "sobbings of the place" (2.122), and by the song of an invisible bird. The Boy of Winander experiences quiet amid tumult, and also the usurpation of a voice over silence: "when a lengthened pause / Of silence came . . . Then sometimes . . . the voice / Of mountain torrents . . ." (5.379–80, 381, 383–84). The opening of Book 7 illustrates the sound/silence interpenetration, as it begins by recalling the poet's "not audible" song (7.11). But a "choir of redbreasts" (7.21) sings to him and he in turn "whispers" (7.28) to the birds that he and they "will chant together" (7.31). "Silence touched me here," Wordsworth writes, "no less than sound had done before" (7.36–37).

The alternation of sound and silence, or of voice and echo, is significant for the way in which it characterizes a nature that both listens and responds to the poet (see Martin 190–92). But one sometimes feels that the disjunction between voice and response in Wordsworth is too great, that he makes too much of "low breathings" (1.323) or murmurings or whisperings. There is often the sense, in Coleridge's words, of "a disproportion of thought to the circumstance," or what Coleridge called "mental bombast, as distinguished from verbal" (*Biographia* 258). Yet it might equally be called *hermeneutical* bombast, in which the meaning seems excessive to the linguistic experience. To have the experience but to miss the meaning is the very condition of Wordsworth's great poetry. And to approach the meaning (to complete Eliot's figure) is to approach "the hiding-places of man's power" (12.279), where "powerful feelings" overflow and emotions are "recollected" in a form of self-interpretation (*Prose* 1:127, 149). Consider the following example of a "mute dialogue" (2.268) between one individual and nature. The passage, taken from Book 7 of *The Excursion* (395–481), also stands as an epitaph at the end of Wordsworth's third essay upon epitaphs (*Prose* 2:94–96).

A man loses "the precious gift of hearing" (*Ex.* 7.402) in his childhood. All nature therefore becomes "soundless" (*Ex.* 7.405) to him, "silent as a picture" (*Ex.* 7.415). Yet despite his affliction, Wordsworth's Pastor tells his audience, he serves a good and useful life. After almost sixty-five years of living in utter silence, the man dies and is carried "to the profounder stillness of the grave" (*Ex.* 7.468). The concluding lines of the deaf man's story show nature surviving in a manner that is not a usurpation, but a triumph nonetheless:

> —And yon tall pine-tree, whose composing sound
> Was wasted on the good Man's living ear,
> Hath now its own peculiar sanctity;
> And, at the touch of every wandering breeze,
> Murmurs, not idly, o'er his peaceful grave.
> (*Ex.* 7.477–81)

The reversals in this epitaph are curious. The Pastor speaks of the man's "living ear," but the epithet is ironic: while he lived, the man's ears were dead; now he is dead, they live: the pine tree "murmurs, not idly." "Not idly": that is, the dead can hear nature? This presents an unsettling doctrine: not the frightful notion of lying listening in the grave! Coleridge might have said (cf. *Biographia* 262). The "peculiar sanctity" of the pine's murmurs lies in the appropriateness of the mute dialogue between the deaf man's grave and the voice of nature, in the "tender fiction" in which the voice of this world is heard in the next.

Though deaf, the man was not completely bereft of hearing a "voice" in his life. Books, his "ready comrades" (*Ex.* 7.440), spoke to him rememberable things:

> Their familiar voice,
> Even to old age, with unabated charm
> Beguiled his leisure hours; refreshed his thoughts;
> Beyond its natural elevation raised
> His introverted spirit; and bestowed
> Upon his life an outward dignity. . . .
> (*Ex.* 7.442–47)

"Beguiled," "refreshed," "raised," "bestowed"—all these things the "voice" of books did. This trope of a voice that is really a letter, a speaking book, anticipates our exploration of the written word, but it also draws our attention to the fact that the effect of books, especially their refreshing and raising, is similar to the effects of nature and the "spots of time." The reason is not far to seek. As one who was, like Wordsworth, "a daily wanderer among woods and fields" (*Prelude* 5.587), the deaf man experiences in the voice of books "the great Nature that exists in works / Of mighty Poets" (5.594–95).[9]

For Wordsworth, the most vocal forms of nature are the streams, waterfalls, rivers, and lakes. In "Tintern Abbey" we hear the "sounding cataract" (76). In *The Prelude* Wordsworth compares his habit of composing aloud to "a river murmuring / And talking to itself" (4.119–20). Book 8 has the "wild brooks prattling from invisible haunts" (67) and later the contrast with the more powerful "Atlantic's voice" (217). In the climactic Snowdon episode, we hear "the roar of waters, torrents, streams / Innumerable, roaring with one voice!" (14.59–60). Water almost inevitably is figured as voice; conversely, when Wordsworth begins with the vocal element in a descriptive passage, he often insinuates a natural trope of water, turning his verse into "vocal streams" (14.146). On Snowdon again he perceives "the emblem of a mind" that is "intent to hear / Its voices issuing forth to silent light / In one continuous stream" (14.70, 72–74). The Leech-gatherer's voice is "like a stream / Scarce heard" (107–08). These tropes of voice and water amount to a way of reading Wordsworth's poetry that deserves explicit formulation; and if we revise Geoffrey Hartman's phenomenological equation on Wordsworth, transposing it into its rhetorical aspect, we shall glimpse a theory of voice in Wordsworth. Hartman correctly writes: "*In the imagination of Wordsworth everything tends to the image and sound of universal waters*" (*Unmediated Vision* 43). But we must alter this theorem thus: *In the language of Wordsworth the sound of waters tends to the image of voice.*

Dorothy Wordsworth's Grasmere journal for 29 April 1802 beautifully illustrates the collocation of the vocal sound of waters with an epitaphic consciousness:

> Afterwards William lay, and I lay in the trench under the fence—he with his eyes shut and listening to the waterfalls and the Birds. There was no one waterfall above another—it was a sound of waters in the air—the voice of the air. William heard me breathing and rustling now and then but we both lay still, and unseen by one another. He thought that it would be as sweet thus to lie so in the grave, to hear the *peaceful* sounds of the earth and just to know that our dear friends were near. (117)

Similar examples of Wordsworth's turn to voice in figuring nature—"this mighty sum / Of things for ever speaking" ("Tables Turned" 25–26); "the speaking face of earth and heaven" (5.13); "the earth / And common face of Nature spake to me / Rememberable things" (1.585–86)—could be multiplied considerably; not only water but wind, trees, birds, even flowers are "speaking monuments" (8.172). "The Pansy at my feet / Doth the same tale repeat," he says ("Intimations" 54–55). The notion of a monument, a "speaking monument," implies a past event—a history, as it were, of departed things: "But there's a Tree, of many, one; / A single field which I have looked upon; / Both of them speak of something that is gone" ("Intimations" 51–53). The voice of nature *is* like an epitaphic voice; nature itself is like one giant epitaph, one complex memorial text to be conned by human beings. But how do all these voices in nature—all these whisperings, murmurings, utterings, prattlings, breathings and echoings—affect Wordsworth? What is their rhetorical function?

It might suffice to show that they "haunt" Wordsworth. The voice of the "sounding cataract" in "Tintern Abbey," he says, "haunted me like a passion" (76–77). In "The Tuft of Primroses" he remarks: "Those voices! . . . these sighs / These whispers that pursue or meet me . . ." (521–24). But I wish to go one step further and suggest that the haunting voice of nature is also sometimes a usurping voice: in the episode of the nurse's song, in the overlap of voice and epitaph, in the baffling of the Boy of Winander when his "mimic hootings" are unreturned (5.373), in the moment in youth when the physical ear is "o'ercome" by the song of nature, in the uncanny extravagance of the mountain echoes in Book 1 that take up the voices of the skaters and return them frighteningly, there is always the sense of a recurrent "alien sound," as Wordsworth calls it (1.443), unable or unwilling to harmonize perfectly with the human voice. Yet Wordsworth, strangely, is haunted and usurped by a voice that is also a letter. "Ye Presences of Nature!" (1.464), he writes,

> Haunting me thus among my boyish sports,
> On caves and trees, upon the woods and hills,
> Impressed upon all forms the characters
> Of danger or desire. . . .
> (1.469–72)

These "Presences" are indicated not by a voice but by writing, by the memorial "characters" inscribed on "the surface of the universal earth" (1.473). In phenomenological terms this usurpation of a human or even a natural voice by "monumental letters" in nature (12.241) may signify the ascendance of a self-consciousness over an unself-consciousness, or the Wordsworthian split into "two consciousnesses" (2.32)—"myself / And . . . some other Being" (2.32–33). In rhetorical terms, the usurpation marks the "interchangeable supremacy" (14.84) of voice and letter in Wordsworth's poetry, with speech and writing competing for presence in the midst of difference. In such strength of usurpation, when voice becomes writing, Wordsworth's text acknowledges the passing from living voice to the dead letter but seeks to outlive this death through the epitaphic permanence of writing that aspires to the phonocentric immediacy of speech. The voice of Wordsworth's poetry is always the voice to be accomplished in writing.

III

—The monumental letters were inscribed
The Prelude

At the end of *The Prelude* Wordsworth looks back over his poem and regrets that "much hath been omitted . . . of books how much!" (14.312, 313). In fact, a considerable portion of the poem is devoted to books, to book tropes, and to the relation of man-made books to the book of nature. While crossing the Alps Wordsworth declares that "with such a book / Before our eyes, we could not choose but read" (6.543–44); earlier he finds illustrations for "Nature's book of rudiments" (3.557) in which he attempts to discover the moral lessons encoded in nature—the "lessons of genuine brotherhood, the plain / And universal reason of mankind, / The truths of young and old" (6.545–47).

Since the *liber naturae* is a trope, so also is the act of "reading" it. For Wordsworth, interpreting nature is like the critic's task of interpreting a text: the poet reads the world and the critic reads his reading; both poet and critic try "to detect / Some inner meanings which might harbour there" (8.537–38). Wordsworth stands on the banks of the Wye River, and while gazing at his sister is able to "read / [His] former pleasures in the shooting lights / Of [her] wild eyes" ("Tintern" 117–19). When the French Revolution begins to turn from "a war of self-defence" to "one of conquest" (11.207, 208),

Wordsworth sees, or thinks he sees, that it is doomed to failure. The people of France begin

losing sight of all
Which they had struggled for: and mounted up,
Openly in the eye of earth and heaven,
The scale of liberty. I read her doom. . . .
(11. 208–11)[10]

Just as the poet hears nature's voice while the reader often does not, so Wordsworth reads texts that are kept hidden from his readers. We are told that he reads, and we see his response to the act of reading, but the original writing is not always revealed. Wordsworth's readers sometimes find themselves in the position of the man gazing

Upon a volume whose contents he knows
Are memorable, but from him locked up,
Being written in a tongue he cannot read. . . .
(10.59–61)

The question of the "unreadability" of certain texts is an important one for Wordsworth's poetry, and I hope to demonstrate the rhetorical function of unreadability later in this chapter and in my analysis of the first "spot of time." Here let me illustrate how the interpreter of Wordsworth must read readings, must attend to the translations that mediate the text of nature.

Near the end of *Home at Grasmere* Wordsworth speaks of the "wild appetites and blind desires" (706) that he felt as "an innocent Little-one" (703):

Deep pools, tall trees, black chasms and dizzy crags,
And tottering towers, I loved to stand and read
Their looks forbidding, read and disobey
Sometimes in act, and evermore in thought.
(711–14)

The "looks forbidding" of Nature recall her injunctive voice. To disobey Nature, "sometimes in act, and evermore in thought," presumes a prior command, an imperative pretext, akin to "Stay, stay your sacrilegious hands!" (6.430). Whether written or spoken, the language of Nature has a "forbidding" aspect that implies norms but permits deviations in a manner corresponding to a structuralist model of rhetoric. Disobedience in reading is "misprision," to borrow Harold Bloom's trope; it is the willful error of interpretation. The boy poet loves to stand and misread.

Wordsworth's Prospero-like[11] apostrophe to "Ye Presences of Nature in the sky / And on the earth!" in the first book of *The Prelude* (464–65) roots their "ministry" (1.468) in a specific act of writing. We have already quoted the passage in connection with the haunting voice of nature; let us focus now on its graphological aspects:

can I think
A vulgar hope was yours when ye employed
Such ministry, when ye through many a year
Haunting me thus among my boyish sports,
On caves and trees, upon the woods and hills,
Impressed upon all forms the characters
Of danger or desire. . . ?
(1.466–72)

The word "characters" evokes two images: an alphabet and *dramatis personae*. To *impress* characters, however, is clearly a graphological act; Wordsworth's diction is almost Blakean in its emphasis on the physical process of engraving or inscribing (see, e.g., Blake 38–39). The passage furthermore has links with the epitaphic tradition, though the thought of nature itself being an epitaph, a macro-elegiac text to be read by humans, is barely explicit. Wordsworth tells us that the letters are not elegiac; they are "the characters / Of danger or desire." The text takes us right back to the passage in *Home at Grasmere*, to the "daring feat" and "blind desires" of childhood (710, 706).

Nature can put its mark on physical things—"on caves and trees, upon the woods and hills"—but the "impressing" works also on the insubstantial. What Colin Clarke says of the substantiality of images for Wordsworth is relevant here: if natural imagery, having weight and substance, can, as Clarke maintains (33), lie on the mind, then the mind too must be substantial in order to bear the weight. Thus Wordsworth, having given a physical quality to the immateriality of mind, is able to speak of how "the changeful earth, / And twice five summers on my mind had stamped / The faces of the moving year" (1.559–61). The image has Lockean affiliations, but more interesting from a rhetorical viewpoint is the way that nature's imprinting is humanized. To paraphrase: nature and time stamp faces on the mind. Catachresis? The metaleptic yoking together of stamping and faces (in which the middle term of "characters" is elided) owes something to Wordsworth's earlier metaphorical description of "how Nature . . . peopled the mind" of the poet (1.545–46). Nature imprints characters (as letters) that "people" the mind (as dramatic characters) and bespeak a language of danger or desire.

The one type of imprinting that cannot escape the usurpation of time is the writing of books. After the Apocalypse, Wordsworth wonders, where will books be? His musing takes the rhetorical form of a complaint:

> Oh! why hath not the Mind
> Some element to stamp her image on
> In nature somewhat nearer to her own?
> Why, gifted with such powers to send abroad
> Her spirit, must it lodge in shrines so frail?
> (5.45–49)

Nature can "stamp" its forms on the mind but the mind cannot find a suitable receptacle in nature. One reason is that the "mind of man" is "a thousand times more beautiful" than nature (14.448, 449), and could never hope to find its equal on earth. It must impress its image only on books or poems, "the consecrated works of Bard and Sage" (5.42). But books and poems—or, more generally, words themselves—are "shrines so frail" that they remain sadly incompetent for the task of accepting the mind's imprint. The perishability of books and the "sad incompetence" of language preclude any adequate stamping. "What's in the brain that ink may character?" Shakespeare asks (Sonnet 108).

I turn now to Book 7 of *The Prelude*, which I shall call the book of signs, the book that deals with what David Simpson describes as the "semiotic inferno" of London. There, Simpson writes, "the linguistic metaphor [is] used to suggest exhaustion and overdetermination, the absence of meaning through the very oversupply of possible meanings" (64). Hence the "inferno" is a semiotic, rather than a semantic, structure, declaring a variety of discourses whose meanings are withheld or deferred. The opening of the book is a return to the success of the "glad preamble," which recalls both the triumph of spontaneous overflow and the self-presence of speech. The vocal tropes at the beginning—"I sang / Aloud" (4–5), "I in whispers said" (28), and "ye and I . . . / Will chant together" (29, 31)—and the emphasis on oral composition make the fall into writing in the greater part of Book 7 all the more disturbing: the "man speaking to men" enters a world in which written signs, letters, characters, and symbols seem to prevail. The three parallel, juxtaposed passages on the uses and abuses of oratory that punctuate this book of signs (7.486–572) are conspicuous exceptions to the overwhelming graphological images, and Wordsworth satirizes them to varying degrees, treating them as perversions of the true voice of feeling.

Significantly, Wordsworth begins Book 7 with praise and wonder over the power of names. The schoolmate who returns from a trip to London disappoints Wordsworth, who expected some miraculous transformation to have occurred on his friend's visiting a place whose name evoked imagination far beyond the romance "of airy palaces, and gardens built / By Genii" (7.78–79), beyond the historical excitement "of Rome, / Alcairo, Babylon, or Persepolis" (7.80–81). These names, Wordsworth says, "fell short, far short, / Of what my fond simplicity believed / And thought of London" (7.84–86). The evocativeness of the name of London, for the boy Wordsworth, is richer than "Fairy-land" (7.98), yet it also conjures up a *failure* of naming:

> Above all, one thought
> Baffled my understanding: how men lived
> Even next-door neighbours, as we say, yet still
> Strangers, nor knowing each the other's name.
> (7.115–18)

London, a name above most names, contains the nameless. The casually qualifying phrase "as we say" gives a strong sense of linguistic community to Wordsworth's statement in striking contrast to the baffling anonymity of Londoners; the language of regional idiom ("next-door neighbours, as we say") binds the people of "humble and rustic life" together linguistically (*Prose* 1:125), while even the minimal form of language—naming—is missing in the city.

The apostrophe that follows this passage continues the theme of the denominative power of names, but the way in which that power is characterized undergoes a significant revision between the 1805 and 1850 texts. In the earlier version Wordsworth writes:

> O, wond'rous power of words, how sweet they are
> According to the meaning which they bring!
> (1805:7.121–22)

In the 1850 edition these lines read:

> O, wond'rous power of words, by simple faith
> Licensed to take the meaning that we love!
> (7.119–20)

The introduction of the word "faith" does not mean that Wordsworth has "Christianized" the passage. The revision, in fact, has nothing to do with religion but everything to do with language. The 1850 version shows a progressive acknowledgment of the arbitrary nature of the sign:[12] in the earlier version the words "bring" meaning; in the latter they "take" it. The first version implies a divine or transcendental semantic content, one that is made inherent in the word before it reaches human beings; the second implies a signifier with no intrinsic meaning, only the meaning that humans "by simple faith"—which is to say, by linguistic convention—say it is "licensed" to have. Though Wordsworth is speaking of proper names here, the implications of this passage are applicable to language generally. The "wond'rous power" has become humanized, brought down from a divine or Adamic level of signification to one of immotivation. Though Wordsworth, like all logocentric poets, has great hopes for what language can say and do, what it can communicate as well as perform,[13] he also, like all Romantic poets, has a profound understanding of the incompetence and deficiency involved in the "endless fluctuations and arbitrary associations" of language (*Prose* 3:82). The arbitrary sign determines the limitations as well as the virtues of the "mystery of words" (5.597).

Very early in Book 7 we encounter scenes of reading. The *topos* of the human face as a book lies behind the conjuring passage in which the "monstrous ant-hill" (149) of London rises up at Wordsworth's rhetorical command, and the poet sees

> The comers and the goers face to face,
> Face after face; the string of dazzling wares,
> Shop after shop, with symbols, blazoned names;
> And all the tradesman's honours overhead:
> Here, fronts of houses, like a title-page
> With letters huge inscribed from top to toe. . . .
> (7.156–61)

Perhaps we are reminded of Blake's "London":

> I wander through each chartered street,
> Near where the chartered Thames does flow,

And mark in every face I meet
Marks of weakness, marks of woe.
(26)

"I glance but at a few conspicuous marks," Wordsworth writes, "reading them with quick and curious eye" (7.573, 587). The marks, to Wordsworth, are legible—that is, he finds a semiotic quality in them, though their semantic content is not always disclosed. The fronts of the houses, similarly, are "like a title-page": they are one book Wordsworth can judge by its cover: a joint volume, encyclopedic, author anonymous. But note how the power of rhetoric works noiselessly here to give a human figuration to objects: the title page is inscribed, Wordsworth says, "from top to toe." Now, "from top to toe" is so familiar a metaphorical expression that it is easy to overlook, but when placed alongside the other prosopopoeic tropes (e.g., "overhead"; "fronts of houses"—where "fronts" retains the suggestion of a forehead or face), it is significant for the way in which it turns this passage back to the human form of the opening lines ("face to face, / Face after face"). It is as though Wordsworth wants to make this book speak, to undo the usurpation of the living voice by the dead letter and rediscover a "speaking face of earth and heaven" (5.13). The metaleptic shift from houses to a title page and finally to a human form personifies the city in a way reminiscent of Wordsworth's sonnet "Composed Upon Westminster Bridge" (where "the very houses are asleep"). The poet attempts, not wholly successfully, to humanize the city, to make it meaningful and accessible to him; and he does so, in part, by giving it a human shape but also, in part, by turning it into a text, into writing, into the one distinctively human quality of articulate language.

Wordsworth's reference to the "files of ballads [which] dangle from dead walls" (7.193) in the streets of London recalls his description in Book 1 of nature's habit of impressing or imprinting letters and characters on the landscape—"the characters / Of danger or desire" (471–72). Such scenes of writing can be linked to a pastoral tradition, dating back to Callimachus, of "scratching erotic sentiments into the bark of a tree" (Rosenmeyer 202)—the very thing that Orlando attempts in *As You Like It* by tacking his poems to the trees in the Forest of Arden and by carving names in their trunks. This convention is actually a breach of the pastoral contract between humanity and nature (Rosenmeyer 202–03), a sacrilege of what Karl

Kroeber has called the "ecological holiness" of a *locus amoenus* like Grasmere. "I pray you, mar no more trees with writing love songs in their barks," Jaques says to Orlando (3.2.248). But the ballads in the streets of London parody this convention; instead of representing an attempt (admittedly ecologically perverse) by human beings, through the metonymy of language, to get inside living nature and be at one with it, these poems invert that end: they are, Wordsworth says, "dead letter[s]" (8.297) hanging from "dead walls" (7.193). Is there not something epitaphic about all this dead language? Could not these anonymous bits of verse in the streets of London be, to borrow a phrase from J. Hillis Miller, epitaphs for a dead city ("The Still Heart" 308)? Surely they reflect more than the linguistic "exhaustion" of which Simpson speaks; the poet everywhere sees signs and written characters, but the alphabet is without its transliteration; the signs remain dead to him.

Sometimes the image of writing, by foregrounding the conventionality or arbitrariness of language, throws into relief other conventions—in one case, the conventions of the theater. Describing a play that requires the lead character to become invisible, Wordsworth writes: "Delusion bold! and how can it be wrought? / The garb he wears is black as death, the word / '*Invisible*' flames forth upon his chest" (7.285–87). Writing, in the form of the bare sign, assists in creating the dramatic illusion; written characters collaborate with stage characters. The "delusion bold" that language creates through its arbitrary connection of signifier and signified is here a source of humor for Wordsworth, a "delight" (7.274) that reveals how willingly human beings accept illusions, especially the delusion that the linguistic sign has the power to do, and not just to signify—that it has the "illocutionary force" to make something invisible, and not just to signify the idea of invisibility (Austin 100).

But the one scene of writing in Book 7 that powerfully focuses our concerns with voice and letter is Wordsworth's encounter with a solitary figure. Classified as a "spot of time" by many critics,[14] the moment involves a complex set of echoes of "Resolution and Independence." Wordsworth introduces the episode with a dramatic simile of the multitudinousness of the city:

> As the black storm upon the mountain top
> Sets off the sunbeam in the valley, so
> That huge fermenting mass of humankind

> Serves as a solemn background, or relief,
> To single forms and objects. . . .
> (7.619–23)

The pictorial trope freezes the city as a "spectacle" (7.643), something to be observed, like a painting, relief sculpture, or even a stage performance. The naturalistic opening simile and the diction of "forms and objects" sound like the language of nature again, though the usurping agent here is a text, both human and inscriptive. Here is the short but powerful passage:

> And once, far-travelled in such mood, beyond
> The reach of common indication, lost
> Amid the moving pageant, I was smitten
> Abruptly, with the view (a sight not rare)
> Of a blind Beggar, who, with upright face,
> Stood, propped against a wall, upon his chest
> Wearing a written paper, to explain
> His story, whence he came, and who he was.
> Caught by the spectacle my mind turned round
> As with the might of waters; an apt type
> This label seemed of the utmost we can know,
> Both of ourselves and of the universe;
> And, on the shape of that unmoving man,
> His steadfast face and sightless eyes, I gazed,
> As if admonished from another world.
> (7.635–49)

"Beyond / The reach of common indication": beyond "the reach of words" (3.187)? The double text in the passage, man and paper, is a "label" with a double semantic content, "of ourselves and of the universe"—though this content is not made known to the reader. The content is not important, however, for it is the semiotic, not the semantic, structure of the experience that makes Wordsworth "smitten" and "caught." Both the Beggar and his paper are signs: the man's "unmoving" shape and "steadfast face and sightless eyes" admonish the poet in a language that seems "from another world"; the paper itself, which is intended to explain "his story," gives the reader in the streets of London only a "minimally informative text" (Hertz, "Blockage" 83). The image of a man wearing a text on his chest—like the actor earlier in the book on whose chest "the word / '*Invisible*' flames forth"—suggests a sentimental desire to have language become one with the objects it intends, to make words invoke real things. The placing of a system of signifiers on a paper, and then on the man's chest, reveals the wish for an identity of words and things, not just of signifiers and signifieds, but of signs and objects, or of words and referents. By "wearing a written paper," the man attempts to clothe himself in language: he is the trope of a self seeking pure semiological status. But the Beggar's attempt literally to ornament himself with language, figurally to present himself as a text and not as a referential object, only half succeeds; the text that he wears is an ill-fitting garment. If words are not incarnations but merely garb, ornamentation, or clothing, Wordsworth argues in his third essay on epitaphs, then they will be like "those poisoned vestments, read of in the stories of superstitious times, which had power to consume and to alienate from his right mind the victim who put them on" (*Prose* 2:84–85). The Beggar is in part victimized by his own rhetoric: by merely "wearing" language and not being fully incarnated in it, he repeats the error within all logocentric discourse.

Yet Wordsworth's image of the man wearing the paper does not seem entirely naive. The clothing metaphor, which Wordsworth elsewhere rejects in favor of incarnationist tropes (*Prose* 2:84–85), suggests an awareness of the distance between words and things, an abyss that cannot be bridged by mere appareling, any more than by carving poems in trees (or by writing them on paper, an attenuated form of the same act). Wordsworth uses epistemological terms to couch this visual disjunction between the intentionality of language and the physical objects that language attempts to present: the "label" is a "type" or "emblem," as he says in the 1805 *Prelude*, "of the utmost we can know" (7.618). The original version of these lines in MS X explicitly formulates the episode as a scene of reading (*NP* 260n7):

I thought
That even the very most of what we know,
Both of ourselves and of the universe,
The whole of what is written to our view,
Is but a label on a blind man's chest.

It would perhaps be overstating Wordsworth's response to this sight to say that it embodies a sudden consciousness that whatever is written on the paper cannot "refer" to the man wearing it. Wordsworth's concern is closer to a moral one, to a wish for self-knowledge acquired through such encounters with humanity. But self-knowledge, this scene of reading suggests, cannot be contained by a particular text but can only be intimated through the silence or space between texts, between the Beggar as he is and the paper that tells "who he was." This difference (though in the narrative past) implies a temporal as well as referential disjunction: writing, as representation, lags behind thought and at some distance from the objective referents that the thought intends. Perhaps this semiotic gap is "the utmost we can know," the closest that words can draw to things without being engraved or tattooed on them. Yet, while we might be able to know the "story" of another person, the image of the "label on a blind man's chest" suggests that self-knowledge is not so easily obtained: remember, the blind man cannot read his own history. Two implications: the self must be given its identity partly through the interpretive efforts of others; and all human knowledge—"the very most of what we know"—is but a macrosign ("a label") that posits yet another, inscrutable signified.

Why does the blind Beggar not speak? Is the semiological caesura between body and paper meant in some way to be a function of his blindness, his inability to read imaged as a scene of reading? He better far were mute. The absence of a voice—and the substitution of writing for that voice—sets the Beggar apart from most of Wordsworth's solitaries. Instead of the immediacy of speech, the distanced and deferred mode of writing serves as an epistemological limit, the utmost that language can show. The blindness, a type of muteness, suggests by extension that the Beggar would have to be deaf in order to speak.[15] His characterization recalls the earlier encounter between the poet and the discharged soldier in Book 4: the Beggar is "propped against a wall"; the soldier is supported "from behind, [where] / A milestone propped him" (4.396–97). The Beggar's paper explains "his story"; the poet inquires of the soldier "his history" (4.417). The mode of discourse with the Beggar is writing; with the soldier, "a quiet uncomplaining voice" (4.419). If the blind Beggar's scene of reading exposes the semiological difference between writing and presence, the soldier's voice also leaves something devoutly to be wished:

in all he said
There was a strange half-absence, as of one

> Knowing too well the importance of his theme,
> But feeling it no longer.
> (4.442–45)

Voice as "half-absence" is related to the "label" as half-presence, intending but never reaching its object. The soldier and the Beggar are linked imagistically to each other: they are both motionless and "propped" by a wall or stone. But what is more, their motionlessness and steadied support connect them with the image of Wordsworth's Leech-gatherer: "Himself he propped, limbs, body, and pale face, / Upon a long grey staff of shaven wood . . . Motionless as a cloud the old Man stood" ("Resolution" 71–72, 75). The final lines of the Beggar episode—"I gazed, / As if admonished from another world"—echo "Resolution and Independence" in the description of the Leech-gatherer, who is "like a man from some far region sent, / To give me human strength, by apt admonishment" (111–12). The chastening and subduing effects of the Leech-gatherer and the Beggar associate the episodes with the "spots of time" and their frequent element of "chastisement" (12.311)—with the poet's being figurally "smitten." But the imagistic resemblances between these two figures suggest deeper tropological associations. The Leech-gatherer, who appears "as if he had been reading in a book" (81), is pictured as "not all alive nor dead, / Nor all asleep," but as something halfway between "a huge stone" and a still "sea-beast" (64–65, 57, 62). Wordsworth's explication of this passage in the 1815 Preface at first seems to argue for a metalepsis of stone to sea beast to man, but in fact the rhetoric doubles back on itself in such a way that the man is imaged at the point where stone and beast "unite and coalesce in just comparison" (*Prose* 3:33). The two similes collapsed into the figure of the man allow him to take on the qualities of both images, but it is clear that the figural transformation is a downward metamorphosis: he "is divested of so much of the indications of life and motion" (*Prose* 3:33) that he appears less alive than a sea beast, though not as inanimate as a rock.

An analogous, if not exactly similar, process is at work in the Beggar's description. "The shape of that unmoving man," as Wordsworth calls it, allies him curiously to an inanimate object, one that has to be propped up. The man appears divested of the indications of life: no motion has he now, no force; he neither speaks nor sees. He is his own living epitaph. The "written paper" on his chest takes on lapidary qualities as this stationary figure assumes marmoreal significance. The Beggar and his text are almost explicitly epitaphic: his message is unearthly, "from another world," like the world beyond the grave, and its admonitory tone recalls the imperative and exhortatory mood of epitaphic Nature. The Beggar is not dead, nor all alive, but his state presents an "apt type" (7.644) of what Wordsworth's poetry is forever moving toward: the epitaph, the "memorial" (12.287), the frail shrine of language. The Beggar is a written "speaking monument" (8.172).

Yet a voice is wanting here. Usually Wordsworth's encounters with humanity involve a voice and a person. Think of the Solitary Reaper's song; the voice of the ladies of "Stepping Westward"; the peasant in the Simplon Pass, whose translated reply leads into the great paragraph on imagination; and the discharged soldier again, whose voice, like the voice of the Leech-gatherer, narrates a story that is not as impressive as the physical presence of its narrator. Yet a voice *is* present in the Beggar episode, if only obliquely. The Beggar's label is a written form of utterance that aspires to the innerness of voice. It is an utterance that is not uttered because it has already been "outered" through writing. The label spatializes the voice, making the Beggar no less a "speaking monument." And if, according to our theory of voice in Wordsworth, the sound of universal waters tends to the image of voice, shall the apocalyptic "might of waters" in this passage escape unnoticed and unheard? This "might of waters" contains a mighty "voice / Of sudden admonition" (11.336–37) that is silenced, usurped by the writing of the Beggar. Hence that most intricate evasion of *as*: "my mind turned round / *As* with the might of waters" (emphasis added)—as if the mind were set spinning by a voice and not by a letter. Insofar as the Beggar is a living epitaph, moreover, we hear a voice in the etymology of *epitaphium*, originally a funeral oration. In his first essay on epitaphs, Wordsworth chooses the graphological sense of the word, though he subscribes to the theory of vocal origin. "It need scarcely be said," the 1849–50 final version of the essay begins, "that an epitaph presupposes a Monument, upon which it is to be engraven." Yet in the next paragraph Wordsworth quotes Weever's discourse on *Ancient Funerall Monuments*, which claims that epitaphs were originally oral: "they were first sung at burials, after engraved upon the sepulchres" (*Prose* 2:49, 50).

But Wordsworth's personal definition of the epitaph is even

more instructive. The epitaph, he says, is an "epitomized biography" (*Prose* 2:89). Biography? What does this definition suggest about the relation between the Beggar and his label on the one hand, and the poet and his fourteen-book poem on the other? Can we say that the Beggar is a biographer, an autobiographer, even as he is an epitaphist? The epitomized autobiography written on his paper tells "whence he came, and who he was." Viewed in this way, Wordsworth's meeting with the blind Beggar becomes the image of the poet's encounter with his double, the meeting of autobiographer and autobiographer. Yet this encounter is anything but simple; the blindness, the silence, the impersonality all tend to put in question any attempt to read this scene as a moment of self-possession, as if Wordsworth suddenly acknowledged his double, or the text declared its awareness of this repetition within itself. As soon as the text offers such reflexive readings, based on an implicit model of self-presence, it seems to retract them. The Beggar cannot read his written self, and Wordsworth, for all his celebration of "the mighty world / Of eye, and ear" ("Tintern" 105–06), reveals the spots, silent and blind, that are integral to his rhetoric and that continually push the text from referential into reflexive narrative. "I cannot say what portion is in truth / The naked recollection of that time, / And what may rather have been called to life / By after-meditation," he says (3.613–16). The moment of retrospective silence, however, when one "cannot say," is also the moment of rhetorical response, when the text does say, though reflexively, and with a certain blindness to what it has said. The poem, in its own words, finds a self-answerable style.

Wordsworth's meeting with the Beggar, then, provides the imagistic and thematic correlative of what the language and structure of *The Prelude* have been enacting. The confrontation of the self with itself (or the double of itself) may produce a heightened self-consciousness—even, as Geoffrey Hartman has said, a "*consciousness of self raised to apocalyptic pitch*" (*WP* 17), but this state of mind is in turn, I think, a function of language, a product of a figural foregrounding that repeats language's own self-encounter. Paul de Man, in an essay on Rousseau, once stated this situation in a hypothesis that has far-reaching implications for Wordsworth: "If all language is about language, then the paradigmatic linguistic model is that of an entity that confronts itself" (*Allegories* 153). This is the "narcissistic" moment of language (*Allegories* 152),[16] the point where the poet-autobiographer is "smitten" with his mirror image, an emblem of all he is, the utmost he can know. The epitaphic qualities of the Beggar and his paper reflect on the poet's own scene of writing; *The Prelude* itself appears but a label on a blind man's chest: Wordsworth is composing his own epitaph too. The "single form" of the Beggar draws Wordsworth back to those points "within our souls / Where all stand single" (3.188–89). The poet and his double share a mute dialogue; both of them speak of something that is gone.

But the Beggar wears his text with a *difference*. Blind, mute, and nameless, he is the least egotistical of men, though sufficient to stand as Wordsworth's "second self" ("Michael" 39). Still, questions remain. To what extent is Wordsworth's encounter with his second self also an encounter with his former self—that is, with a precursor? Why is this other self a blind man, accessible only textually? Or perhaps, as Harold Bloom asks in a decidedly different context, "Need we question who this blind man is?" (*Poetry and Repression* 73). John Milton was no beggar, and although he was accessible to Wordsworth only textually—indeed, epitaphically ("Milton! thou shouldst be living at this hour" [*Poems* 1: 579])—the question of the point at which epitaph becomes allusion, naming or invoking an absence, requires separate discussion.

This striking episode in Book 7 is perhaps the clearest and most suggestive example in *The Prelude* of the rhetorical turn known as an "abyss structure" (*mise en abyme*). As James Hulbert, one of Jacques Derrida's translators, has pointed out, "the expression '*mise en abyme*,' originally from heraldry, where it denotes a smaller escutcheon appearing in the center of a larger one, is [used] to refer to a structure in which the whole is represented in miniature in one of its parts" (147–48).[17] The image of the poet writing his autobiographical poem is located in this *mise en abyme* with the Beggar and his label, which also becomes a kind of *mise en scène* for the "pageant" (7.637) or "spectacle" (7.643) of this reflexive drama. The characteristic effect of an abyss structure, either here or in the Simplon Pass, is one of vertigo, a "dizzying, unsettling" (Hulbert 148) experience not unlike Wordsworth's response to the blind man: "my mind turned round / As with the might of waters." The spinning action of the poet's mind suggests precisely this sort of dizziness at being cast into an abyss of epistemological reflexiveness. I am reminded of Shelley's essay "On Life": "We are on that verge where words abandon us, and what wonder if we grow dizzy to look down the dark abyss of—how little we know" (478). Rhetorically the turning round, or "troping," signals an equally disturbing linguistic spin in which writing is thrown back from its referential validity to its self-declaration as language. Perhaps we should not be surprised by this; perhaps we should even expect it, for is it not exquisitely fitting that a so-called "egotistical" poet should produce a "narcissistic" text?

I began this chapter by suggesting that *The Prelude* contains its own allegory of reading. We are closer now to seeing what that allegory is. It consists in the recurrent meetings of the poet with his own image, like the Magus Zoroaster in *Prometheus Unbound*, or in the recurrent foregroundings of the text as a piece of language. Yet these meetings and foregroundings by no means cancel the structure of difference within language, nor do they finally make the text more present to itself. The poem attempts to narrate the life of an actual person but finds itself instead narrating the semiological problems of that narration. Though Wordsworth's text never settles on a single term in the voice-letter alternation, it is accurate to say that voice is an ever-present but often veiled figure, and it bears repeating that in the language of Wordsworth natural phenomena tend to the image of voice. Grammatological images, by contrast, tend to be more situated. But I prefer to remain with the particular insights of the various readings given. The "naturalness" of "a man speaking to men" flows over into the text to create a so-called authentic voice in nature, but scenes of writing, being more "artificial," as it were, are also more instructive about the ways in which the poet translates the landscape, experience, and himself—into language.

—What, a play toward? I'll be an auditor;
An actor too perhaps, if I see cause.
Shakespeare, A Midsummer Night's Dream

THE OUTSIDE AND THE INSIDE: WORDSWORTH'S MIRROR STAGE

4

It is but a short step from examining Wordsworth's tropes of speech and writing, and the corresponding allegories of listening and reading which they imply, to considering the figure in which his reader and listener are combined. That figure is the spectator, whom we have already encountered in the London episodes, and in whom neither eye nor ear is privileged, images of sound and sight in nature combining to make "spectacles" or, specifically, "stage spectacles." The image of the spectator in *The Prelude* thematizes the self-regarding aspect of the text, repeatedly seen in the abyss structures of the blind Beggar, the boy poet of Winander, and the "spots of time." In Wordsworth's language for each of these moments of self-confrontation there is always, to use a Shelleyan metaphor, an "interpenetration" (504) or, to return to our Wordsworthian trope, a "usurpation" of one order of figure by another. The rhetoric of the Wordsworthian usurpation in language is inherently dramatic or "performative," to adapt Austin's term; it involves the fundamental rhetorical situation in which a performer and an audience are present, the very situation that Wordsworth implies when he defines the poet as "a man speaking to men" (*Prose* 1:138). For Wordsworth, the drama of self-encounter, with its "strength / Of usurpation," presents a simultaneous alternation of competing perspectives enacted and observed on a "mirror stage."

By using Jacques Lacan's term "the mirror stage" (*le stade du miroir*),[1] I mean to invoke both the image of reflection and reflexiveness, including reversal, suggested by the mirror metaphor; and the conceit of a dramatic structure implied in one sense of Lacan's "stage." "The *mirror stage*," Lacan writes, "is a drama . . . which manufactures for the subject, caught up in the lure of spatial identification, the succession of phantasies that extends from a fragmented body-image to a form of its totality" ("Mirror" 4). Wordsworth's mirror stage, in its dramatic or "specular" sense, comprises both the performative aspect of "a man speaking to men" and the observational stance of what Coleridge called a *spectator ab extra.*[2] The effect of a reflexive mirror stage, especially in *The Prelude*, may be compared (to alter Swift) to a sort of glass wherein the beholder does generally discover nobody's face but his own. The poet's self-discovery on the narrative or thematic level repeats the self-encounter of the poem on the rhetorical level: once again the "egotistical" poet finds himself in a "narcissistic" text.

An emphasis on the "performative" structure of drama—that is, the relation of actor to spectator—may be distinguished from the Coleridgean (and Keatsian) emphasis on the psychological or sympathetic relation of author to character, especially on the way an author is able to "feel with" his or her character. Wordsworth, however, is not usually thought of as a dramatic poet in this latter sense. Keats's well-known labeling of Wordsworth's style as the "egotistical sublime" (279) would appear to corroborate Coleridge's charge of "ventriloquism" (*Biographia* 258) in asserting Wordsworth's fundamental style of exteriority or projection. Wordsworth ventriloquizes, Coleridge says, by writing in a style in which "the thoughts and diction" of the characters are "indistinguishable" from those of the poet, and thus "two are represented as talking while in truth one man only speaks" (*Biographia* 258). Wordsworth's genius lies in another direction; he is, to recall Coleridge's trope, properly a viewer-from-without, "feeling *for*, but never *with*, [his] characters" (*Table Talk* 210–11).

My own understanding of drama in Wordsworth, however, is different. I would argue, as Coleridge does not, that even the phrase *spectator ab extra* contains a dramatic figure in a performative sense, if not in Coleridge's sympathetic sense. But if Coleridge faults Wordsworth for his "undue predilection for the dramatic form in certain poems" (*Biographia* 258), he also credits him for his rhetorical sensitivity to dramatic tropes in others. Quoting lines from "There was a Boy," Coleridge appends a lengthy footnote in *Biographia Literaria*, Chapter 20, to the verses "the visible scene / Would enter unawares into his mind" (21–22) and "echoes loud / Redoubled and redoubled, concourse wild" (14–15):

Mr Wordsworth's having judiciously adopted 'concourse wild' in this passage for 'a wild scene' as it stood in the former edition, encourages me to hazard a remark which I certainly should not have made in the works of a poet less austerely accurate in the use of words than he is, to his own great honor. It respects the propriety of the word 'scene' even in the sentence in which it is retained. Dryden, and he only in his more careless verses, was the first, as far as my researches have discovered, who for the convenience of rhyme used this word in the vague sense which has been since too current even in our best writers and which (unfortunately, I think) is given as its first explanation in Dr Johnson's Dictionary, and therefore would be taken by an incautious reader as its proper sense. In Shakespeare and Milton the word is never used without some clear reference, proper or metaphorical, to the theatre. Thus Milton:

'Cedar and pine, and fir and branching palm
A sylvan *scene*; and as the ranks ascend
Shade above shade, a woody *theatre*
Of stateliest view.'

I object to any extension of its meaning, because the word is already more equivocal than might be wished; inasmuch as in the limited use which I recommend it may still signify two different things; namely the scenery, and the characters and actions presented on the stage during the presence of particular scenes. It can therefore be preserved from obscurity only by keeping the original signification full in the mind. Thus Milton again:

'Prepare thee for another scene.'

(*Biographia* 233)

Coleridge's footnote alerts the reader to the dramatic aspect of Wordsworth's figural language, often present but hidden in a common expression, even in a single word such as "scene." There are other subtle examples. In the *Norton Prelude* the editors at one point gloss the text in a way that curiously denies a dramatic aspect as much as Coleridge's footnote asserts one. To the word "business" in the second of the "spots of time" they append the note: "I.e., busy-ness, activity" (436). Certainly, in the context of the passage, with

> the wind and sleety rain,
> And all the business of the elements,
> The single sheep, and the one blasted tree,
> And the bleak music of that old stone wall,
> The noise of wood and water . . .
> (12.317–21)

there does appear to be a great deal of activity or "busy-ness," in a general sense, with respect to the weather, the landscape, and especially the poet's mind. But it is not beyond question that "business" here for Wordsworth carries merely the sense of "goings-on," to use a favorite term of Coleridge's;[3] it is arguable, in fact, that he is using the word in the theatrical sense of "stage business," or the actions of actors as distinguished from their dialogue.[4] For Wordsworth to use "business" in this sense is to suggest something specifically dramatic about the experience: the trope personifies the wind and rain, making them characters along with the sheep and tree and wall. The young boy in the "scene" is also a spectator, "straining [his] eyes intensely" (12.303) over the "prospect" of the landscape (12.304), and straining his ears for the sound of the horses over the "bleak music" and "noise" around him. "All these," Wordsworth later recalls, "were kindred spectacles and sounds / To which I oft repaired" (12.324–25). The combination of eye and ear, spectacle and sound, places the boy in a starkly sublime natural theater, a *theatrum mundi*, as Curtius might call it (138–44), of which Wordsworth is the boy-spectator within and the unaccommodated man without. The scene is more one of drama and conflict (meteorological as well as phenomenological) than of general "activity" or commotion.

A parallel example occurs in the Ravine of Gondo. After another catalogue of natural elements in conflict,

> Winds thwarting winds, bewildered and forlorn,
> The torrents shooting from the clear blue sky,
> The rocks that muttered close upon our ears,
> Black drizzling crags that spake by the wayside
> As if a voice were in them, the sick sight
> And giddy prospect of the raving stream,
> The unfettered clouds and region of the Heavens,
> Tumult and peace, the darkness and the light . . .
> (6.628–35)

Wordsworth compares these speaking elements to the "characters of the great Apocalypse" (6.638). In the last chapter we saw that "characters" can have a distinctly graphological connotation: these spectacles are like a proleptic epitaph for the end of things. Yet, should it not also be urged that "characters" has the equally valid connotation of an actor in a role? The boy on the hill in Book 12 tropes the elements as characters in a solemn drama; is this not the case here as well? These characters are part of the book of nature, but they are also part of a book of revelation. Wordsworth would have known, from his reading of Milton not least, the Renaissance tradition of interpreting the Apocalypse of St. John as a drama. Milton, in the preface to *Samson Agonistes* and in the second book of *The Reason of Church Government*, alludes to the German theologian David Pareus to support his effort to give Biblical sanction to the genre of drama. Milton writes that "the Apocalypse of St. John is the majestic image of a high and stately tragedy . . . and this my opinion the grave authority of Pareus, commenting that book, is sufficient to confirm" (669; see also 549). Pareus's commentary includes a detailed description of the business of the "*Propheticall Drama*" of Revelation (Milton 669n171), and the conclusion: "I more truly may say touching the Revelation, that it seemes unto mee, the Lord Iesus revealed the same unto Iohn by his Angell, after the manner of a *Drammaticall Representation*" (Milton 669n170). Wordsworth's "characters of the great Apocalypse" may originate in a sacred drama, but they are adapted to a natural spectacle in which imaginative perception replaces divine revelation and external dramatic structure yields to the deeper, internal drama of words.

My concern in this chapter is not with Wordsworth's dramatic technique or narrative method—Stephen Parrish has already explored that area sufficiently with respect to *Lyrical Ballads* (80–148)—but rather, as these first examples show, with the implications of his dramatic language, with his tropes of drama, theater, spectacle, and performance. I am not concerned, therefore, to take issue with John Jones, who argues that Wordsworth's "talent was not only undramatic in its kind, but in a positive sense the denial of drama" (61). Jones may be right in the sense of Wordsworth's failure to identify with his characters (although even this interpretation deserves rethinking), but there is nothing undramatic about Wordsworth's rhetoric. Let me show how the dance of *difference* in language is fundamentally for Wordsworth the operation of a mirror stage on which the reader sees the simultaneous alternation of hierarchical oppositions such as subject/object, inside/outside, and, in our specific figures under consideration, spectator/actor.

One might expect a text like *The Prelude* to encourage such rhetorical reversals partly because the terms of subject and object in the poem are already identified in the self as both character and author. Similarly, according to this view, what is perceived as being "outside" is also "inside," the perceiver and the perceived being one and the same. In the terms here, terms that both Frederick Garber and Martin Price have used in a different sense,[5] the spectator is thus also the actor, and what he watches is himself performing. Yet, leaving aside Garber's and Price's views of doubleness as fusion or identity rather than difference and usurpation, how is the alternation of the subject with the object accomplished in the text? In rhetorical terms, how is Wordsworth both inside and outside the drama of his mind, differentially spectator and spectacle in the theater of language?

Parrish's suggestion that a "dramatic dimension" in Wordsworth provides "esthetic distance" between the poet and reality (14) can be applied to *The Prelude* as well as to *Lyrical Ballads*. With *The Prelude*, however, the mechanism of "distancing" is anything but innocent. Does Wordsworth, by employing tropes of a mirror stage, implicate himself in a simple hierarchical favoring of distance over proximity, in which distance, exteriority, perspective, specularity, and objectivity define the poet as a *spectator ab extra* of the growth of his own mind? Partly—but the Wordsworthian "counter-spirit" (*Prose* 2:85) of language in such moments suggests that each distancing, each exteriorizing, each dramatizing locates the poet within the abyss of his own viewing, creating a *mise en abyme* that is also a *mise en scène*.

Paul de Man, in a seminal essay on Romantic allegory and symbol, has demonstrated the tension that exists between different valorizations of subject and object. His deconstruction of the Romantic symbol is relevant to the question we are addressing here. De Man writes:

> The assertion of a radical priority of the subject over objective nature is not easily compatible with the poetic praxis of the romantic poets, who all gave a great deal of importance to the presence of nature. . . . One can find numerous quotations

> and examples that plead for the predominance, in romantic poetry, of an analogical imagination that is founded on the priority of natural substances over the consciousness of the self. ("Rhetoric of Temporality" 180–81)

With Wordsworth, what I shall call the competing valorizations of subject and object are easily located. We have already seen how *The Prelude*, in its form of autobiography, attempts a fusion of subject and object, but such an identification is never achieved in the form of a simple presence. Every repetition has its difference, and at those points where subject and object seem most to coincide there is always a silent rhetorical struggle between them for ontological as well as figural priority. Evidence of Wordsworth's privileging of the subject over the object, or of the inside over the outside, can be seen in his emphasis on the "spontaneous" aspect of his poetry (*Prose* 1:127, 149)—which M. H. Abrams takes as the motto for an "expressive" orientation of art (*Mirror* 22)—in his choice of topic as the growth of a poet's *mind*, and in his declaration of theme as "what passed within [him]" (3.176). Yet the competing priority of object over subject, of outside over inside, is everywhere found in Wordsworth as well, in his joy experienced in "the beautiful and permanent forms of nature" (*Prose* 1:125)—what de Man calls "the ontological stability of the natural object" ("Intentional Structure" 69)—in his stress on the powers of "Observation and Description" in poetry (*Prose* 3:26), and, most elementally, in his rhetoric of the epitaph, in which fixed object and speaking subject interinhabit each other. Nowhere is the "interchangeable supremacy" (14.84) of these competing perspectives so elaborately seen as in the rhetoric of a mirror stage, where the trope of a distanced spectator can be deconstructed to reveal its performative supplement already within. Let us read Wordsworth's performative language in three distinct moments in *The Prelude*: Cambridge, London, and France. In each case we shall discover a Wordsworthian counter-spirit of language working to turn the text inside out. Though there may not be any "*hors-texte*," as Derrida has claimed (*Grammatology* 158), there is undeniably a pull within language to get outside language. But inevitably the figure outside the text turns into the text, entering it while attempting to maintain its exteriority. Wordsworth's desire for distance revolves on a performative trope that measures itself according to the poet's interpenetration of what we might call, after Poulet, an "interior distance."

Cambridge

The opening of Book 3 of *The Prelude* asserts a heroic status which is quickly undermined. The 1805 version describes when the poet first

> saw
> The long-backed chapel of King's College rear
> His pinnacles above the dusky groves.
> (1805:3.3–5)

The intertext here is *Paradise Lost*, the passage the same as the one echoed in Book 14 when Wordsworth, reaching the top of Snowdon, recalls Milton's account of creation, when "the Mountains huge appear / Emergent, and thir broad bare backs upheave / Into the Clouds" (7.285–87).[6] Historically as well as intertextually the speaker is entering Milton's territory—his university, his sphere of influence—and Wordsworth responds by announcing the challenge of his new "heroic argument" (3.184) in contrast to Milton's. Book 3 is in many ways Milton's book; and there is the sense, in Wordsworth's unusually self-conscious stance vis-à-vis his experience at Cambridge that he is at some pains to keep himself at arm's length from Milton. There is something threatening about Cambridge, as suggested by the whirling images of the "eddy's force" (3.14) and the vertigo of the mind (3.624–28) that frame the entire book. It is as if Wordsworth fears to be swept into the abyss, overwhelmed by the Miltonic underpresence; hence his struggle to portray himself as maintaining a "safe" distance in rhetorical as well as psychological terms. Yet I am reluctant to assign a biographical motivation to what is fundamentally a linguistic phenomenon in which figures of exteriority compete with figures of interiority, though a complex Miltonic intertextuality is undoubtedly at issue here as well.

Having invoked the Miltonic voice in the context of pinnacles, mountain-climbing, and creation—Wordsworth retraces his life up to "an eminence" (3.171) and speaks "of genius, power, / Creation and divinity itself" (3.173–74)—the poet undercuts the heroic with the mock-heroic in the line "And at the *Hoop* alighted, famous Inn" (3.17). The function of this gentle self-parody, which many readers, including Matthew Arnold, have misunderstood,[7] is central to our concerns here and later in the poem. The effect of the self-mockery is to "distance" Wordsworth, to exteriorize him from the world he sees. The overwhelming impression of Wordsworth's account of his undergraduate years at Cambridge is that he remained "detached /

Internally from academic cares" (6.25–26), on the periphery of university life, outside an inner circle of community, "feeling that [he] was not for that hour, / Nor for that place" (3.81–82). In other words, in the language really used by men and women today, he was not "into" school. But we can overturn the author's palpable intention to portray himself as not "into" the scene, and show that he is inside even as he claims to be outside.

The first trope that follows the introduction again appears to provide a figural distance between the speaker and the other students: "I was the Dreamer, they the Dream" (3.30). The specular structure of the double metaphor suggests something of the spectator/actor combination; the poet as dreamer stands back and views his own dream. We do not need a Keats here to tell us that the poet and the dreamer are distinct, for Wordsworth's text silently does that: the poet is not the dreamer, for the man speaking to men creates a text that is uttered or outered, made outside of himself; the dreamer, however, cannot get outside the text of his own unconscious without ceasing to be a dreamer. Sleeping and dreaming provide surface images of separation, but at a deeper level they constitute a rhetoric of interiority. Thus when Wordsworth, to demonstrate his detachment, his "loose and careless mind" (3.29), says "I was the Dreamer, they the Dream," the statement can be read as reversing the intended externalizing gesture, for no dream exists except within a dreamer. The objects and feelings that Wordsworth describes are not distanced from him; they are within him and he within them: Wordsworth participates in something which is thought to be exterior but which is seen to be interior. He passes into his own dream.

"I roamed / Delighted through the motley spectacle," he says (3.30–31), describing Cambridge life, but the awkward difference between the scene and its principal actor is obvious in the lines that follow:

> Gowns grave, or gaudy, doctors, students, streets,
> Courts, cloisters, flocks of churches, gateways, towers:
> Migration strange for a stripling of the hills,
> A northern villager.
>
> (3.32–35)

The "motley spectacle" is an ironic drama of foolishness, with doctors and students taking the parts of jesters. The speaker is above such nonsense; the naturalistic metaphors by which he chooses to characterize himself—"migration," associated with birds and animals as well as people (perhaps suggested by the *flocks* of churches?), and "stripling of the hills"—stress the contrast between the natural "villager" and the motley world of Cambridge. But Wordsworth's reversal comes suddenly; his "change" (3.35) from external spectator into internal actor seems magical, the act of "some Fairy's wand" (3.36)—as it should seem in the midst of a "dream." "Behold me," Wordsworth says, "rich in moneys, and attired / In splendid garb, with hose of silk, and hair / Powdered like rimy trees" (3.37–39). Outwardly, the change represents his initiation into Cambridge life, his being costumed to enter the "spectacle" of which he is both viewer and participant. Yet a self-mocking tone persists in excluding the poet from his drama, making him still a spectator, though in costume: "My lordly dressing-gown, I pass it by" (3.40).

To Wordsworth, Cambridge was a "dazzling show" (3.90) that gradually "ceased to dazzle" (3.91) him. The key trope of the university as a "show," with all its theatrical connotations, recurs about a hundred lines later:

> It hath been told, that when the first delight
> That flashed upon me from this novel show
> Had failed, the mind returned into herself;
> Yet true it is, that I had made a change
> In climate, and my nature's outward coat. . . .
> (3.204–08)

The "change / In climate" recalls the earlier "migration" metaphor, emphasizing the attitude of displacement. The moment when "the mind returned into herself," an intratextual reference to the business of the mind's "into herself returning" (3.96), forms a variation of the interior/exterior pattern in the book: the mind, exercising what Wordsworth in *The Excursion* calls its "*excursive* power" (4.1263), sends itself abroad and participates in the spectacle; when the show loses its delight, the imagination withdraws its projection. But this introversion, which is also an introspection, a seeking for those "points . . . within our souls / Where all stand single" (3.188–89), is at the same time an outward joining with community, personal "community with highest truth" (3.126) and social community of "companionships, / Friendships, acquaintances" (3.249–50). Still,

Wordsworth declares that his theme is "what passed within" him (3.176), not "outward things / Done visibly" (3.176–77). The rhetoric makes it difficult to distinguish between the two sides.

The performative trope linking drama and dream is made explicit after Wordsworth's account of his non-academic pastimes. He writes: "Such was the tenor of the second act / In this new life. Imagination slept" (3.259–60). In the 1805 version it is "the opening act / In this new life" (3.259–60), but the rhetorical significance is the same: the poet imposes the fragment of a dramatic structure on the events of his life, and yet that structure proceeds from a source that is not dependent on those events for its drama. Hence the mind again returns into itself, creating the image of the solitary poet who is

> Like a lone shepherd on a promontory
> Who lacking occupation looks far forth
> Into the boundless sea, and rather makes
> Than finds what he beholds.
> (3.516–19)

The specularity of the simile ("like a lone shepherd on a promontory") is consistent with the figural language used throughout the book; the creating of a vision by a lone poet on an eminence describes the theme not just of Book 3 but of the whole poem: the transformation of Cambridge into spectacle and show (second act) belies any sleeping imagination. Yet the vision, once created, does not work to exclude the creator; he enters it as he creates it, and stands as a subject in an object of his own making.

The memory of certain theatrical elements of Cambridge life causes Wordsworth to compare his drama with others:

> At this day
> I smile, in many a mountain solitude
> Conjuring up scenes as obsolete in freaks
> Of character, in points of wit as broad,
> As aught by wooden images performed
> For entertainment of the gaping crowd
> At wake or fair.
> (3.570–76)

Like the lawyers and politicians of London, who are, as Wordsworth discovers in Book 7, performers on "that great stage" (7.491) of Parliament and the courts, the "grave Elders" (3.545) of the university—men who are described, dramatically, as "grotesque / In character" (3.545–46)—are compared to puppet shows of the kind that Wordsworth also encounters in London. Cambridge is a stylized comedy of manners in which Wordsworth is reluctant to be involved; it is also something of a masque, though one in which he is likewise uninterested:

> The surfaces of artificial life
> And manners finely wrought, the delicate race
> Of colours, lurking, gleaming up and down
> Through that state arras woven with silk and gold;
> This wily interchange of snaky hues,
> Willingly or unwillingly revealed,
> I neither knew nor cared for. . . .
> (3.562–68)

De Selincourt is right to think that Spenser surely stands behind this "arras" that displays a masque-like variety of colors and pictures (531–32); the metaphor of Cambridge as a tapestry or "elaborate fabric" (3.570) turns the experience into a tableau, another spectacle to be observed. From tropes of stage and arras Wordsworth shifts to a different specular moment, that of reading a book, "Nature's book of rudiments" (3.557), in which he views characters as letters rather than as actors in a play. The structure of exteriority in all these figures is clear; as Neil Hertz says of Wordsworth in Book 7, so here "the poet adopts the showman's stance" ("Blockage" 81), actually "conjuring up" (3.572) his dramatic scenes. The poet is a conjurer, a dramaturge, a viewer standing outside the drama he has made.

Yet in a deliberately casual statement Wordsworth immediately reverses the situation and places himself within the *mise en scène*. "I play the loiterer," he says (3.582). Play? Wordsworth is playing a role? Indeed he is, but if the veil of familiarity masks the performative trope in the expression "I play," Wordsworth's catalogue of fellow actors in the mirror spectacle of Cambridge makes it more explicit:

> And here was Labour, his own bondslave; Hope,
> That never set the pains against the prize;
> Idleness halting with his weary clog,
> And poor misguided Shame, and witless Fear,
> And simple Pleasure foraging for Death;
> Honour misplaced, and Dignity astray;
> Feuds, factions, flatteries, enmity, and guile;

Murmuring submission, and bald government,
(The idol weak as the idolator),
And Decency and Custom starving Truth,
And blind Authority beating with his staff
The child that might have led him; Emptiness
Followed as of good omen, and meek Worth
Left to herself unheard of and unknown.
(3.598–611)

The passage reads like the program for a *commedia dell'arte*. We should remember, in the midst of all these personified nouns, that the part of loiterer is played by Wordsworth. Through this "pageant" (3.588) or "motley spectacle" (here expressing a strong moral sentiment), Wordsworth wanders "as through a wide museum" (3.620): he is both spectator and exhibit, curiously, for even as he goes "through" he seems to be outside. He is the "artless rustic" (3.599), yet he is the astonishingly artful writer-director of the whole production; he has, in fact, "called to life" (3.615) everything that he sees. There is a hint at the end of the book that the poet feels the dizzying effect of his doubling of roles at university—that is, as the strayed reveler from those revels of which he is in truth the master. The spinning, vertiginous effect of the "eddy's force" of Cambridge, which at the beginning of the book seems "to suck" Wordsworth "in" (3.14), is felt again at the end when the poet's head "turns round and cannot right itself" (3.626) amid the "barren sense / Of gay confusion" (3.627–28). Likewise, in Book 7, when Wordsworth sees the blind Beggar, his "mind turn[s] round / As with the might of waters" (7.643–44). The verbal echo suggests deeper similarities. The specular moment of Cambridge, when the poet first sees himself in the allegorical drama of his own making, has overtones of the "spots of time": though originally unsettling, it is a moment "whence profit may be drawn in times to come" (3.631).

London

The rhetorical structure of Book 7 elevates the underlying tropes of drama and spectacle to the level of explicit thematic description. Book 7, Neil Hertz has commented, "is the book of spectacle, theatricality, oratory, advertising, and *ad hoc* showmanship." It presents, he continues, "the sometimes exhilarating, sometimes baffling proliferation, not merely of sights and sounds, objects and people, but of consciously chosen and exhibited modes of representation" ("Blockage" 79). Such terms as scene, show, spectacle, drama, stage, and their variations, occur more than two dozen times in the book.

Wordsworth's strategy in using a figural language of drama here is much the same as in Book 3: the trivialization of the sights and sounds of London is another "distancing" technique to make him the passer-by, the on-looker. He is certainly that much, as his catalogues of attractions make clear. Early on, however, he encounters an arresting sight:

> A raree-show is here,
> With children gathered round; another street
> Presents a company of dancing dogs,
> Or dromedary, with an antic pair
> Of monkeys on his back; a minstrel band
> Of Savoyards; or, single and alone,
> An English ballad-singer.
> (7.174–80)

Need we ask whom this "English ballad-singer" is a double of? Wordsworth is forever the spectator, "single and alone," yet he has the uncanny habit of running into himself wherever he goes. Every moment of self-encounter, as *mise en abyme*, is also a mirror stage, a *mise en scène*, in which actor and spectator simultaneously compete for priority.

Richard D. Altick's book *The Shows of London* gives the reader a good idea of the kinds of sights Wordsworth might have been referring to when he writes:

> At leisure, then, I viewed, from day to day,
> The spectacles within doors,—birds and beasts
> Of every nature, and strange plants convened
> From every clime; and, next, those sights that ape
> The absolute presence of reality,
> Expressing, as in mirror, sea and land,
> And what earth is, and what she has to show.
> (7.229–35)

This last line sounds familiar. "Earth has not anything to show more fair" ("Westminster Bridge") than London itself—at least, when it is sleeping or, as J. Hillis Miller has suggested, when it is dead, that is, when "all that mighty heart is lying still."[8] The introduction of an explicit mimetic or representational element in the multi-media shows of London—"sights that ape / The absolute presence of reality"—builds on the spectator/spectacle structure. It throws into relief the contrast between the external mimesis of the city ("as in mirror") and the internal drama of Wordsworth's poem—what mind is and what she has to show. The merging of drama as presentation and mimesis as re-presentation is seen again in Wordsworth's misquote of *Hamlet*. He writes:

> Here, too, were 'forms and pressures of the time,'
> Rough, bold, as Grecian comedy displayed
> When Art was young; dramas of living men,
> And recent things yet warm with life. . . .
> (7.288–91)

The intertextual appeal of these lines suggests that Wordsworth is thinking of mimesis in terms of reference to a transcendental signified ("the absolute presence of reality"); his simile of the mirror to image this realistic reflexiveness, particularly in the *Hamlet* context, also suggests that the mimesis is topical, historical, referential. The end of stage-playing, Hamlet says, is "to hold, as 'twere, the mirror up to nature; to show virtue her own feature, scorn her own image, and the very age and body of the time his form and pressure" (3.2.19–23). The dramatic mimesis of *The Prelude* thus has two dimensions—one that hopes to present an absolute reality, and another that attempts to re-present a topical actuality, especially a history of departed things, or of "recent things yet warm with life." Wordsworth's language is revealing, for "things yet warm with life" seems a periphrasis for things that have just died: the prosopopoeia gives time itself a very age and body. Here, in his observations on drama and mimesis, even as in his practice in the lyric, Wordsworth's tendency is again toward the epitaph, toward things yet warm with life that need their memorial.

The section of Book 7 that treats the difference between presentation and re-presentation works to characterize the poet as the spectator before the mirror of reality, that is, as the detached observer of a mediated object, but it also prepares the reader for the competing movement that places Wordsworth before the same mirror in which the reflection is only of himself. This interiorization is accomplished in the Maid of Buttermere passage that follows the catalogue of "things yet warm with life" that serve as suitable dramatic topics. But Wordsworth's personal interest in the story of Mary Robinson[9]—"a story drawn / From our own ground," as he says (7.296–97)—makes him call it "too serious theme for that light place" (7.295) of Sadler's Wells; the apostrophe to Coleridge at this point in the narrative also has the effect of personalizing the moment. The text's underlying inclination toward epitaph surfaces here in the "memorial tribute" (7.316) to Mary of Buttermere and in the echoes of "Lycidas" that we noted in Chapter 2: "For we [Wordsworth and Mary] were nursed, as almost might be said, / On the same mountains" (1805:7.341–42). By invoking "Lycidas" Wordsworth in effect casts Mary in the role of elegiac object: "This memorial verse / Comes from the Poet's heart, and is her due" (1805:7.339–40). The Norton editors note that "despite the seeming implication of 'memorial' . . . Mary lived on, and married a local farmer" (*NP* 244), but such commentary seems to go out of its way to deny the very implication that it senses. This is indeed a monumental text. Wordsworth describes Mary as a mother who is so closely identified with her dead child, and who is cast in such a quiet, static, even marmoreal, role as to be virtually lifeless herself. The Maid of Buttermere is another "living epitaph." The digression on Mary results in a moment of "blockage," as Hertz would say, a rising-up of apostrophe:

> From this memorial tribute to my theme
> I was returning, when, with sundry forms
> Commingled—shapes which met me in the way
> That we must tread—thy image rose again,
> Maiden of Buttermere! She lives in peace
> Upon the spot where she was born and reared;
> Without contamination doth she live
> In quietness, without anxiety:
> Beside the mountain chapel, sleeps in earth
> Her new-born infant, fearless as a lamb. . . .
> (7.316–25)

The rising-up of the image comes athwart Wordsworth in a way that looks back to the apotheosis of imagination in Book 6. The close proximity of "spot" and "contamination" links the idea of place to a moral content, but the surface rhetoric emphatically denies any connection: "Upon the spot . . . Without contamination . . . without anxiety." In the 1805 text a complementary moment of arrest occurs, a "crossing" of the poet's path by the memory of another mother and child:

mid the numerous scenes which they
Have left behind them, foremost I am crossed
Here by remembrance of two figures. . . .
(7.364–66)

The forward narrative movement of Wordsworth is thus twice stopped by images of memory, first by Mary of Buttermere and her child, and now by a London mother's son, who provides an unnatural contrast to Mary Robinson's "nameless babe" (7.380). The description of this other "lovely Boy" (7.336, 367) who is placed on public view on a board, "*his* little stage in the vast theatre" (7.358) of London, is ambiguous, though its function as an example of Wordsworth's detaching himself from a local or personal perspective and again distancing himself to the vantage point of spectator seems clear. The little child is "surrounded with a throng / Of chance spectators, chiefly dissolute men / And shameless women" (7.359–61); he is "like one of those who walked with hair unsinged / Amid the fiery furnace" (7.369–70) of Daniel 3. Innocence amid experience, purity amid debauchery, unself-consciousness amid "wretched" (7.368) consciousness: the child seems like the object of a regressive desire of Wordsworth's. But the specular structure of the experience also suggests that the child can be read as another double of Wordsworth himself, not as something he once was and would like to be again, but as something he is now. The child in the theater is a figure for Wordsworth in London. "Neither vice nor guilt, / Debasement undergone by body or mind, / Nor all the misery forced upon [his] sight" (8.645–47) in the streets of London can overthrow Wordsworth's trust in humanity; the poet walks through a fiery furnace—akin to the semiotic inferno that Simpson mentions (64)—and comes out unscathed:

From those sad scenes when meditation turned,
Lo! every thing that was indeed divine
Retained its purity inviolate,
Nay brighter shone, by this portentous gloom
Set off. . . .
(8.654–58)

Like Adam in the closing books of *Paradise Lost*, Wordsworth in London is "yet in Paradise / Though fallen from bliss" (8.659–60). The child's experience, however, is different: the "little Actor" ("Intimations" 103) becomes trapped in the role to which Wordsworth's imagination assigns him, the *puer aeternus*: "He hath since / Appeared to me oft times as if embalmed / By Nature" (1805:7.398–400). This astonishing image of the arresting of innocence, and its embalming by nature, would have horrified Blake. Wordsworth conjectures that even if he were grown to manhood, the child might have felt a power of thanatos equal to the one implied in the poet's response to the boy, "till he could look / With envy on [the] nameless babe that sleeps, / Beside the mountain chapel, undisturbed" (7.379–81). The envying of the dead by the living is a convention not foreign to elegy—consider the close of Shelley's "Adonais"[10]—but in the context of the Buttermere interlude the regressive desire, projected onto a character but still emanating from the speaker himself, serves both to involve and to dislocate the poet.

What is remarkable in these episodes is their muted epitaphic style. Wordsworth, as epitaphist, gazes on Mary and her child, even as he looks, in Book 5, on the Boy of Winander, "a long half hour together" (5.396); the London boy, similarly, is imagined to stare at a grave "with envy." The poet is admittedly a spectator, but to the extent that he identifies himself with the Boy of Winander, with his childhood neighbor Mary, and with the inviolate child in London, he is also a participant in this epitaphic spectacle, standing proleptically over his own grave, or the graves of second selves. If, as Geoffrey Hartman has said, "the poet who stands at the child's grave knows that consciousness is always *of* death, a confrontation of the self with a buried self" (*WP* 22), then the intentional structure of the mirror stage in *The Prelude* is analogous to the figure of epitaph, in which what is thought to be a buried voice becomes a "speaking monument" (8.172).

There is a consistency in Wordsworth's favoring the "casual incidents" (7.402) of real life over the "measured passions of the stage" (7.405): we perceive an analogy to his privileging of "the language really used by men" over the artificial passions of poetic diction (see *Prose* 1:123–27). We also recall how the "great stage" (7.491) of Parliament rivals the drama of the traditional playhouses later in Book 7. "Yet was the theatre my dear delight," protests Wordsworth (7.407), attempting to redress the wavering balance between indoor and outdoor dramas. But in another reversal he steps back and celebrates the occasional breaking of dramatic illusion indoors; he views the theatricality as theatricality, and the usurping power of the mind to suspend its disbelief gives him joy:

> When at a country-playhouse, some rude barn
> Tricked out for that proud use, if I perchance
> Caught, on a summer evening through a chink
> In the old wall, an unexpected glimpse
> Of daylight, the bare thought of where I was
> Gladdened me more than if I had been led
> Into a dazzling cave of romance. . . .
> (7.449–55)

What has priority here? He knows that the play is a play, but does the consciousness of illusion usurp the illusion itself? Wordsworth is a spectator of a drama; his self-consciousness makes him realize that he is also *in* a drama, within a dramatic construct ("some rude barn / Tricked out"); and his consciousness of that consciousness—his reflection—in turn makes him a supra-spectator, a phenomenological *spectator ab extra*. There is no end, no ultimate term in this *mise en abyme* of spectator-participant regressions. If, as Husserl said (120, 242), all consciousness is intentional, that is, conscious *of* something, the spectator is faced with an actor; every actor presupposes a spectator. The two figures enjoy a mutual usurpation of encounter.

Let me pause here to venture some theoretical considerations. I have shown how Wordsworth's text repeatedly offers moments when the speaking or writing subject confronts objects and characters which it perceives to be external to or different from itself, but no sooner is the exteriority of these moments asserted than we begin to see how they contain aspects of interiority. It is as if for Wordsworth there really is no "world of the other," to use Frederick Garber's phrase (14), except as that world is shown to be always already within the world of the self. If this interpenetration constitutes a *mise en abyme* in Wordsworth's poetry, it is an abyss which the poet himself struggled over. "I was often unable," he writes of his childhood in the note to the "Intimations Ode," "to think of external things as having external existence, and I communed with all that I saw as something not apart from, but inherent in, my own immaterial nature" (*Poems* 1:978). This often-quoted passage can be read not only as a description of Wordsworth's feelings in childhood, but also as an account of his experience at Cambridge, for the binary opposition of inside and outside that Wordsworth denies here, declaring the "external" to be "inherent," recalls the subtext of his claim: "I was the Dreamer, they the Dream." The numerous characters that Wordsworth meets, observes, or apostrophizes in *The Prelude* thus serve a dual function, as they assert a difference between the poet and his object of encounter, but a difference that is also a repetition or doubling of the figure of the poet himself. In other words, the totalized, "egotistically sublime" self becomes ventriloquized into a multiplicity of selves, each of which presents in miniature a reflection of Wordsworth. The reflection is not a literal one, of course, and it inevitably involves some distortion and reversal, but it nevertheless offers the poet an image of potential self-knowledge. The crucial point is that self-knowledge, the object of the "rigorous inquisition" (1.148) that begins *The Prelude*, is never revealed as presence, but as difference; and yet the paradox is that this imagistic difference (here in the form of distance or exteriority) is always subject to a rhetorical interference that insinuates images of presence into the midst of difference. Two examples which are beyond our scope here, but which would focus the play of self and other in *The Prelude*, are the images of Coleridge and Dorothy. To what extent are these figures—the one, as we saw in Chapter 2, a negative double of the poet, the other a former self that he hears and reads in "Tintern Abbey"—"second selves" of Wordsworth, and how do they fit the pattern of reciprocity between inside and outside?

Let me pursue a second implication of Wordsworth's mirror stage, following a hint from Harold Bloom. According to his *Map of Misreading*, alternations of inside and outside belong to a psychic defense strategy in which the poet attempts to mask his belatedness, his exteriority or derivativeness vis-à-vis a precursor poet (84).[11] "It is no accident," Bloom writes, "that so many important poems of the last two hundred years conclude with an imagistic movement from inside/outside polarities to early/late reversals" (*Map* 101). We will see such a movement in Book 9, where the poet's spatially peripheral, psychically indifferent relation to the French Revolution is translated into the image of a late spectator. But do the reversals that I have been describing here conform to Bloom's strategy, and, if so, how is such a strategy related to the encounter of the self with itself? It might be answered that in Wordsworth's scene of encounter, just as in Freud's scene of lovemaking, there are always four people present: the subject, the object, the precursor, and the reader. Not all are discretely present; sometimes all four seem to crowd into one, as when Wordsworth re-reads his former textual self in his later poetry. Let us consider such an encounter between self and text in *The Prelude*.

The central reflexive episode in the book of London is Wordsworth's meeting with the blind Beggar, in whom the tropes of mirror and stage are subtly joined. Though we saw the episode as a scene of reading in which the self meets itself and discovers in that meeting an epistemological limit ("the utmost we can know" [7.645]) derived from a semiological structure (a "label" on a blind man's chest [7.645]), we may restate the encounter now in performative terms. The Beggar is an autobiographer, like the poet, but he is also associated with the role of actor, specifically with the actual actor some four hundred lines earlier who also wears a written text on his chest (the word "*Invisible*" [7.287]). The actor sees, but is not supposed to be seen; the Beggar cannot see, but wishes to be seen, even read, like a text. He is to be seen as a character in a drama, and to be read like the characters on his paper. Is the Beggar any different from all the other dramas that the poet sees in London? Wordsworth does call the blind man a "spectacle" (7.643), one in a "moving pageant" (7.637). Sure enough, there is also something dream-like about the encounter; it is like "a second-sight procession, such as glides / Over still mountains, or appears in dreams" (7.633–34). "In such mood" (7.635) Wordsworth wanders as through a dream, spectator of the "solemn background" (7.622) of the city that throws into relief single, foregrounded characters. Insofar as the Beggar is both a dramatic character and the rhetorical double of the poet himself, we may see to what point, and how, Wordsworth is at once alternately viewer and participant in the same drama—not just autobiographer meeting autobiographer, but actor confronting actor, spectator observing actor, spectator encountering (sightless) spectator. The rhetoric suggests a theater and its double in language.

Can we express this doubling strictly on the level of words? It is related, I suggest, to the reflexive structure of language generally. "Though reared upon the base of outward things," Wordsworth writes, "structures like these the excited spirit mainly / Builds for herself" (7.650, 651–52). These scenes of doubling and encounter, while possessing a referential "base of outward things," continually usurps that base by thematizing language's preoccupation with itself through the image of a mirror stage. But before pursuing these conclusions too far, let us complete our demonstration of the competing movements of interiority and exteriority in books 9 to 11 of *The Prelude*.

France

When we turn to the books on France, we expect the rhetoric of drama to expand to epic proportions. If there were one period in his life that Wordsworth might wish to "distance," it would be his experience in the French Revolution: it is "passion over-near [himself], / Reality too close and too intense" (11.57–58), and therefore would seem to need aesthetic deferral. But we find here, as in the earlier books, that the alternating pattern of proximity and distance is at work, that even as the poet attempts to place himself outside his experience the text keeps locating him within it.

Book 9 opens by setting itself in relation to the poet's sojourn in London. His explicit reference to the great city displays the inner/outer simultaneity that we have been tracing. The 1805 version shows Wordsworth

> in the midst of things, it seemed,
> Looking as from a distance on the world
> That moved about me. . . .
> (1805: 9.23–25)

By 1850 this paradoxical movement from center ("in the midst") to circumference ("as from a distance") and back to center ("the world / That moved about me") is condensed to its rhetorical trope of oxymoron: Wordsworth calls London simply a "crowded solitude" (9.29). He is in the midst of things, yet he observes as from afar; he is "single and alone" (7.179), yet surrounded by multitudinousness; he is inside and outside, spectator and actor, center and circumference of his experience. But in Paris the intentional distancing of the poet is doubled through the ear as well as through the eye, not only by means of the specular structure of the moment but by means of its linguistic incomprehensibility. The French city is a "hubbub wild" (9.58), more a Babel than a Pandemonium (Potts 323), and Wordsworth is conventionally by now, the audience: "I stared and listened, with a stranger's ears" (9.57). Early in Book 10 he returns to the problem of the French language—his "half-learnt speech" (9.192)—as a strategy of exteriority, a proof of his peripheral existence; he gazes on the events in France

> as doth a man
> Upon a volume whose contents he knows

> Are memorable, but from him locked up,
> Being written in a tongue he cannot read. . . .
> (10.58–61)

This scene of non-reading (itself a reading or misreading) looks ahead to the first "spot of time," but also serves here to ground Wordsworth's response in a thoroughly linguistic trope.

Similarly, his initial response to the Revolution is one of "indifference" (9.91). He writes:

> by novelties in speech,
> Domestic manners, customs, gestures, looks,
> And all the attire of ordinary life,
> Attention was engrossed; and, thus amused,
> I stood, 'mid those concussions, unconcerned,
> Tranquil almost, and careless as a flower. . . .
> (9.82–87)

"Amused . . . unconcerned . . . careless": the downplaying of any psychic investment in France cannot be missed. But watch how Wordsworth moves from "indifference" to enthusiasm, a reversal perhaps already anticipated in the word "engrossed" above. The pivot is a significant stage metaphor that includes an explicit pattern of inside/outside, early/late rhetorical shifts. Wordsworth says that by entering France he

> had abruptly passed
> Into a theatre, whose stage was filled
> And busy with an action far advanced.
> (9.93–95)

In other words, he is a late theater-goer, arriving *in medias res* and having missed the early acts. But such an interpretation recognizes only one half of the significance of Wordsworth's theatrical metaphor, and it perpetuates his own myth of exteriority. Many critics who have read Book 9 in this way accept Wordsworth's gesture of exteriority, seeing in it those mocking qualities—specifically, of mock-romance[12]—which here, no less than in the mock-heroic gestures at the beginning of Book 3, create a sense of detachment. Such a reading explicitly subscribes to the drama of separation and belatedness that Wordsworth's surface text offers. Wordsworth is everywhere the innocent *spectator ab extra!*

But the doubleness of the theater trope suggests that the opposing view can be urged—that in fact Wordsworth can be read as an actor already in the *mise en scène* of the unfolding drama of France. We see him in costume—"in the guise / Of an enthusiast . . . affecting more emotion than [he] felt" (9.70–71, 73)—which is exactly what an actor does. What's France to him, or he to France, that he should thus feel for her? And yet this costuming and this acting serve to turn Wordsworth into a spectator; his entering the Revolutionary cause, his in-volvement, is curiously a withdrawal, a retirement that is also a sallying forth: "I gradually withdrew / Into a noisier world, and thus ere long / Became a patriot" (9.121–23).

Wordsworth clearly begins in France as an outsider of the French Revolution. But he is equally an outsider on his native soil: when England and France declare war on each other, Wordsworth feels the "shock" (10.268) of "a conflict of sensations without name" (10.290) that leaves him "like an uninvited guest" (10.297) in the English community of national faith. The competing movement of interiority follows, however, displacing Wordsworth by a nightmarish dream-work that involves the alternation of spectator and actor, or dreamer and dreamed. The catalogue of "ghastly visions . . . of despair / And tyranny, and implements of death" (10.402–03) places Wordsworth outside his own dream, but the text again achieves its reversal, locating him as one of the victims in that dream. We are tipped off to the changing drama by the word "scene," with all its theatricality, as Coleridge noted:

> Then suddenly the scene
> Changed, and the unbroken dream entangled me
> In long orations, which I strove to plead
> Before unjust tribunals. . . .
> (10.409–12)

Suddenly Wordsworth is before the audience; he is the spectator become actor, now on "that great stage" (7.491) of the courts of the mind where, like the lawyers of Book 7, he must plead his case.

From his historical vantage point as retrospective poet, Wordsworth can view his experiences in the Revolution with a certain temporal detachment. Describing his first visit to "the town of Arras" (10.498), birthplace of Robespierre, Wordsworth recalls how he entered it during the town's celebrations of the first anniversary of the fall of the Bastille (6.345–74; 10.491–98). When he was in the town, there was joy, but now from his perspective he is "driven to think" (10.490) of the atrocities that Arras afterwards suffered. From participant in 1790 to retrospective poet in 1804: not only has he changed, but the town of Arras has been the innocent victim of a corresponding change:

> As Lear reproached the winds—I could almost
> Have quarrelled with that blameless spectacle
> For lingering yet an image in my mind
> To mock me under such a strange reverse.
> (10.507–10)

"A strange reverse": if Wordsworth had wanted to trope this experience as a drama or a "spectacle," what better place could he have chosen than "Arras," whose very name suggests something dramatic or masque-like, as in the "state arras" of Cambridge (3.565), which recalls the tapestries in Book 3 of *The Faerie Queene*, where Spenser also names the town of Arras (3.1.34)? Nor is Milton far away. While Wordsworth uses the word "arras" only twice in his poetry—in the sense of tapestry and as the proper name—Milton uses it but once, in a passage we have already cited in Chapter 2 as the likely intertext for *Descriptive Sketches.*[13]

The closing episode of Book 10 glances back to the business of voice and text in the Simplon Pass, and looks ahead to the first of the "spots of time." Wordsworth, now back in England, walks through a landscape suffused with celestial light to visit the grave of a former schoolteacher. He reads "with tender pleasure" the epitaph from Gray "graven / Upon his tombstone" (10.546–47), and recalls his teacher's hopes for him to become a poet. Recollecting the loss of his "faithful guide" (10.537), seeing "the turf that covered him" (10.540), and reading his epitaph—actions which resemble the first "spot" in Book 12, in which the boy similarly loses his "guide" (12.230), sees a place of death, and reads a name—Wordsworth withdraws to a vantage point from where he views the landscape "spotted with a variegated crowd / Of vehicles and travellers" (10.563–64). As in the first "spot" on the hill, Wordsworth here longs "to paint [the] scene" (10.569) of "visionary dreariness" (12.256), but he is usurped upon by a voice from a traveler who informs him that "'Robespierre is dead!'" (10.573). The 1805 version, in which this announcement occurs in indirect speech—"that, *Robespierre was dead*" (1805:10.536)—illustrates a close rhetorical similarity to the peasant's speech in the Alps in Book 6.

Book 10 ends with a "hymn of triumph" (10.580) by Wordsworth in immediate response to the news of Robespierre's death, thus making a present joy the matter of his song. The final line of the book—"We beat with thundering hoofs the level sand" (10.603)—which, as many critics have noted, is taken verbatim from Book 2.137, not only places Wordsworth back in childhood, but makes him, through the self-echo, a *spectator ab extra* of that childhood, an audience where he once was the player. Wordsworth experiences a similar feeling in another significant self-echo at Book 11.243–44, where he quotes a verse and a half from his play *The Borderers* (1495–96). In both cases the subject has become an object, one that is able to be quoted, adapted, revised, or reprised; Wordsworth becomes his own dramatic intertext.

Aside from the rhetorical structuring of spectator and actor in the books on France, there is the question of their dramatic allusiveness. Wordsworth quotes, echoes, refers, or alludes to a number of plays, including *King Lear*, *Macbeth*, *Hamlet*, *Romeo and Juliet*, *As You Like It*, *Richard III*, *A Midsummer Night's Dream*, *Samson Agonistes*, and his own play *The Borderers*, almost as if such intertextuality could appropriate a sense of drama for his experience in France. Sometimes the allusiveness casts the poet in a drama, as it does early in Book 10 when he describes himself, separated from the September massacres of 1792 "by one little month" (10.74)—perhaps from *Hamlet* 1.2.147—hearing "a voice that cried, / To the whole city, 'Sleep no more'" (10.86–87). The latter quotation points to Macbeth, who hears a voice crying "Sleep no more! / Macbeth does murder sleep" (2.2.34–35) immediately following his murder of Duncan; Wordsworth, also hearing a voice, seems ambiguously associated with Macbeth, and also with his guilt that prompts the voice, or with the guilt of the city to whom the voice in Paris speaks.[14] Or consider this transposed echo of *Hamlet*: to the "wild theories" (11.189) of political partisans, Wordsworth says, "I had but lent a careless ear, assured / That time was ready to set all things right" (11.191–92). The surface rhetoric implies the detached speaker, with his "careless" attitude and his deferring action of investing "time" with the responsibility of setting history right. But the intertextual rhetoric shows that the superficial carelessness is really a calculated swerving from an original responsibility that is the speaker's. Hamlet's speech, the hintertext of this passage (perhaps with *Julius Caesar* 3.2.78 in the background), displays the unavoidable recognition that he has the pivotal role in his real-life drama: "The time is out of joint. O, cursed spite, / That ever I was born to set it right!" (1.5.188–89). The contradiction between surface and intertext in Wordsworth is also expressed by the difference between the competing roles of spectator and player implicit in these texts.

Surely, it would be over-literalizing the trope of a mirror stage in the books on France to suggest that, in addition to employing a rhetoric of theatricality, books 9 to 11 also possess a dramatic structure, that in a specific way they correspond to the protasis, epitasis, and catastrophe of an actual drama. To demonstrate that the books embody a dramatic structure of beginning, middle, and end would again trace the allegorization of language from the level of trope to the level of literal narrative. It is perhaps expecting too much; yet, in the closing movement of Book 11 Wordsworth explicitly tropes the conclusion of the French Revolution—the crowning of Napoleon—as a "catastrophe" (11.357) associated, as Jonathan Wordsworth has said, with "a piece of cheap theatrical machinery" (*NP* 410n4):

the catastrophe (for so they dream,
And nothing else), when, finally to close
And rivet down the gains of France, a Pope
Is summoned in, to crown an Emperor—
This last opprobrium, when we see a people,
That once looked up in faith, as if to Heaven
For manna, take a lesson from the dog
Returning to his vomit; when the sun
That rose in splendour, was alive, and moved
In exultation with a living pomp
Of clouds—his glory's natural retinue—
Hath dropped all functions by the gods bestowed,
And, turned into a gewgaw, a machine,
Sets like an Opera phantom.
(11.357–70)

We are almost back in London, with the spectacles and gewgaws and raree-shows that Wordsworth everywhere sees. But here the dramatic rhetoric does not merely involve the actor/audience trope; it also suggests a dramatic structure, in which the catastrophe or *denouement* is coterminous with the final book on France, as though France were a self-contained tragedy in structural as well as rhetorical terms. Viewed in this way, Wordsworth's peripeteia is achieved, with Dorothy's help, as a "return" to nature; and his anagnorisis, his moment of recognition, is—what else?—a self-recognition, "a saving intercourse / With my true self" (11.341–42). An attempt to see books 9 to 11 as containing a dramatic structure, however, seems contradicted by the poet, who wishes that he could give a truly dramatic form to his experiences in the Revolution:

> Share with me, Friend! the wish
> That some dramatic tale, endued with shapes
> Livelier, and flinging out less guarded words
> Than suit the work we fashion, might set forth
> What then I learned, or think I learned, of truth. . . .
> (11.282–86)

This is the voice of the incipient ventriloquist, wanting to make his "thoughts and diction" (*Biographia* 258) those of his characters. The conclusion of the books on France may contain its own catastrophe—both as resolution and as debacle—but the poem has three books yet to go, and what appears here as a failed political climax will be superseded by a so-called imaginative restoration.

"One always inhabits, and all the more when one does not suspect it" (*Grammatology* 24). Derrida's statement has particular relevance to the specular structure of *The Prelude*. My readings of Cambridge, London, and France, in their effort to demonstrate that Wordsworth, when he professes to be in the external, detached position of spectator, can be shown to be at the same time in an internal, involved role of actor, raise questions about the function of reversals and doublings in the autobiographical translation of a self into language. What does this simultaneous alternation, this variance in the surface rhetoric, mean in semiological terms? What is the significance of the competing rhetorical movements, of the "tension between gesture and statement" (*Grammatology* 30) in the image of a mirror stage? One answer, already hinted at, may be given in terms of language's own competing valorizations of referentiality and reflexivity. Just when we think that language is pointing us to the "outside" world, to the referential world, to *res*, we discover that it is directing us "inside" again, to the structure of its own discourse, to *verba* and not to thing. Whether we view the inside/outside doubleness of language as a difference between "sense and reference" (Frege), "intransitivity" and "transitivity" (Bloomfield 312), or "centripetal" and "centrifugal" contexts (Frye, *Anatomy* 73–82; *Code* 58–61), we cannot escape the knowledge that rhetoric is in a semiotic sense what it has always been complained of being in an ethical sense: equivocal, duplicitous, even two-faced. Thus language's Janus-like preoccupation with its competing perspectives becomes thematized in the inner/outer, spectator/actor, proximity/distance structures in Wordsworth's text, in which rhetoric's self-regarding aspect is repeated in the poet's self-encounters, in his recurrent tendency to view himself as an audience does an actor, and yet still remain the audience. If language's self-concern is semiological narcissism—that is, if it involves a mirror—it also involves a stage, a radically dramatic moment in which the *spectator ab extra* gazes on himself as "the man speaking to men." The rhetorical reversals which the text performs on itself, never settling on a single, ultimate term in the alternation, but always existing within a system of difference, a "strength / Of usurpation," constitute, in a sublimely egotistical sense, the figural language in which the poet defines himself.

—Spots where a word, ghost-like, survives
"In the Sound of Mull"

MONUMENTAL WRITING: WORDSWORTH AND THE LIFE OF WORDS

5

Shoshana Felman, in an essay mapping out the "limits and possibilities" of psychoanalytic approaches to reading poetry, discerns in the work of Jacques Lacan "a type of reading that is methodologically unprecedented in the whole history of literary criticism."[1] Lacan's method, she says, operates as "an analysis of the signifier as opposed to an analysis of the signified" (140)—a method which thus subverts "the history of reading [that] has accustomed us to the assumption—usually unquestioned—that reading is finding meaning, that interpretation—of whatever method—can dwell but on the meaningful" (141). "An analysis not of the signified but of the signifier" (140)—of what Lacan calls "a pure signifier" (*le pur signifiant*: *Ecrits* 16)—becomes a radically alternative method of reading by means of a rhetorical or semiotic displacement within the sign itself.

But can we really do such a thing as separate the signifier from the signified for the purposes of analysis? Saussure tells us that the linguistic sign is like a sheet of paper, and we cannot cut one side without cutting the other (113). What is more, it is difficult, not to say impossible, to think of a signified that is not also a signifier, the Lacanian "bar" between the two sides often being, as Terry Eagleton among others has shown, more a membrane than a barrier (128). Any attempt to divide or "analyze" the sign in this way must recognize that while it produces a "pure signifier," and therefore an object suitable for rhetorical description, it also insinuates the return of the signified, the "meaning" that is repressed by such an interpretive method. To put it another way, any analysis that is "opposed to" another analysis—as in Felman's "analysis of the signifier as opposed to an analysis of the signified"—courts its own deconstruction by repudiating a term that can be divorced or excluded, but not without intrinsically disturbing the exclusive term.

To call such a method of interpretation "psychoanalytic" perhaps excites resistance. There is, for example, Derrida's charge that "despite appearances, the deconstruction of logocentrism is not a psychoanalysis of philosophy" (*Writing and Difference* 196). But Derrida's statement, taken from an essay that is itself a resistance to Lacan—at least, written under the sign of Lacan and in opposition to it[2]—seems to depend on a radically different, and in a curious way more popular, notion of psychoanalysis than Lacan's. Yet if it is possible to psychoanalyze the linguistic sign, the reason is not just because "the unconscious is structured like a language," as Lacan famously put it,[3] but also because language has its own "unconscious," an economy or system of differences which Derrida shows is something other than analogous to the deep structure of the mind. In contrast to the traditional psychoanalytic approach to an author (in which the text is read as the manifest expression of a consciousness, as a psychic symptom or perhaps a cure), or the similar approach to a character (in which the focus, for Wordsworth's poetry, might be on the aetiology of Idiot Boys or hysterical mothers), Felman's reading of Lacan points the way to what may be called a *semiotic psychoanalysis*: that is, an unprecedented interpretation of a signifier, not in opposition to its signified, but rather despite it, especially despite the appearance that any deconstruction of the sign is not a psychoanalysis of semiotics.

In Wordsworth there is an exemplary occasion on which it is possible to free up the signifier, to cut it adrift and allow it to float away from a semantic or referential anchor. We can do this because Wordsworth's text has already done it through a series of erasures of both signifier and signified, and their provisional replacement by a corresponding series of intertexts. At such a point in Wordsworth's poetry, we are able to observe the effect of certain rhetorical functions whose power derives from the give-and-take of the erasure and indelibility of a "monumental writing" (1805 *Prelude* 11.295). While even the heuristic separation of signifier from signified is not without its theoretical as well as practical problems, I propose to read the first "spot of time" in *The Prelude* with the assumption, in Felman's words, "that the signifier can be analyzed in its effects without its signified being known" (141). If, as Stuart Schneiderman says, "the theory of psychoanalysis can be constructed out of the empty grave and the signifier" (7), then Wordsworth's first "spot of time" would seem to present itself for a semiotic psychoanalysis in a most exemplary way.

I

—No Epitaph ought to be written upon a bad Man, except for a warning.

Essays Upon Epitaphs

In the 1799 *Prelude* the gibbet episode stands amidst a configuration of four dead people: the drowned man, the gibbeted criminal, the murdered wife, and the buried father. The passage linking the first and second of these figures is significant, despite its deletion from later versions of the text:

I might advert
To numerous accidents in flood or field,
Quarry or moor, or 'mid the winter snows
Distresses and disasters, tragic facts
Of rural history, that impressed my mind
With images to which in following years
Far other feelings were attached—with forms
That yet exist with independent life,
And, like their archetypes, know no decay.
(1.279–87)

What I want to focus on here is the intertextual rhetoric of these lines, which readers have noted owe something to Othello's speech before Brabantio and the Duke in Act 1.3.[4] Othello says:

Her father lov'd me, oft invited me,
Still question'd me the story of my life,
From year to year; the battles, sieges, fortunes,
That I have pass'd:
I ran it through, even from my boyish days,
To the very moment that he bade me tell it.
Wherein I spake of most disastrous chances,
Of moving accidents by flood and field;
Of hair-breadth scapes i'th'imminent deadly breach;
Of being taken by the insolent foe;
And sold to slavery, and my redemption thence,
And with it all my travel's history;

> Wherein of antres vast, and deserts idle,
> Rough quarries, rocks and hills, whose heads touch heaven
> It was my hint to speak. . . .

This speech haunted Wordsworth, for he reappropriated it on numerous occasions, including the opening of the second part of "Hart-Leap Well": "The moving accident is not my trade . . ." (97).[5] The underpresence of *Othello* in the 1799 *Prelude*, however, goes beyond the echo of "accidents in flood or field"; the phrase "quarry or moor" looks back to Shakespeare's noble Moor and his description of "rough quarries, rocks and hills," and Wordsworth's adverting specifically to *tragic* facts reinforces a Shakespearean connection. Even Othello's phrase "the story of my life," a common enough trope, finds its way into *The Prelude* by 1805, at 1.667 (1850: 1.639). But other echoes persist in the gibbet scene. Only twenty lines after this passage, in the account of his experience in the first "spot of time," Wordsworth writes:

> down the rough and stony moor
> I led my horse, and stumbling on, at length
> Came to a bottom, where in former times
> A man, the murderer of his wife, was hung
> In irons.
> (1799:1.306–10)

Does Wordsworth's intertextual rhetoric suggest who this "man, the murderer of his wife," might be? The transmuted figure of Othello resurfaces here in a trace of that play which was, Wordsworth says in his "Personal Talk," "pre-eminently dear" (40): the story of "the gentle Lady married to the Moor" (41). But what is equally significant is that when the connecting passage "I might advert . . ." was dropped for the 1805 *Prelude*, so too was the detail that this particular man had murdered his wife. The *Othello* intertext arises only to be effaced, leaving but scattered echoes "down the rough and stony moor."

In the 1850 *Prelude* the child encounters a text, engraven characters in the turf. But that is not what originally confronted him; the 1799 poem renders a radically different experience:

> Mouldered was the gibbet-mast;
> The bones were gone, the iron and the wood;
> Only a long green ridge of turf remained
> Whose shape was like a grave.
> (1799:1.310–13)

The simile of the grave is tentative, though not unmotivated. But by 1850 this "ridge of turf" has evolved into language:

on the turf,
Hard by, soon after that fell deed was wrought,
Some unknown hand had carved the murderer's name.
The monumental letters were inscribed
In times long past; but still, from year to year,
By superstition of the neighbourhood,
The grass is cleared away, and to that hour
The characters were fresh and visible. . . .
(12.238–45)

From a grave into writing: the "monumental letters" are an epitaph for an effaced tomb. They are the metonymy of an absence, a word put for something that the text cancels. The grave is *sous rature*.

In this "scene of proper names," as Derrida might say (*Grammatology* 112), or this "scene of nomination," as Geoffrey Hartman might call it (*Saving* 101), the name that Wordsworth sees is a minimal epitaphic text, less even than the blind Beggar's "label" in Book 7, even less than the usual epitaphic form. "The most numerous class of sepulchral Inscriptions," Wordsworth writes in the third essay on epitaphs, "do indeed record nothing else but the name of the buried Person, but that he was born upon one day and died upon another" (*Prose* 2:93). The name and dates, he says, echoing Gray's "Elegy," constitute a "frail memorial" (*Prose* 2:93). But here there are no dates in the turf, no record of either birth or death, for the name is an epitaph *for an already dead man*. That is to say, the murderer was not *hanged* in this place; he was "hung in iron chains"—in other words, after his execution his body was "gibbeted" or exposed to public view as a warning. Wordsworth's own description of the practice of gibbeting in *An Unpublished Tour* (composed 1811–12; see *Prose* 2:128) provides a stark gloss on the poem:

> Adjoining to this Pool . . . formerly stood a gibbet, upon which the body of some atrocious Criminal had been hung in Chains near the spot where his crime had been committed. Part of the Irons & some of the wood work remained in my memory. Think of a human figure tossing about in the air in one of these sweet Valleys. . . . It seems as if no sense of humanity, no feeling for rural beauty could have existed in the

> minds of those who among their woods & fields could tolerate such a spectacle. . . . [T]he croaking of the carrion Crow & the Raven attracted by the suspended corpse, must have made a dismal chorus for the ears of Passengers, while the circumstances of the murder were yet fresh in memory. . . . [I]t would be well if this odious custom of exposing the Bodies of Criminals, of whatever description, were abandoned & all traces of this relic of barbarism had disappeared from the land. . . . Whom can the ignominy of this exposure deter from wickedness? Surely not those from whose hand the most inhuman cruelties are to be apprehended! There is no place which a hardened villain would prefer for the perpetration of a murder to the foot of a gibbet, if it lay within his choice. . . .
>
> No vestiges probably now remain of the object which led me to these reflections. . . .
>
> (*Prose* 2:333–34)[6]

The name remains; but the bare proper noun seems bereft of its referent, divested of its temporality; it is a text almost without a context: it appears to have been created at some point in time, yet does not seem to exist within time. It is a form "that yet exist[s] with independent life," but a life that is not of this world. Like its "archetype," its transcendental signifier in the imagination, the name is a text that knows no decay.

The endurance of language, its durability, is emphasized by the repeated references to the distant past, to the moment when the name may be supposed to have been written—"in former times"; "soon after that fell deed"; "in times long past"—which contrasts with the present moment of the boy's scene of reading: "But still, from year to year," Wordsworth writes, "The grass is cleared away, and to that hour / The characters were fresh and visible." A man dies; his body, even his grave disappears; but Wordsworth is smitten by a word "that shall not pass away" ("Power of Sound" 224).

"Fresh" characters, after all those years? The 1805 text is even more insistent: "to *this* hour," Wordsworth says, "the letters *are* all fresh and visible" (11.298–99; emphasis added). The grammar points, on the one hand, to a mere hyperbole for the indelibility of these letters, their stubborn permanence within a landscape where man (his bones), the works of man (the gibbet mast), and nature itself (the very grass) are subject to chance and change. But the word "fresh," on the other hand, can be read not figurally as hyperbole but literally as a description of something that is not outside nature, not beyond its sphere of activity, but rather is part of nature, participating in its very life: a *perennial* text which, like the grass around it, remains fresh "from year to year." We begin to detect in these lines a sub-audible transposition, or metaplasm, whose effect is a solemn intertextuality. The usurping ear wants to hear that these characters were *flesh* instead of "fresh"—not the metonym of an absence, not the trace of an effaced grave, but the embodied presence of a word amid the transient splendor of the grass that is "cleared away": "And the Word was made flesh" (John 1:14); "all flesh is grass" (Isaiah 40:6). But the literal and figural readings are at odds: how can this text be eternal, that is, supra-natural, having an undecaying permanence; and at the same time natural, having a freshness or immediacy? How is it that this earth-writing is able to withstand the usurpation of time, remaining "visible" when it should have faded or become hidden?

The name is indeed an uncanny inscription. It wants no mediation in its intentionality, no blind Beggar's "written paper" this time, no tombstone to come between itself and the dust in which it is carved. Like the Beggar's label, however, it strives toward the semiological status of an index through its contiguity with the obliterated grave containing the murderer's remains.[7] Yet despite this sentimental trick of engraving signs in their objective referents, there is still a difference between the murderer and his name; the "turf," or "green sod," as 1805 has it (11.302), on which the letters are carved is yet a type of appareling, a medium that intervenes in the intentional structure of the man and his name. Instead of "wearing a written paper" (7.641), the murderer is covered by a garment of earth, a shroud of the dust to which he will insensibly return. He lives in a "turf-clad grave" ("To May" 56). The turf is superficial, a surface text containing a "deep" meaning or hidden semantic content. But this "content" disappears, leaving only surface impressions—what Cynthia Chase has called a "residue" of writing. Wordsworth, she says, misprisioning McLuhan, "comes upon a code without a message, a spot where the medium is the message: letters" (553–54).

Still, this observation does not explain the boy's terrified response to the letters, a variation of Wordsworth's own "Letter-

Phobia" (*EY* 436).[8] Epitaphs, we recall, were a potential comfort to Wordsworth—even epitaphs that seem to have a life of their own. In one of the brief elegies addressed to Matthew, Wordsworth writes:

> Carved, Mathew, with a master's skill,
> Thy name is on the hawthorn tree,
> 'Twill live, and yet it seemed that still
> I owed another verse to thee.
> (Gill 145)

The engraven, living name of Matthew, through its assimilation to a language of nature, is an obvious, if inadequate, consolation. But there is something about the murderer's epitaph that is vexing. Geoffrey Hartman suggests that the characters in the turf scare the boy because they imply an indestructible consciousness in nature and in man (*Unmediated Vision* 130). Leslie Brisman says that "the inscription *represents* death" (319). In *Scepticism and Poetry* D. G. James speaks of "terrifying intimations of 'otherness'" in the midst of this dreary scene (158–59). And Thomas Weiskel arrives, "by no doubt too great a jump as yet, at the equation writing = death, or more exactly, the recognition of a signifier = the intimation of death" (178). Is there a common textual ground for these divergent interpretations, something in Wordsworth's words themselves that would account for the boy's inability to pass this fatal name unalarmed?

We may note, first of all, that the child is not alone in his fear and awe of this place and this word. His reaction is framed within a significant social context: "the superstition of the neighbourhood." Evidently more than one person has been affected by this manuscript—so much so, that certain annual rites are performed to give prominence to the engraven name ("the grass is cleared away"). Now as we have seen in the passage from Wordsworth's *Unpublished Tour*, gibbetings were not uncommon in his day, and there is nothing in the text of an historical or even anecdotal nature by which we might expect the neighbourhood to be more superstitious in this case than in any other. What the evidence points to, in this murder mystery, is the displacement of one spectacle by another, a metonym or meta-name being put for the gibbeted man himself: dead letters for a dead man—and yet letters with a strange afterlife. (The common noun "name" [12.240] is already a meta-name for the actual proper noun.) But what is implied by such an exchange or displacement? How does a hanged man—a haltered traveler if ever there were one—relate to name and place? The purpose of a gibbet, we noted, was to hold up the corpse of an executed criminal as a warning or *exemplum horrendum* to society, but what function do these letters serve?

We need at once to remember that they are "monumental" letters—that is, epitaphic characters that *admonish* as well as commemorate, the word monumental being derived from the Latin *monere*, to warn. The letters are a "chastisement" (12.311) of the little boy. They are a sign, but a danger sign. But the epithet "monumental" carries associations of not only moral or psychological admonition, but physical magnitude as well. It is as if these monumental "characters / Of danger or desire" (1.471–72) are also colossal characters, larger-than-life signifiers. As such, they are tropes in the hyperbolical rhetoric of the boy's imagination, but tropes that we have encountered before. Back in Book 7, the bewildering book of signs, Wordsworth in London reads the face of the city "like a title-page / With letters huge inscribed" (7.160–61); he confronts "advertisements, of giant size" in the streets (7.194). In the poem "To Joanna" the Vicar asks Wordsworth why he, "like a Runic Priest, in characters / Of formidable size had chiselled out / Some uncouth name upon the native rock" (28–30). Just as primitive man, associating ideas in a state of excitement, perceived, according to Rousseau, other men as giants (12–13), the young boy here spies monumental letters whose immensity reflects the enormity of the "fell deed" of which they are the memorial.

But there is something else in Wordsworth's rhetoric that makes the writing unearthly. It is his statement that "soon after that fell deed was wrought, / Some unknown hand had carved the murderer's name." The first question raised here involves the referent of the phrase "that fell deed." Which fell deed? The murder, the execution, or the gibbeting? From the grammar of the passage, not to mention Wordsworth's opinions vigorously put forward in *An Unpublished Tour*, one suspects that the referent is the fact that "a murderer had been hung in iron chains"—although the word "fell," meaning savage, inhuman, causing death, could clearly refer to the two previous events in this causal chain. A reading of the word "fell" might stop here with its forensic connotations (fell, felony, Wordsworth as "fell destroyer" [1805:1.318], *felo-de-se*), though the adjective provokes other resonances in its noun and verb forms too (fall, fell, "bare fell" [6.235], "fell / A spirit of pleasure and youth's golden gleam" [12.265–66]).

There is, however, another puzzling contrast in these verses, namely the opposition between the frailty and impermanence of iron, wood, and bone, and the durability and firmness of the "turf, / Hard by." The difference hinges on the word "wrought." The text suggests that soon after the fell deed of hanging a dead man "in iron chains" (12.236), in an "iron case" (12.238), was wrought—that is, perhaps, soon after the deed was wrought to make a "wrought-iron" case—the name was carved. Such a reading posits yet another displacement, a metonymic substitution in which the building of the iron case is put for the actual gibbeting. First a deed is wrought in iron and then a name is wrought in the turf; both are fashioned by hammering or chiseling. We might expect that in the transumption of the fell deed by the monumental letters there would be an accommodating rhetorical effect similar to the one the boy experiences in the drowned man episode in Book 5; we might think, that is, that the name

> hallowed the sad spectacle
> With decoration of ideal grace;
> A dignity, a smoothness, like the words
> Of Grecian art, and purest poesy.
> (5.456–59)

But the boy in the first "spot of time" experiences no smoothness, but a stammering, alliterative impulse: "I fled, / Faltering and faint, and ignorant of the road" (12.246–47).

Based on the recurrent pattern of encounter in Wordsworth's poetry outlined in the two previous chapters, one's expectation in this episode might be for the boy to meet a person and a voice; instead, he meets the trace of a corpse and a written text, where trace and text, from 1799 to 1805, gradually merge. Originally he sees a grave, or a shape "like a grave" (1799:1.313); now he reads letters. The voice that should speak to the boy appears to be silenced by death and/or writing. "Silence," Wordsworth writes in *A Letter to a Friend of Robert Burns* (1816), "is a privilege of the grave" (*Prose* 3:121) and, it might seem, an intrinsic feature of writing, but for Wordsworth the undying life of these "dead letters" makes them a type of natural "speaking monument" (8.172).

But I must trope my own vocal figure here through a rhetoric of grammar, for the "voice" in the scene is not really absent or silent, but only *passive*. The shift in grammatical voice from the surrounding narrative to the gibbet encounter and back to the narrative raises certain questions. Wordsworth begins in the active voice—"I led my horse, and, stumbling on, at length / Came to a bottom"—and resumes this voice in "I fled. . . ." But of the nine verbs that occur between these verses, four are passive, and three more are intransitive or copula. The effect is not one of stasis, but just its opposite: a catalogue of goings-on, but in a curiously detached way. The verbs are: (passive) "had been hung," "was wrought," "were inscribed," "is cleared"; (intransitive) "had mouldered"; (copula) "were" (twice). The critic that is concerned to address the question of language might in an elementary way ask: Who is the "doer" of all this action? The grammar declines to say. These things—hanging, working, inscribing, clearing—are done, but by whom? We need not assume that they are all done by the same person, but the absence of a specified performer adds to their hermeneutical mystery.

A more important question concerns the chirographic text itself. Who is the author of these letters? Wordsworth replies: "Some unknown hand." The commonplace synecdoche implies an anonymous author, but it also has the effect of disembodying that author, particularly of reducing him to an uncouth hand. It is a powerful trope in this case, since it involves a chiasmic linguistic substitution as well: a nameless writer writing a name. Does the anonymity of the text help to explain the supernatural aura surrounding it—the fact, for example, that there is a "superstition of the neighbourhood" concerning it? The monumental name, we saw, is an unearthly warning, and Wordsworth reads it "as if admonished from another world" (7.649). But what is this unspecified hand—a ghost-writer writing a ghost-word?

Under other circumstances, the letters would not be as puzzling; they would be read—that is, interpreted—simply as an excerpt from the book of nature, as yet another example of the "characters / Of danger or desire" (1.471–72) that nature everywhere impresses. But it is the *literal* insistence of the letters, and their creation by an "unknown hand," that make this scene, like the blind Beggar's, problematic. Because the letters are so legible, so easy to read, they are difficult to interpret. Despite their hermeneutical resistance, however, they do convey a meaning to the ears if not to the eyes. The image of an unknown hand inscribing a warning for all to see but only one to interpret has an intertextual as well as experiential provenance; Wordsworth can read the handwriting on the turf, and the message is danger. I allude to Wordsworth's remarkable biblical hintertext:

> In the same hour came forth fingers of a man's hand, and wrote over against the candlestick upon the plaister of the wall of the king's palace; and the king saw the part of the hand that wrote. Then the king's countenance was changed, and his thoughts troubled him, so that the joints of his loins were loosed, and his knees smote one against another. . . . Then came in all the king's wise men: but they could not read the writing, nor make known to the king the interpretation thereof. . . .
>
> Then Daniel answered and said before the king . . . I will read the writing unto the king, and make known to him the interpretation. . . . O Belshazzar . . . [thou] hast lifted up thyself against the Lord of heaven; and they have brought the vessels of his house before thee, and thou, and thy lords, thy wives, and thy concubines, have drunk wine in them; and thou hast praised the gods of silver, and gold, of brass, iron, wood, and stone, which see not, nor hear, nor know: and the God in whose hand thy breath is, and whose are all thy ways, hast thou not glorified: Then was the part of the hand sent from him; and this writing was written.
>
> And this is the writing that was written, MENE, MENE, TEKEL, UPHARSIN. This is the interpretation of the thing: MENE; God hath numbered thy kingdom, and finished it. TEKEL; thou art weighed in the balances, and art found wanting. PERES; thy kingdom is divided, and given to the Medes and Persians. Then commanded Belshazzar, and they clothed Daniel with scarlet, and put a chain of gold about his neck, and made a proclamation concerning him, that he should be the third ruler in the kingdom. In that night was Belshazzar the king of the Chaldeans slain.
>
> (Daniel 5:5–30)[9]

Can we suggest that the "unknown hand" in the first "spot of time" is, like the hand in the Book of Daniel, from God? Yet what would such a thing mean? The admonitory aspect seems clear enough in both cases, but it is the literalness of the divine handwriting, arbitrary signs rather than natural symbols, which perplexes—and yet which helps to ground both the supernatural quality of the letters and the strange fact that the neighborhood superstition is focused on the name rather than the once-exposed man. The fatal handwriting says not *Ecce homo*, but *Ecce signum*!

Because the signifier in this case is a proper name, we might expect to profit by a consideration of it in terms of its reference—that is, its status as what Searle would call a "definite referring expression" (72–96, 162–74). But here, as with the Beggar's label, the problem is not one of reference, despite the fact that what the proper name refers to no longer exists (see Searle 77). Wordsworth has no hesitation in connecting the name with the murderer; he takes it for granted, since there are no other contextual or explanatory markers in the turf, that the letters spell "the murderer's name." Here, but not only here, we sense the interpretive disjunction between the little boy's experience and the retrospective poet's rendering of it: just how much the child knows—that is, how much he knows about the history of the place, the murder, the identity of the murderer, whether at about five years of age he can indeed read the letters as more than just letters—and how much more the mature poet knows are questions we can ask but not answer. Yet one feels that the power of the scene derives less from its referential aspect than from its semiotic structure, less from the identity of the murderer than from his name as such.

Nevertheless, there is a natural if somewhat irritating desire to know exactly what name was carved on the turf. Ernest de Selincourt, among others, has attempted to solve the puzzle, but one feels that such inquiry tends to miss the point.[10] Nor is intertextuality of much help here. Is it Othello's name that Wordsworth sees? Specific guesswork of this kind needs to be supplemented by a consideration of the semiosis of the passage—that is, the way in which the text uses the name to signify. Such a semiotic reading would assume "that the signifier [the name] can be analyzed in its effects without its signified [the particular name] being known" (Felman 141).

Yet if we persist in asking, along with Roland Barthes, "Who wrote?"[11] we verge on a theoretical space in which writing, the author, and death are intertwined. We may hear Michel Foucault replying "What difference does it make who wrote?"[12], but the question nevertheless seems relevant to Wordsworth. What Foucault says about this matrix of writing, authorship, and death, especially the Western notion of writing "as something designed to ward off death" (142), helps articulate our concerns with the monumental letters. Foucault states:

> Writing [in Western culture] has become linked to sacrifice, even to the sacrifice of life. . . . The work, which once had the duty of providing immortality, now possesses the right to kill, to be its author's murderer. . . . As a result, the mark of the writer is reduced to nothing more than the singularity of his absence; he must assume the role of the dead man in the game of writing.
>
> (142–43)

In this first "spot of time" the author has disappeared or died. Wordsworth does not know who he or she is; but the reader guesses that s/he is something between a sky-writer and a grave-digger. The question of authorship is not trivial, since the relation of writer to text in the case of the name reflects on the situation of the poet and his poem. Reflects in a certain way: as we recall from Book 7, when Wordsworth sees the Beggar's label his mind turns round as if in response to the self-reflexive aspect of the encounter. Here, the boy sees a plain, unvarnished inscription, but the effect is similarly one of confusion and admonition. It is as if the moving power of the name implies another self-referential moment, a transfigured recognition scene in which "a casual glance" (12.246)—Latin: *casualis*, from *casus*, chance or casualty—fixes on the "disastrous chances, / Of moving accidents by flood and field" (*Othello* 1.3.134–35). If, in this "casual" anagnorisis, there is a correspondence between the murderer and his name on the one hand, and the poet and his autobiographical poem on the other, it is grounded in the intertextual encounter of what may be called the murderer's "literary remains" and the poet's "posthumous text." The name forms a proleptic analogy in Wordsworth's mind as he looks ahead to his own "destin'd Urn"

("Lycidas" 20), which he imagines in Book 6 of *The Prelude*—"such a daring thought, that I might leave / Some monument behind me which pure hearts / Should reverence" (6.55–57). Or Milton's own version—that "I might perhaps leave something so written to aftertimes, as they should not willingly let it die" (668). The neighborhood in this scene is unwilling to let the name die; its superstition and the boy's fear form a correspondent "reverence." But by invoking these examples from Milton and Wordsworth, I might seem to be assuming that the memorial left behind in the case of the murderer, as in *The Reason of Church Government* and *The Prelude*, is in some way autobiographical—that is, pointing back from the text to its absent author, as though author and murderer, in this case, *were the same person*.

Is the name an autograph—the apocalyptic signature of a dead man reaching back from beyond the grave to write his own name in the turf? "He had a name written, that no man knew, but he himself" (Revelation 19:12). From a "grave" (1799) into "engraven" (1805): Wordsworth's frivolous yet motivated play on words suggests a substitution that is evolutionary as well as paronomastic. The word "grave," in its derivation from the Anglo-Saxon *grafan*, to dig, connotes both the act of inscribing and a place of burial; to en-grave, therefore, means both to carve and to inter (Latin: *in terra*). But "grave" also has a Latin derivation, from *gravis*, meaning heavy or weighty; perhaps this clarifies Wordsworth's claim that the "renovating virtue" (12.210) of the "spots of time" is to overcome not only "false opinion and contentious thought" (12.211), but "aught of heavier or more deadly weight" (12.212). The "Intimations Ode" evokes the same echoes. "Mighty Prophet! Seer blest!" Wordsworth writes in the 1807 version (114),

> To whom the grave
> Is but a lonely bed without the sense or sight
> Of day or the warm light
> A place of thought where we in waiting lie. . .
>
> . . . Full soon thy Soul shall have her earthly freight,
> And custom lie upon thee with a weight,
> Heavy as frost, and deep almost as life!
> (Gill 300)

As periphrasis, these last three lines skirt or perhaps stand astride the trope of a grave. But the murderer's name cannot escape its own figuration. Inscribed *in terra*, "on the turf," the name seems to represent a logo-taphia, or word-burial; it is not an intertext, but an *interred text*. And yet this murderer's epitaph, a floating signifier despite its interment, commemorates anything but the death of language, for the name is undecaying, a resurrected word "from year to year."

"From year to year": that's what Othello says in Act 1: "Her father lov'd me, oft invited me, / Still question'd me the story of my life, / From year to year. . . ." The Shakespearean echo exposes a figure who as well as being creator and destroyer of "the story of [his] life" is also "the murderer of his wife" (1799 *Prelude* 1.309). Othello emerges as an exemplary autobiographer-murderer, as one in whom language and life compete for priority, with fatal consequences. "Forthwith shall be brought down / Through later years the story of my life," Wordsworth says (1.638–39). The potentially overdetermined relation between autobiography and murder, even self-murder, in *Othello* acts as a powerful intertext for yet another "fell deed."

One need not take literally the idea that the murderer carved his own name—though by committing murder in the first place he did in a sense sign his own death warrant—to read certain autobiographical features in the scene. I do not insist on the self-nomination of Wordsworth's rhetoric here, but its very suggestiveness persuades by showing how the abyss structure (*mise en abyme*) of this first "spot of time" brings together the power of the man and the power of the monument. Whether the "unknown hand" is the murderer's or another's, or whether "that fell deed" is the gibbeting or the murder, the possibility of a self-reflexive reading remains with this bare inscription. As epitaph, the name is an "epitomized biography" (*Prose* 2:89). Reading Wordsworth reading the name, an emblem of his own name, one sees analogically the rhetorical condensation (synecdoche) of the poet's written life to a name, a meta-name like "Wordsworth," whereby cause and effect change places (metonymy). Wordsworth's poem recognizes the proleptic displacement of a life by letters, specifically by autobiographical letters that spell out a text whose bottom line is a proper name.[13]

If language usurps life in this way—if, as Foucault claims, a written work is licensed to kill, "to be its author's murderer," and hence the author is required to "assume the role of the dead man in the game of writing"—then Wordsworth's experience in the first "spot of time" has disturbing semiotic as well as thematic implications. Error, murder, an effaced grave, a graven image, death, language—these are puzzling and traumatic associations for the critic as well as for the five-year-old boy. In a climactic passage that hopes to give "profoundest knowledge" (12.221) of the mind and the senses—in short, of the self—what the text gradually reveals is that *language* is lord and master, and life itself the obedient servant of its will. The role that Wordsworth assumes in this game is epitaphist, and the only knowledge that he wins, it appears, is that self-knowledge is withheld, not to be possessed directly, but mediated (displaced or condensed) through words. At "bottom" (12.235), of course, there is a name, but a name that by analogy seems to cancel the self rather than renovate it. What is totem to the superstitious neighborhood is taboo to the little boy. The name is not a "lucky word."

And yet it still has power to charm. "When, in the blessed hours / Of early love" (12.261–62), Wordsworth writes, recalling an experience recounted in Book 6,

> I roamed, in daily presence of this scene,
> Upon the naked pool and dreary crags,
> And on the melancholy beacon, fell
> A spirit of pleasure and youth's golden gleam;
> And think ye not with radiance more sublime
> For these remembrances, and for the power
> They had left behind?
> (12.263–69)

What it means for "remembrances" to leave power behind is what the "spots of time" dramatize but do not explain. That power which is left behind, is it inscribed, as in the sense of being deposited as self-evident residue, as intertext or self-echo, or is it rather forgotten or repressed—that is, left far behind? The "mystery of words" (5.597) points in contradictory directions at once. To "leave / Some monument behind" (6.55–56) is the poet's hope, but even this hope is fraught with an epitaphic sense of loss, a leaving behind as both presence and absence. Though the name speaks of something that is gone (life), Wordsworth finds strength in what remains behind (letters).

II

—*Every poem an epitaph*
T. S. Eliot, "Little Gidding"

My concern in this chapter has been to analyze the effect of a "monumental writing" (1805:11.295) we cannot read. One result has been to describe the gibbet episode almost as if it belonged to a different version of a "life and letters" genre. Or perhaps it should be regarded as a disfigured example of Wordsworth's "Poems on the Naming of Places." The text has Shakespearean affinities in its "tragic facts / Of rural history" (1799:1.282–83), and although these intertextual affiliations are variously erased and rewritten from 1799 to 1850, Wordsworth's rhetoric indicates the continuous underpresence of Shakespeare. *Othello* stands as an intertext not only in terms of its placement of autobiography within tragedy, even as Wordsworth inverts this relation and places "tragic facts" within his autobiography, but also in terms of its rhetorical entanglement of autobiography and (self-)murder.

What is perhaps so moving in this episode is the effect of displacement involved in the name. What name? It does not matter. The identity of the murderer is not important, not *meaningful.*[14] The text cancels the direct name, so that the reader sees only a nominal effect, *un effet du nom*, that has suggestive self-reflexive implications. A man is displaced, even effaced, by a name, by the effect of naming—which is allegorical of an aspect of autobiography. Wordsworth tropes himself as he writes *The Prelude*, turning flesh into word, putting effect in place of cause, substituting the misnomer "Wordsworth" for the proper noun that is his name. The autobiographical text, which might have been expected to present a life, insteads usurps it, so "consumed with that which it was nourished by" that it creates a shroud of words that both obliterates and preserves a "buried life." It is as if the writing of *The Prelude*—or, what is more, its publication in his lifetime—would have signaled death for Wordsworth; not immortality, as traditionally thought, but a "strength / Of usurpation" (6.599–600) demonstrating that the letter kills.

But Wordsworth's text is not undone so easily. To say even proverbially that "the letter kills" is to give a prosopopoeic life to language. Still, the "decaying, never to be decayed" (6.625) life of words is always in a sense an afterlife—that is, posthumous, belated, always already epitaphic. As such, it seems to be missing something: a referent, a meaning or a signified, maybe even an author. Wordsworth's reading of the name allegorizes the critic's response to a text that gives and takes away a life in letters.

Immediate are the acts of God, more swift
Than time or motion, but to human ears
Cannot without process of speech be told,
So told as earthly notion can receive.
Milton, Paradise Lost

I gotta use words when I talk to you.
T. S. Eliot, Sweeney Agonistes

USURPATION, RHETORIC, IMAGINATION

6

In his note to "The Thorn," Wordsworth shows his awareness of the double difficulty involved in the (literary) use of language:

> Now every man must know that an attempt is rarely made to communicate impassioned feelings without something of an accompanying consciousness of the inadequateness of our own powers, or the deficiencies of language. (Brett and Jones 289)

These two factors, the "deficiencies" of language and the "inadequateness" of the language user, are related to the interpretive problem, expressed by Jacques Derrida, of that "certain relationship, unperceived by the writer, between what he commands and what he does not command of the patterns of the language that he uses" (*Grammatology* 158)—though Wordsworth's interest here seems to be more on what he does *not* command than on what he does. "'Tis here," he says of one particular "impassioned feeling" in *Home at Grasmere* (137), "'Tis, but I cannot name it" (142). The "deficiencies" of language, "a thing subject to endless fluctuations and arbitrary associations" (*Prose* 3:82), cause it to fall short of a descriptive adequacy even in the fundamental act of naming. The name, like the murderer's in the first "spot of time," lies "far hidden from the reach of words" (3.187).

The limitations of poetry and poets, however, are not for Wordsworth a sudden discovery, full of frustration or despair. Indeed, the personal inability of a poet to communicate immaculately his "impassioned feelings" is often a conventional strategy: Milton's "forc't fingers rude" apologetically begin "Lycidas" (4); Coleridge compares his lyric ode on "Dejection" to a lute "which better far were mute" (18); and Wordsworth, in his dedicatory sonnet to *The*

Excursion, tropes the poem as his "imperfect," though not "premature," offering (*Poems* 2:35). The convention of affected modesty calls for an element of diffidence in the poet, and occasionally Wordsworth will "blame"—to speak in the rhetoric of complaint—his own skill in using language. While he never exclaims, as Prufrock does, "It is impossible to say just what I mean!" (104), he does at one point confess: "My drift I fear / Is scarcely obvious" (5.293–94), but even here the statement is less an admission of personal ineptitude than a strategic resting place. For Wordsworth, as for the other Romantic poets, the alleged reason for the impotence of the poet is more often an inherent fault of language itself, an incapacity in the very stuff of poetry. As Herbert Lindenberger puts it, "it is the resources of the language itself, not his own resources, which [Wordsworth] sees fit to blame" (308).[1]

Not one of Shakespeare's sonnets contains such a complaint against language; there the lament of the poet is always for his want of "skill" (#106) in his "poor rude lines" (#32) inspired by a Muse that is "tongue-tied" (#85) or "sick" (#79) or bereft of "invention" (#105). Chiding the Muse in this conventional way is a trope for the deferred sense of the ineptitude of the poet, but the possibility that some of the fault ought to lie with the medium of language never emerges in the sonnet sequence. Critics today, however, are pointing out more and more the radical limitations of language as a communicative force, but they are only restating what the Romantics knew and demonstrated so well.

A central question addressed in this final chapter involves the way in which the "deficiencies" of language for Wordsworth function as part of an "allegory of reading"—by which I mean, to recall Paul de Man's phrase again, a linguistic structure whose literal or narrative level simultaneously repeats its rhetorical substructure, so that what seems "literal" or thematic is already "allegorical" of its own figurality. The question of a what a text is "about," in these terms, correspondingly shifts from a concern with referential meaning to a concern with rhetorical foregrounding; and such a shift is especially apparent in a poem like *The Prelude*, which offers itself as the autobiography of a poet's imagination, but which is forced repeatedly to meditate on the "deficiencies" of its translation of a self into language.

Where these rhetorical difficulties are often clearly seen is in what Wordsworth calls an act of "usurpation" (*Prelude* 6.600), which characteristically involves a trope of "unfathering"—that is, the putting in question of a figural father, source, "light of sense" (6.600), or point of reference in order to liberate the power of the imagination. For the purposes of rhetorical analysis, however, "usurpation" may be described in terms such as Saussure uses in the introduction to his *Course in General Linguistics*, where, as Derrida has shown at length, the hierarchical placement of "authentic" speech over "derivative" writing is put in doubt by the deconstructive power of writing to usurp speech (*Grammatology* 27–73). To what extent are the thematic (i.e., autobiographical, optical, phenomenological) usurpations or unfatherings in *The Prelude* repetitions of a linguistic usurpation of writing over speech? Moreover, how does the text use the *topos* of linguistic deficiency as part of its overall rhetorical strategy? By focusing on two significant moments in books 6 and 12 we can show to what point, and how, these questions of theme and allegory are aspects of the more fundamental Wordsworthian question of language.

Saussure and a Paradigm of Usurpation

Early in the introduction to his *Course in General Linguistics*, Saussure devotes a chapter to the "Graphic Representation of Language," in which he asserts that speech alone constitutes the proper object of study for linguistics, and that writing, speech's "graphic representation," is secondary and derivative. His observations are useful for the reading of Wordsworth's language that we will undertake. Saussure writes:

> Language and writing are two distinct systems of signs; the second exists for the sole purpose of representing the first. The linguistic object is not both the written and the spoken forms of words; the spoken forms alone constitute the object. (23–24)

This clear hierarchy, in which speech is privileged as prior and authentic, and writing is devalued as removed and incidental, seems confidently asserted by Saussure. But in the next sentence he opens up the possibility of a complete undoing of this hierarchy, a deconstruction of the entire project of linguistics as he had envisioned it:

> But the spoken word is so intimately bound to its written image that the latter manages to usurp the main role. (24)

What is the nature of the Saussurean usurpation? First of all, Saussure conceives of it in dramatic tropes: the "role" of speech is upstaged by writing. But later he alters his metaphors: "The graphic form of words," he writes, "strikes us as being something permanent and stable, better suited than sound to account for the unity of language throughout time" (25). Again, while "language is constantly evolving . . . writing tends to remain stable" (27). The apparent stability of writing, however, is actually a destabilizing force within "language," by which Saussure means speech, because it raises problems in two particular areas: pronunciation and spelling. Whereas initially the sound of a word (pronunciation) might by convention determine its graphic representation (spelling), gradually the situation is reversed and the orthography of a word dictates its sound; writing determines speech. "Some Parisians," Saussure complains, "already pronounce the 't' in *sept femmes*," and there will come "the day when even the last two letters of *vingt* 'twenty' will be pronounced—truly an orthographic monstrosity" (32).

Saussure's conclusion is emphatic: "Writing obscures language; it is not a guise for language but a disguise" (30). "The tyranny of writing," he calls it (31). But this tyranny must be confronted:

> Writing, though unrelated to its inner system, is used continually to represent language. We cannot simply disregard it. We must be acquainted with its usefulness, shortcomings, and dangers. (23)

To turn briefly now to Derrida's deconstruction of Saussure, we may recall that Derrida puts in question this structure of inner/outer systems, or original/derivative modes. Writing, for Derrida, means more than the popular notion of graphic representation: "In general," he says, "[it] covers the entire field of linguistic signs" (*Grammatology* 44). In the tone of Saussure's argument against writing, Derrida detects an aim "at more than a theoretical error, more than a moral fault: at a sort of stain and primarily at a sin" (*Grammatology* 34). Sin, Derrida says, constitutes "the inversion of the natural relationship between the soul and the body through passion" (*Grammatology* 34); hence in this Saussurean usurpation or inversion of speech and writing Derrida uncovers "the original sin of writing" (*Grammatology* 35), which I take to be a sin against origins, a reversing of authority.

The word "usurpation," for Derrida as for Saussure and Wordsworth, has strong historical and political overtones that figure in the idea of usurpation in language. "Saussure," Derrida writes, "is faithful to the tradition that has always associated writing with the fatal violence of the political institution" (*Grammatology* 36). He concludes:

> Finally, the "usurpation" of which Saussure speaks, the violence by which writing would substitute itself for its own origin, for that which ought not only to have engendered it but to have been engendered from itself—such a reversal of power cannot be an accidental aberration. Usurpation necessarily refers us to a profound possibility of essence. (*Grammatology* 39–40)

But that "essence" turns out to be an "absence"; writing itself, says Derrida, is the name of two absences, that of the "signatory" and that of the "referent" (*Grammatology* 40–41). Thus in place of a rhetoric of essence, origin, and derivation, Derrida puts Saussure's own notion of linguistic "difference," that is, the structure of interdependence or non-coincidence by which words acquire linguistic value or identity. "Language," Saussure writes, "is a system of interdependent terms in which the value of each term results solely from the simultaneous presence of the others" (114). He elaborates:

> Concepts [in language] are purely differential and defined not by their positive content but negatively by their relations with the other terms of the system. Their most precise characteristic is in being what the others are not. . . . A segment of language can never in the final analysis be based on anything except its non-coincidence with the rest. *Arbitrary* and *differential* are two correlative qualities. (117–18)

According to Saussure, "in language there are only differences *without positive terms*" (120). Thus writing, for Derrida, is not derivative of speech if one intends speech as a positive origin, center, or essence, because both speech and writing are constituted by the same structure of absence, difference, and non-coincidence; they both belong within a larger "grammatological" concept of writing, "the entire field of linguistic signs," or what Derrida calls an "arche-writing" (*Grammatology* 56).[2]

While Derrida is concerned to point out these contradictory aspects of Saussure's linguistic theory, there is a more specific question to be asked regarding a different deconstructive moment in Saussure's text. We have seen Saussure describe writing in terms of both a usurpation and a tyranny, but at what point does usurpation turn into tyranny? When does the pretender become ruler? Or is writing a usurper and a tyrant at the same time? The spatial overtones, however, are opposite: the power of a tyrant comes from above and is directed downwards; the usurper works from below or within and presumes to a new height. Or does Saussure have a distinctly dialectical process in mind, as if language begins with the *ancien régime* of speech, then subversive, revolutionary writing usurps the originary state to become the new tyrant of language?

The greatest usurper of all, of course, is Satan, the demonic revolutionary who attempts to usurp the authority of God's voice. If we read Satan's revolt in heaven, not, as Harold Bloom has done, "as an allegory of the dilemma of the modern poet, at his strongest" (*Anxiety* 20), but as an allegory of the Saussurean usurpation in language, then Satan's sin becomes the "sin of writing," the belated and secondary attempt to take the place of a God whose voice is pure *kerygma*. That Satan's revolt is "belated" (Bloom's key term) in a linguistic sense suggests that a theory for the anxiety of influence may actually be a trope for a deeper phenomenon at the level of language. Satan's attempted usurpation, in addition to being a rhetorical "sin of writing," also has suggestive thematic associations in his repudiation of the Father—his "un-fathering"—a trope that becomes significant for Wordsworth in the Alps and the "spots of time." Satan is not a literal writer, of course; his performance in Eve's temptation scene, for example, is clearly oratorical, emphasizing the power of speech as one of the gifts of the forbidden fruit. But he is an under-writer, in the sense of accuser, who attempts to reverse the body/spirit relation in a way analogous to the Saussurean model. The sin of usurpation is a Satanic act, but more fundamentally a rhetorical problem. The issues we have raised here will provide part of our conceptual framework as we now consider the business of usurpation in Wordsworth, first by a reading of key passages in Book 6, and then by a closer interrogation of language in the "spots of time."

"A Bad Five Minutes in the Alps" (Leslie Stephen)

Ever since W. G. Fraser in 1929 offered the interpretation that Wordsworth's experience of "Imagination" in Book 6 occurred during composition in 1804, critical examination of the passage has tended to follow his lead. Wordsworth's moment of insight, "when the light of sense / Goes out" (6.600–01), this interpretation suggests, took place as the emotion that the poet had felt in the Simplon Pass was "recollected in tranquillity" (*Prose* 1:149), resulting in the "spontaneous overflow of powerful feelings" (*Prose* 1:127, 149) in lines 592–616. Some of the early versions of this important section of *The Prelude* do suggest the experience of "Imagination" thwarting composition temporarily. The 1805 version reads:

> Imagination! lifting up itself
> Before the eye and progress of my song. . . .
> (6.525–26)

MSS D and E, which both Fraser and Havens cite, read:

> Imagination—here that awful Power
> Before the retrospective Song rose up. . . .
> (de Selincourt 208)

The first revised version of MS E (MS E^2), however, has:

> Imagination at that moment rose
> The awful Power before my mental eye. . . .
> (de Selincourt 208)

And by the second revision to MS E (MS E^3), which finally stands in the 1850 edition, we have:

> Imagination—here the Power so called
> Through sad incompetence of human speech,
> That awful Power rose from the mind's abyss. . . .
> (6.592–94)

It is true that in the earliest attempts to recount his experience, Wordsworth does appear to indicate that the moment occurred in the midst of his poem—his "retrospective Song"—but it is also true that the successive revisions of this passage remove a specific temporal reference, and locate the experience of "Imagination" less and less in the act of poetic composition and more and more in the narrative structure of the original account. In fact, the one MS that Fraser does not quote (MS E^2) arguably locates the experience back in 1790: "Imagination *at that moment* rose" (de Selincourt 208; emphasis added). The localizing antecedent of the demonstrative adjective "that" would be the "moment" of the peasant's telling the travelers that they "*had crossed the Alps*" (6.591). Jonathan Wordsworth, with other evidence, has argued that the "impressive juxtaposition" of "*we had crossed the Alps*" and "Imagination—here the Power so called" is "a second thought" (*NP* 216). In the original MS WW, he says, the simile of the cave (later 1805:8.711–27) separates these two verse paragraphs—thus putting in doubt the notion that "Imagination" rose during the composition of these very lines on the Alps, or that it rose as a narratologically disjunctive force. Recent reconsiderations have confirmed this view. Robert A. Brinkley writes that "Wordsworth has revised his account of the Simplon Pass incident so that the affirmation of his soul's glory will become an interpretation of his Alpine experience" (123). Susan Luther argues that Wordsworth's revisions make the account applicable "to 1790 as well as to 1804" (258).

Yet the older view that the passage refers to the temporality of writing still has its supporters. John T. Ogden, commenting on these lines, suggests, like Fraser, "that the imagination arose in the process of composition." Ogden goes on to argue that in the 1850 edition, "the poet has lost his temporal orientation, as the original experience turns into a metaphor for his present emotional experience" ("Distance" 255).[3] The temporal orientation that Ogden discusses is certainly less clear in the 1850 poem than in the earlier MSS, but that is not because the poet has "lost" it. On the contrary, the removal of explicit temporal references is part of a rhetorical tendency by Wordsworth to create the sense of an experience not bound by time or place that fertilizes and sustains the poet throughout the composition of the poem. The diction of the passage points to the literal climb and descent as well as to the experience during composition. The "lonely traveller" (6.596) is at once the speaker in the Alps and the retrospective poet; the "unfathered vapour" (6.595) is both the mountain mists and the temporary confusion felt by the poet "when the light of sense / Goes out" (6.600–01).[4] The abyss of the mind corresponds to the abyss in the mountains to which the poet must descend; and the "hope . . . effort, and expectation, and desire" (6.606–07) all refer to the concrete, actual climb as well as to the poet's apocalyptic vision. The rhetoric thus looks in two directions: upwards to the climb, and downwards to the descent; outwards to the actual world, and inwards to "the invisible world" (6.602).

It is not until the second revision of MS E—a late revision, occurring sometime after 1839 (de Selincourt xxiv, 208)—that the notion of the inadequacy of language enters. What the reader gains is a new sense of the awfulness of the experience: through revision the power grows in impressiveness as Wordsworth's ability adequately to describe it declines. The 1805 version of this passage begins:

> Imagination! lifting up itself
> Before the eye and progress of my song

Like an unfathered vapour—here that Power,
In all the might of its endowments, came
Athwart me. . . .
(6.525–29)

The faintly nautical overtones of the metaphor the "Power . . . came / Athwart me" suggest the image of Wordsworth as a sailor, the poem as a ship, confronted by an obstacle. Such a nautical image, as Curtius has splendidly pointed out, is conventional in poetry: "The epic poet voyages over the open sea in a great ship, the lyric poet on a river in a small boat . . . the poet becomes the sailor, his mind or work the boat" (128, 129; cf. Lindenberger 306). "Our little bark / On a strong river boldly hath been launched," Wordsworth writes in Book 4 (559–60), in a characteristic blending of lyric and heroic elements. The first epic simile in the poem likewise involves a nautical image; Wordsworth compares himself, in the manner of Curtius' lyric mode, to "one who hangs down-bending from the side / Of a slow-moving boat, upon the breast / Of a still water" (4.256–58); yet the fact that this lyrical imagery is expressed in an *epic* simile again suggests a blending of genres. Wordsworth needs "sea-room" to tell his story.

The word "athwart" need not have the connotation of a nautical journey—the journey metaphor is also grounded in the pedestrian figure of the "lonely traveller"—but there are other tropes to suggest the image of a ship. The power that comes athwart the poet shows him that it "harbours" (6.603) in infinitude; thus the external "banners militant" (6.609) are not concerned to attest the mind's "prowess" (6.611), which remains hidden in another water image, "the mighty flood of Nile" (6.614). After hearing the peasant's "tidings" (6.618), the poet experiences a "melancholy slackening" (6.617); the "proud full sail of his great verse," as Shakespeare would say (Sonnet 86), drops down. Though "athwart" is removed by 1850, an echo of it remains, heard in the "winds thwarting winds, bewildered and forlorn" (6.628) later in the passage.

Wordsworth gives the name "Imagination" to the power that rises from the mind's abyss because he is so baffled by it that he cannot think of any other word to describe it. Even by 1839 Wordsworth must not have been satisfied with his choice. The "sad incompetence of human speech"—or what he elsewhere calls sheer "poverty of language" (*Prose* 3:82)—ostensibly prevents him from articulating the experience more precisely; and yet, does not the admittedly ineffable nature of the moment—language articulating its inarticulateness—strive toward a logocentric adequacy even in its deficiency? In Book 5 Wordsworth laments the mind's inability adequately to realize its power in language or in natural objects; both media remain "shrines so frail" (5.49) that they can only give what Shelley would call "a feeble shadow" of the mind's original conceptions (504). Between the conception and the creation falls the shadow.

Usurpation

It is easy to take Wordsworth at his word and accept his labeling of the power as "Imagination." But if we recognize his own hesitancy in giving such a name to the power, we may wish to be more tentative. We may even wish to suggest that the "awful Power" is not the "Imagination" at all, but a psychic power that lies behind and within the faculty of imagination. Imagination takes the raw power and refines it, modifies it, directs it toward a creative end. The power without the refining and controlling function of the imagination becomes "a tempest, a redundant energy, / Vexing its own creation" (1.37–38). Precisely what is involved in the transmission of power through the imagination may be traced using the analogue of Wordsworth's "correspondent breeze" (1.35).

In his definitive essay on the metaphor of the correspondent breeze, M. H. Abrams adds a comment about the Stoic concept of the World Soul:

> The poet Lucan said that Apollo founded the Delphic oracle at a huge chasm where "the earth breathed forth divine truth, and . . . gave out a wind that spoke"; and he suggested that the Pythian priestess stationed there is inspired by inhaling the very breath of the World Soul. (45)

Although Abrams does not discuss this vocal, vaporous aspect of the metaphorical breeze in relation to Wordsworth, its applicability to *The Prelude* is tantalizing. Whereas at the Delphic oracle the earth breathes forth a wind, in Book 6 the mind's abyss issues forth the "unfathered vapour." In both cases, the vapor is oracular: at Delphi it utters "divine truth"; in the Simplon Pass it creates an inner breeze that is felt and transmitted by the poet through language. In this sense, what the process suggests is an internalized reversal of the correspondent breeze; the effect of the "awful Power" is to set in motion the imagination of the poet, to create a psychic wave that becomes actualized in the text. Whereas in the correspondent breeze trope, as Wordsworth employs it, the process of transmission is from an external breeze that is natural and beneficent to an internal breeze that is psychic and vexing (at least, in Book 1), in the Simplon Pass the process is reversed: the internal, raw power rises and is transmitted through the imagination into an actual, external poem. Now in the moment of usurpation the power bypasses the refining and transmitting function of the imagination and presents itself directly to the senses, at which point they become overloaded and "the light of sense / Goes out." But it goes out "with a flash" (6.601), which is to say, with a sudden intensification of sense that reveals "the invisible world." The raw psychic power floods the senses of the poet from within in an instantaneous burst of energy that puts the light of sense out, but not before the light itself is able to illumine the very power that is about to overpower it. The effect is like lightning, like Shelley's image of "the cloud of mind . . . discharging its collected lightning" (134). Thus the "invisible world" that is revealed is not a transcendent world that exists beyond nature; it is the invisible world of the mind's abyss, and what is revealed there is the potentiality contained within the hiding places of the mind: "something evermore about to be" (6.608).

In other words, the Alps episode is a clear example in *The Prelude* when "the hiding-places of man's power / Open" (12.279–80), and the poet glimpses their invisible world without being consumed or annihilated. The power itself is involuntary, as Wordsworth implies in Book 12: "the hiding-places of man's power / Open; I would approach them, but they close" (12.280). The power must be mediated, therefore, through language; for Wordsworth, I think, there is no "unmediated vision," in Geoffrey Hartman's phrase. Shelley adapts the image of a mediating principle in "Adonais," although in that poem more so than in any other of Shelley's the medium is also a barrier:

> Life, like a dome of many-coloured glass,
> Stains the white radiance of Eternity,
> Until Death tramples it to fragments.—Die,
> If thou wouldst be with that which thou dost seek!
> (462–65)

It is difficult to imagine Wordsworth writing this last verse, but there is, nevertheless, a similarity between his and Shelley's depictions of power. The "white radiance" corresponds to the "awful Power" in the mind's abyss; the imagination, which gives a "colouring" to objects, as Wordsworth says in the Preface to *Lyrical Ballads* (*Prose* 1:123), is the "dome of many-coloured glass." Usurpation is the smashing of the dome, which is to say, the bypass of imagination and the overpowering of sense.

Now insofar as Wordsworth does not come into naked contact with his psychic power, he might appear to validate Harold Bloom's notion of "Wordsworth's resistance to his own imaginative emancipation" (what Bloom calls the "hidden tragedy" of *The Prelude* [*Visionary Company* 155]), and to confirm Geoffrey Hartman's theory of Wordsworth's avoidance of apocalypse (*WP* 61, 226, 254). But the poet, in fact, tells us that he is not resisting anything at all:

> I was lost;
> Halted *without an effort* to break through. . . .
> (6.596–97; emphasis added)

He makes no effort to resist the power, but instead surrenders to it and finds it glorious:

> to my conscious soul I now can say—
> 'I recognize thy glory'; in such strength
> Of usurpation, when the light of sense
> Goes out, but with a flash that has revealed
> The invisible world, doth greatness make abode. . . .
> (6.598–602)

The power rises from the mind's abyss to fertilize his imagination even as a "fount of Abyssinian clouds" feeds the river Nile "to fertilize the whole Egyptian plain" (6.615, 616). Whereas the power in the mind rises from below, the nourishment of the clouds descends from above: power rising is the same as power descending. This completes the motif of the poet's discovery that his "future course" is "downwards, with the current of that stream" (6.585). His mistaken "hopes that pointed to the clouds" (6.587) in the climbing of the Alps are redirected downwards to "humble and rustic life" (*Prose* 1:125). By linking the power rising from the mind's abyss to the clouds descending to the Egyptian plain, Wordsworth provides a naturalistic trope of the workings of his own mind. On the literal level of the climb, his proper course is not up but down, which on the level of mind becomes expressed not as a journey toward something above and beyond but below and within, like an abyss. The fertilizing clouds provide the imagistic and linguistic key, for they are specifically "Abyss-inian" clouds.[5] In the pun Wordsworth indicates the two directions of up and down, transcendence and descendence, and the correct choice of the path that leads downwards and inwards to his psychic source.

Let us consider the idea of usurpation more closely. In the Prospectus Wordsworth announces his intention to proclaim that the mind of man and the external world are exquisitely fitted to each other. At the opening of *The Prelude*, however, the poet is anxiously searching for this very sort of cooperation that threatens to turn, on the one hand, into a "vain perplexity" (1.266) that foils poetry or, on the other hand, into what Patrick Holland calls "an abyss of self-consciousness" that usurps the outer world (21). The "gentle breeze" of the first line of the poem awakens within the poet "a correspondent breeze" that becomes "a tempest, a redundant energy / Vexing its own creation" (1.37–38). The poet's attempt to come to terms with this redundant energy forms the imaginative action of the first book, as Wordsworth believes that the "discordant elements" in his own mind may be reconciled through the "dark / Inscrutable workmanship" (1.343, 341–42) of his imagination. The dramatized fumbling for a theme is not exactly conventional, as Hartman has pointed out (*WP* 38), and yet the convention of affected modesty is manipulated in such a way as to belie the inept performance, and thus make the discovery of the proper theme all the more dramatic.

One connotation of the word "usurpation" which we explored in Derrida's reading of Saussure suggests that there may be something unlawful about the mind's overloading of sense, an arrogance and even a violence to its power. A displaced form of this violence is apparent in the fragment called "Nutting," originally intended as part of *The Prelude*, but published instead in the *Lyrical Ballads* in 1800 (de Selincourt xxvii). The speaker of the poem ravages a hazel tree and afterwards feels "a sense of pain" (52) for his violent act. An intertextual note may add to our understanding of usurpation here. We said earlier that the great usurper is Satan, the demonic pretender to the throne of God. He is present in this fragment, though by means of a series of transformations. The speaker describes his difficult journey in search of the hazel tree:

O'er pathless rocks,
Through beds of matted fern, and tangled thickets,

> Forcing my way, I came to one dear nook
> Unvisited. . . .
>
> (14–17)

The language transumes Satan's journey through Chaos in quest of Paradise:

> O'er bog or steep, through strait, rough, dense, or rare,
> With head, hands, wings, or feet pursues his way,
> And swims or sinks, or wades, or creeps, or flies. . . .
>
> (*PL* 2.948–50)

Wordsworth goes on to recount how he came to a secret place

> where not a broken bough
> Drooped with its withered leaves, ungracious sign
> Of devastation; but the hazels rose
> Tall and erect, with tempting clusters hung,
> A virgin scene!
>
> (17–21)

The "virgin scene" very much resembles Paradise, and Wordsworth is self-consciously a type of Satanic intruder. The lines echo the tempting of Eve in Book 9 of *Paradise Lost*, especially Satan's fictitious description of his eating the forbidden apples (*PL* 9.575–612). Wordsworth's phrase "tempting clusters hung" echoes Satan's sight of "where plenty hung / Tempting so nigh" (*PL* 9.594–95), while the text's insistence on the absence of a "broken bough" and "withered leaves" in the scene may be contrasted with the bough that Eve breaks off to take to Adam (*PL* 9.850–51) and the withered petals ("ungracious sign / Of devastation!") of the garland that Adam makes for Eve (*PL* 9.892–93). But what is perhaps more curious is the "sweet reluctant amorous delay" (*PL* 4.311) of Wordsworth after finding the hazel nuts; instead of seeking an immediate gratification, he delays and defers with a "wise restraint / Voluptuous" (23–24). By contrast, "to satisfy the sharp desire I had," Satan says, "I resolv'd / Not to defer" (*PL* 9.584, 585–86).

The intertextual rhetoric of "Nutting" thus resonates with the act of original sin in the boy's behavior. The usurpation in "Nutting" reaches back to a Miltonic analogue in which the old Usurper himself plays the crucial role. Usurpation, for Wordsworth, always has elements of a Satanic act about it, a demonic or criminal intent, a temptation not to be withstood: the sin of usurpation.

The word "unfathered" likewise requires comment. The word

is usually interpreted as meaning "with no apparent source" (Havens, *Mind* 428),[6] and is thus associated again with Satan, who fancies himself as being unfathered, that is, "self-begot, self-rais'd" (*PL* 5.860). "We know no time when we were not as now," Satan says (*PL* 5.859). But "unfathered" can mean not only lacking a father but, in a more active sense, having lost a father, being de-fathered, in the same way that Macbeth is "unmann'd in folly" at the sight of Banquo's ghost (3.4.73). "Unfathered" is a Shakespearean word (it never occurs in Milton's poetry); Shakespeare uses it in both the senses of never having had and having lost a father. When in 2 *Henry IV* he speaks of "unfather'd heirs and loathly births of nature" (4.4.122), the word "unfather'd" suggests the idea of a bastard, as it arguably does in Sonnet 124, in which the speaker's love "might for fortune's bastard be unfather'd." But as Rollins points out in his variorum edition of Shakespeare's sonnets, critics have read "unfather'd" in Sonnet 124 as meaning both "without a *true* father" and "deprived of a father"—that is, orphaned (1:312). This second meaning is certainly present in Sonnet 97, in which we have the lines "Yet this abundant issue seemed to me, / But hope of orphans, and unfathered fruit." Alastair Fowler, however, has suggested that both meanings are present in this latter instance, both the bastard and the orphan (112).

Wordsworth uses "fathered" in a related sense in Book 3 of *The Prelude*: Cambridge scholars are like caterpillars eating "with keen devouring noise / Not to be tracked or fathered" (3.456–57)—that is, perhaps, not to be traced to a source.[7] In the Alps passage, if we read "unfathered" as meaning without a source, then we tend to ascribe supernatural characteristics to imagination, since the "unfathered vapour" is a simile for "Imagination." Yet the poet has already located the power: "that awful Power rose from the mind's abyss." On the other hand, if we take the sense as that of a vapor that has just lost its father, is perhaps in search of another father, then by virtue of the simile "Imagination" becomes a force cut off from its source, from "the light of sense" that contributes to its going out. Deprived of "nature and the language of the sense" ("Tintern" 108), imagination is "unfathered."

Yet how is the unfathering related to usurpation? Is the situation as Oedipal as its rhetoric suggests? Oedipus encounters and kills a traveler on the road outside Thebes, and by doing so unfathers himself. The child is father of the man, naturally, but the poet fathers himself, satanically, by writing a poem about his genesis. If the "strength / Of usurpation" is then the power to unfather, it is also the power to overturn what Wordsworth calls the "subjugation" (*Poems* 1: 978) of the mind to the limitations of the material, sensory world.

Considered as a trope not only for imagination but for language itself, "unfathered vapour" verges on oxymoron. Vapor is naturally associated with the breath of speech, with voice, and hence with the presence of the breather or speaker. But a breath that is unfathered, cut off from its source, makes this figure of speech sound like a figure of writing—that is, a trope for the form of language in which the sender of the message is absent from the context of the message. Wordsworth's "unfathered vapour" becomes a "wandering utterance" (cf. "On the Power of Sound" 169), and imagination begins to take on grammatological connotations.

Usurpation has other implications. The diction and imagery of the passage preceding the "spots of time" in Book 12 are striking in their concrete depiction of the tyranny of the senses, especially sight. Echoing a passage in Book 3 in which the speaker declares that as a child "the bodily eye" (3.158) did "bind [his] feelings even as in a chain" (3.169), Wordsworth in Book 12 calls "the bodily eye" the "most despotic of our senses" (12.129) (cf. Coleridge's "despotism of the eye" in *Biographia Literaria* [62]) and the imagery of tyranny that follows is impressive. The process of binding, which recurs throughout Romantic literature in various forms, would have here a negative implication for Blake: the binder would be a Tirzah-figure, a mother of the mortal part of the poet. The binding that Wordsworth has in mind, however, is not a binding of "Nostrils Eyes & Ears" (Blake 30), but of the feelings, as by natural piety. He speaks of the "absolute dominion" (12.131) of the eye, of the "wider empire for the sight" (12.145), of the "thraldom of that sense" (12.150); and he contrasts himself, subservient to sense in his youth, to his future wife, a maid "who escaped these bonds" (12.152) of astonishing power.

Given such rhetoric of the power and dictatorship of sight in *The Prelude*, it is appropriate that Wordsworth describe his moment in the Simplon as a "usurpation" or overthrow of the government of the senses—at least, as a radical de-privileging of the eye. Nature calls forth an imagination that comes into full play only when the language of the sense is not perceived; vision is clearest when the eye is made quiet; the ear hears best when it sleeps undisturbed. But usurpation yet retains the connotation of a wrongful act; Wordsworth's desire to clutch at the nearest wall or tree hovers somewhere in the background (*Poems* 1:978). To his "conscious soul" the poet can say, "I recognize thy glory,"

> in such strength
> Of usurpation, when the light of sense
> Goes out, but with a flash that has revealed
> The invisible world, doth greatness make abode,
> There harbours, whether we be young or old.
> Our destiny, our being's heart and home
> Is with infinitude, and only there;
> With hope it is, hope that can never die,
> Effort, and expectation, and desire,
> And something evermore about to be.
> (6.599–608)

Greatness makes abode not in the act of usurpation but in the *strength* of usurpation. Humanity's "destiny" is linked to its own imaginative strength. Our home is not in "the invisible world"; it is with the power that is able to reveal that world by imaging itself (imperfectly) in language.

Through the conscious recognition of the spiritual glory and strength that reside in his mind, and through his attempts to communicate that power, the speaker is able to say that the soul "seeks for no trophies, struggles for no spoils / That may attest her prowess" (6.610–11): other palms are won; the consciousness is enough; the soul is "blest in thoughts / That are their own perfection and reward" (6.611–12). Paradoxically, the outward and visible expression of humanity's infinite strength belies itself as "beatitude" (6.613), even as the "exterior semblance" of the child in the "Intimations Ode" belies the "Soul's immensity" (109–10). Although not for the Shelley of "Mont Blanc," for Wordsworth here the power, while serene and remote insofar as it lies in the hiding places of the mind, is not entirely inaccessible; it can be approached—even made self-present, as Wordsworth hopes—through the articulate imagination and the "sensuous incarnation" of language (*Prose* 3:65). "I would give," he says in Book 12, "as far as words can give, / Substance and life to what I feel" (12.282–84).

Error and Voice

If, as Cynthia Chase has said, Book 5 is the "book of accidents" (547), then Book 6 is the book of error. It concerns both the wanderings of Wordsworth and the ways in which by indirections he finds directions out. "Juvenile errors are my theme," he says in Book 11 (54). But if, in *The Prelude*'s allegory of reading, what happens on the thematic level is a simultaneous repetition of an occurrence on the linguistic level, then the theme of error, wandering, deviation from a path plays out the more fundamental deviations of figural language itself.

What are the errors of language in the Simplon passage? The most conspicuous, of course, is the word "Imagination," which is "so called / Through sad incompetence of human speech." There is the suggestion of a doubling of error here: "incompetence" chooses a name, and "Imagination" becomes a so-called power. Given its questionable accuracy as a name, "Imagination" is hardly a metaphor for the power; it is not identified with the power, but is a name put for the power: it is a meta-name, or metonym. The metonymic status of so-called "Imagination" makes clear the disjunction between word and thing, and conveys the tentativeness of the entire meta-naming process. But why is it the "incompetence" of speech that designates imagination thus?

We might return to the Chomskyan distinction, mentioned in Chapter 3, between linguistic competence and linguistic performance (Chomsky 4), for Wordsworth seems to a surprising degree consistent with Chomsky's theory when he says that it is the incompetence, and not the unsatisfactory performance of the poet, that gives to the power the label of "Imagination." In other words, the naming of the power lies beyond the ability of language itself, not just beyond the particular eloquence of one person: it lies beyond "the reach of words" (3.187). Had Wordsworth said that the name was the result of the sad performance of the poet, he would have reiterated the convention of affected modesty; he makes himself worthy of his Romantic stature, however, by shifting the question of language to the questionableness of language, to the limits of language's competence. Wordsworth reformulates the problem in the 1815 Essay Supplementary. In response to our question, "Why is it the 'incompetence' of language that designates imagination thus?" Wordsworth flatly replies: "Poverty of language is the primary cause of the use which we make of the word, Imagination" (*Prose* 3:81).

It is thus debatable whether the "Imagination" passage should hold the privileged position that it generally does in Wordsworth commentary. Structurally, the experience of an obstacle rising up to block the poet should be familiar. In Book 4 Wordsworth speaks of those moments of poetic composition when "some lovely Image in the song rose up / Full-formed, like Venus rising from the sea" (4.113–14); later in the same book he says: "The memory of one particular hour / Doth here rise up against me" (4.308–09)—where the trope of rising up against is synonymous with a usurpation. In the book of London, Wordsworth commands the city: "Rise up, thou monstrous ant-hill!" (7.149); the Maiden of Buttermere's image later rises twice to meet and block the poet (7.295–320). We could multiply examples of risings: the drowned man, who rises up out of the lake (5.448–50); the "fair trains of imagery" that rise up before the poet in the Prospectus (3); the rising morn that arrests Wordsworth in his dedication scene (4.323–38); the mistaken rising of the moon, and not the sun, on Snowdon (14.5–6, 39–42); and the dream of the Arab, in which, Wordsworth says, "certain thoughts / Beset me, and to height unusual rose" (5.61–62). What results from this last rising up is a moment when the poet's light of sense likewise goes out, and he passes into a dream.

Blocking images are always coming athwart Wordsworth.[8] But the Simplon Pass episode should be familiar in other ways—not least, in the context of an act of usurpation. The abyss experience of the Simplon, with its "strength / Of usurpation," has a precedent only a hundred lines earlier in the episode of the Chartreuse. There Wordsworth speaks of a

'conquest over sense, hourly achieved
Through faith and meditative reason, resting
Upon the word of heaven-imparted truth,
Calmly triumphant; and for humbler claim
Of that imaginative impulse sent
From these majestic floods, yon shining cliffs,
The untransmuted shapes of many worlds,
Cerulean ether's pure inhabitants,
These forests unapproachable by death,
That shall endure as long as man endures,
To think, to hope, to worship and to feel,

To struggle, to be lost within himself
In trepidation, from the blank abyss
To look with bodily eyes and be consoled.'
(6.458–71)

Havens describes these lines as "obscure" (*Mind* 424), but they nevertheless do bear arguable relation to the "Imagination" passage. Two aspects in particular invite comparison: the theme, religious but expressed in terms that are not explicitly religious, of a "conquest over sense" that rests upon an imparted word; and the matter of achieving a complementary consolation through the will and the senses. The "forests unapproachable by death" give the poet an intimation of his own immortality, and though these natural symbols of immutability have a "humbler claim" on the mind than "faith and meditative reason" do, they nevertheless contain an "imaginative impulse" analogous to "the word of heaven-imparted truth." The consolation proposed in the final lines depends on a return to the senses ("bodily eyes") from within the abyss of the conquest over sense.

Now in the Simplon passage a number of these details are reiterated. The "conquest over sense" becomes a "usurpation, when the light of sense / Goes out" (6.600–01); "the word of heaven-imparted truth" becomes the words of a human-imparted answer by a peasant; "the forests unapproachable by death" are transformed into "woods decaying, never to be decayed" (6.625); the work that man has to do "to think, to hope, to worship and to feel, / To struggle" becomes the "hope that can never die, / Effort, and expectation, and desire" (6.606–07); and the experience of man's being "lost within himself" changes into direct statement: "I was lost" (6.596). The "blank abyss"—which surely owes something to Milton's "universal blanc" (*PL* 3.48), which similarly is recompensed by "things invisible" (*PL* 3.55)—is altered to the "mind's abyss" (6.594); both abysses involve things seen (with "bodily eyes") and unseen ("the invisible world"). A final correspondence concerns the metonym of "Imagination": at the Chartreuse Wordsworth feels an "imaginative impulse sent / From these majestic floods"—that is, from nature; in the Simplon Pass, "Imagination" comes from the mind.

Structurally, then, these two episodes are strikingly similar. Perhaps the Chartreuse, instead of the Ravine of Gondo, should be regarded as what Abrams calls Wordsworth's "complementary revelation" ("Portrait" 214); it prepares the reader for its analogous version in the poet's encounter with the peasant. Under the question of language, let us see to what extent the "Imagination" passage depends on an imparted word corresponding to "the word of heaven-imparted truth."

Jonathan Wordsworth has observed that in MS WW the crossing of the Alps and the passage on "Imagination" are separated by the simile of the cave from Book 8 ("As when a traveller hath from open day . . ." [1805:8.711]), which Wordsworth wrote, perhaps, "in an attempt to define [his] sense of anticlimax at having unknowingly crossed the Alps" (*NP* 304). That intervening passage, in which the poet describes the interior of an underground cave where chiaroscuro effects dominate, ends in a curious trope: "the scene before him stands in perfect view / Exposed, and lifeless as a written book!" (8.575–76). This simile of the dead letter, which Wordsworth uses earlier in Book 8 (297), stands in marked contrast to the rhetoric of presence of the peasant whose voice corrects the travelers. The writing simile was relocated, and Wordsworth's response to the peasant's response became a lament for the incompetence of human speech.

Is there a usurpation here? Speech seems to outlast writing in the growth of this passage. The meeting with the peasant emphasizes the oral/aural aspects of the encounter; strangely, Wordsworth gives us no matter-of-fact description of the peasant's appearance. "A peasant met us," he says, "from whose mouth we learned / That . . . we must descend" (6.579–80, 581). The travelers "grieved to hear" (6.586) what the peasant had to say:

> We questioned him again and yet again;
> But every word that from the peasant's lips
> Came in reply, translated by our feelings,
> Ended in this,—*that we had crossed the Alps.*
> (6.588–91)

Mouth, hearing, words, lips, questioning, reply, translation—the diction clearly emphasizes the vocal nature of the transaction. The participial phrase "translated by our feelings" introduces a profound mediating element: insofar as the peasant's words are a text, Wordsworth is an interpreter, both as a reader of texts and as a linguistic translator, and his interpretation/translation a periphrasis of the text; hence the indirect speech—"*that we had crossed the Alps.*" Like the voice of nature, the peasant's speech is partially hidden from the reader; the poet is also a mediator, and the poem the text of a text.

The episode with the peasant, like the encounter with the blind Beggar, is thus an instance of interpretation, when the linguistic performance of one person in one language is translated through the sad incompetence of another person in another language. In a relatively late poem, "After Leaving Italy, Continued," Wordsworth presents a surprising parallel in his account of his departure from Italy on his tour of 1837. To demonstrate his rapture over the Italian landscape, he offers proof of his reluctance to leave the country:

witness that unwelcome shock
That followed the first sound of German speech,
Caught the far-winding barrier Alps among.
In that announcement, greeting seemed to mock
Parting; the casual word had power to reach
My heart, and filled that heart with conflict strong.
(*Poems* 2:864)

The note to Isabella Fenwick makes the parallel to *The Prelude* even clearer: "It was only by the accidental sound of a few German words I was aware that we had quitted Italy" (*Poems* 2:1067). "*That we had crossed the Alps*," we hear. It is only by the accidental words of the peasant that the travelers in Book 6 discover where they are; despite their errors in language, through interpretation they realize their mistaken direction. A similar voice/shock effect is felt: the poet confronts a vocal text, he translates, and "Imagination" rises. The same error of 1790 is repeated in 1837. The German words are "unwelcome"; Wordsworth is "loth to believe what [he] so grieved to hear" (6.586). The greeting of the Germans seems to "mock" the parting from Italy; the crossing of a threshold marks the completion of one tour and the beginning of another.

The journey across the Alps seems guided by error and disappointment. Wordsworth grieves when he sees Mont Blanc (6.523–28), but he then proceeds to relate a "far different dejection . . . a deep and genuine sadness" (1805:6.491, 492) resulting from what he calls his "underthirst / Of vigour" (6.558–59):

And from that source how different a sadness
Would issue, let one incident make known.
(6.560–61)

What follows is the Simplon episode, and what "issues" from an under-source is not "sadness" but a "sad incompetence of human speech" that both celebrates and deplores the so-called errors of "Imagination."

My earlier suggestion that the word "Imagination" is but a metonym for an "awful Power" in the mind has a certain phenomenological appeal, however fallacious such an hypothesis might be according to faculty psychology. But I want to reformulate my approach now in terms of the Saussurean usurpation outlined at the beginning of this chapter. There we saw that writing usurps speech; what is the analogous usurpation here? We might be tempted to say that imagination usurps sense, but from our reading of the rhetorical structure of the whole passage we know that it is actually a voice, a vocal text, that usurps upon the poet. *Language* usurps sense in this passage; and if "Imagination" is put for the power that usurps, we may say that here "Imagination" is but a trope for language. The naming of the power is the naming of language; language *is* power; and for language thus to talk about itself is to enter an abyss of linguistic reflexiveness unequalled in *The Prelude*. The text comes face to face with its awful power of language, and calls that power "Imagination."

Mind and Language in the "Spots of Time"

After his description of the first "spot of time," Wordsworth concludes with the following apostrophe:

> Oh! mystery of man, from what a depth
> Proceed thy honours. I am lost, but see
> In simple childhood something of the base
> On which thy greatness stands; but this I feel,
> That from thyself it comes, that thou must give,
> Else never canst receive. The days gone by
> Return upon me almost from the dawn
> Of life: the hiding-places of man's power
> Open; I would approach them, but they close.
> I see by glimpses now; when age comes on,
> May scarcely see at all; and I would give,
> While yet we may, as far as words can give,
> Substance and life to what I feel, enshrining,
> Such is my hope, the spirit of the Past
> For future restoration.
>
> (12.272–86)

The poet initially addresses himself to the "mystery of man," and during the course of the passage he attempts to locate and define—and by locating and defining to put himself in touch with—"the hiding-places of man's power." As this phrase suggests, there is something elusive about the power, where it resides, what its function is, and Wordsworth attempts to track it down by imaging it in a number of ways. Basil Willey offers one solution to the mystery when he says that "certain memories are the 'hiding-places of man's power'; memories, that is, of former successful exertions of imaginative strength" (307). But the power does not exist only in the past; it also makes abode in the realm of "something evermore about to be."

What is this "mystery of man"? Another secret? Or is it, like the "mystery of words" (5.597), also related to the sense of mystery as craft? "What a piece of work is a man!" Hamlet says (2.2.300). Wordsworth begins by troping the "honours" of man as something that proceeds from a great depth or abyss that is active and creative. Where he sees such activity and creativity clearly exampled is in childhood, and that becomes part of the "base" on which the power is founded:

I am lost, but see
In simple childhood something of the base
On which thy greatness stands; but this I feel,
That from thyself it comes, that thou must give,
Else never canst receive.

"Something of the base": childhood can provide an image of only part of the foundation of man's imaginative greatness; the rest of the foundation, in Wordsworth's architectonic metaphor, must be sought elsewhere. Man's "greatness" is not equated with childhood, nor even located there: it dwells apart only to ground itself partially on the actual human base in childhood. Eventually, however, as the "Intimations Ode" records, childhood becomes simply another frail shrine, like books, to the glory of the mind of man.

Geoffrey Hartman is right to note the ambiguity of the parallel clauses beginning "but see" and "but this I feel" (*WP* 217–18). What the poet can "see" is that childhood offers an imagistic base, admittedly inadequate, for the greatness of man; what he can "feel," however, is that in whatever way he images the power, it is personal and dynamic: ". . . from thyself it comes . . . thou must give, / Else never canst receive." But is the giving so absolutely prior? Can the poet in fact give of something that he has never received? Or does he merely give of an already given, as nature calls forth and strengthens a pre-existing imagination? "I would give," he continues, "while yet we may, as far as words can give, / Substance and life to what I feel." It is difficult not to hear the tentativeness of such short, hesitant clauses. The very manner in which the poet says that he wishes to give "substance and life" to impassioned feeling implies, apart from his logocentric desire to give "sensuous incarnation" (*Prose* 3:65) to his passion—to have it become word and dwell among men—a self-conscious recognition of the extreme tenuousness, even impossibility, of such an endeavour: language is forever declaring its difference from passion. As a poet, Wordsworth can give flesh to the imagination only "as far as words can give" an image of its truth, and ultimately for Wordsworth as for Shelley, "the deep truth is imageless" (Shelley 175).

Whereas in the Alps passage man's greatness abides in the "strength / Of usurpation," here we find that "simple childhood" provides a concrete support for greatness too. The lines that follow, however, direct our attention away from these architectural metaphors to a new series of tropes: journey, entrance, return:

> The days gone by
> Return upon me almost from the dawn
> Of life: the hiding-places of man's power
> Open. . . .

The phrasing and punctuation are important here. Does the colon imply an identity between the clauses on either side of it—that is, that the "return" constitutes the opening? The syntactical parallelism would seem to support this reading: the structure of "the days gone by / Return" aligns itself with "the hiding places . . . / Open." Or is there also the suggestion of a cause-and-effect relation, that the returning of past days functions as a key that opens the hiding-places? If we accept the first possibility, then the passage equates memory with power, and we are back to Willey's argument;[9] if we take the second, then man's power yet dwells apart, distinct from the predeterminations of memory. The precise workings of "the hiding-places of man's power" may be clarified by an analogy in Shelley's *Defence of Poetry*.

Shelley says that "the mind in creation is as a fading coal, which some invisible influence, like an inconstant wind, awakens to transitory brightness." He further describes these "evanescent visitations" as "always arising unforeseen and departing unbidden" (503–04). The case may be applied to the "mystery of man." When Wordsworth says that "the hiding-places of man's power / Open," the analogy implies that the "fading coal" is awakened "to transitory brightness," and that the poet is able, as he affirms, to "see by glimpses" into the mystery. When the coal fades back into dimness, the hiding places close. Like Shelley's "visitations," a word paralleling Wordsworth's "visitings of imaginative power" (12.203), or his "visitings / Of awful promise" (1805:6.533–34), the hiding places open "unforeseen" and close "unbidden."

Comparison of the 1805 and 1850 texts of *The Prelude* indicates, through Wordsworth's rhetorical revisions, his shifting attitude to the power. In the earlier version he writes:

> the hiding-places of my power
> Seem open; I approach, and then they close. . . .
> (1805:11.336–37)

The 1850 edition changes this to the following:

> the hiding-places of man's power
> Open; I would approach them, but they close.
> I see by glimpses now. . . .
> (12.279–81)

The later version is more universal in its attribution of the power ("man's power," not "my power"). The stasis of "seem open" in 1805 changes to the active verb "open" in 1850 to give a symmetrical verbal frame to the line ("open . . . close"). The focus shifts from the speaker's subjective perception implied in the verb "seem" to the active opening and closing of the hiding places themselves. But the most significant change is the shift from the present indicative ("I approach") to the conditional ("I would approach"), accompanied by a corresponding shift in conjunctions: "and" (1805) . . . "but" (1850). The modified parataxis of "I approach, and then they close" does not suggest, because of the impartial conjunction "and," any clear relation, except sequential, between the speaker's approach and the closing of the hiding places; in the second version, however, the opening and closing are clearly something over which the poet has no control: they open, and just when he "would approach them," they close of their apparent own free will—they depart "unbidden," as in Shelley's analogy. What Jacques Lacan says about the psychoanalytic implications of Plato's allegory of the cave applies here to Wordsworth's hiding places. "This is an entrance," Lacan writes, "which you never reach until the moment they're about to close . . . the only way of getting [the cave] to open up is to call out from the inside" (Bowie 119). Or as Malcolm Bowie has paraphrased Lacan: "Whenever we arrive at the cave of the unconscious, it is always closing time; the only way we have of gaining access is to be inside already" (119). In Chapter 4 I showed how, in Wordsworth's figural language of a mirror stage, the speaker is both inside and outside a spectacle of his own making; can we overturn Wordsworth's confession of his "stinted powers" (5.517) here and show that he is already inside the hiding places, perhaps always already there in a sense, indeed most so when he least suspects? Such a deconstruction would first involve the reversal of such valorized terms as inside, hiding place, abyss, imagination, mystery, power, and depth, and their reformulation within a system of usurpation, in which a hiding place is both constituted by the approach made toward it and effaced by that approach too, in which the approach makes possible a hiding place that invites and resists its own discovery. Wordsworth is not merely the *spectator ab extra* of his hiding places, seeing "by glimpses" into them; they are inside him in the first place, and what he must do is not so much enter them as to have them exit him, and realize their "power" in language.

Wordsworth makes it clear that the two incidents recorded in Book 12 are not the only "spots of time"; on the contrary, "such moments / Are scattered everywhere" (12.223–24), throughout the poem as well as life, and take "their date / From our first childhood" (12.224–25).[10] Both incidents present compressed versions of the quest-romance pattern that we saw at work with Coleridge in Chapter 2. In his journey toward the hills, the boy in the first "spot" is by "some mischance" (12.231) or error separated from his "encourager and guide" (12.230). Evelyn Shakir has noted that this motif of desertion is present in both "spots" as well as in the dream of the Arab: ". . . in each instance the child, lost and terrified, is deserted by a mounted rider whom he depends on as his guide" (160). In other words, he is "unfathered" as the traveler in the Alps is; the echo of "I was lost" (6.596) in "I am lost" (12.273) points to this connection between the two passages. "Through fear" (12.232) he dismounts his horse, and instead of continuing the ascent "towards the hills" (12.228), he stumbles downward until he comes to "a bottom" (12.235). The moment of arrest, which Hartman has shown is typical of Wordsworth's imaginative experiences, is present, as are the characteristic feeling of separation and the thought of loss or death (*WP* 17). Although the hanged man is no longer there, the child is shocked to see the murderer's name carved in the turf. The "light of sense" almost goes out; the boy flees, "faltering and faint, and ignorant of the road" (12.247). One error leads to another, but ends in a restoration:

> Then, reascending the bare common, saw
> A naked pool that lay beneath the hills,
> The beacon on the summit, and more near,
> A girl, who bore a pitcher on her head,
> And seemed with difficult steps to force her way
> Against the blowing wind.
> (12.248–53)

The same details ("naked pool . . . beacon . . . girl") are first seen in Book 6 in a somewhat different context, in which the poet is speaking of a period in his life later than that of Book 12, when he and "another maid" (6.224) used to wander through the countryside:

> O'er paths and fields
> In all that neighbourhood, through narrow lanes
> Of eglantine, and through the shady woods,
> And o'er the Border Beacon, and the waste
> Of naked pools, and common crags that lay
> Exposed on the bare fell, were scattered love,
> The spirit of pleasure, and youth's golden gleam.
> (6.230–36)

This last line is echoed almost verbatim in the "spots of time" sequence (12.266), and throws into relief an interesting structural inversion in Wordsworth's narrative. Both Bloom and Onorato make note of the echo as an example of "feeling com[ing] in aid / Of feeling" (12.269–70);[11] we might prefer to describe the repetition as an instance of those "images to which in following years / Far other feelings were attached" (1799 *Prelude* 1.284–85). Structurally, Book 6 comes in aid of Book 12 through the help of the verbal echo, but in terms of the poet's development the incident in Book 12 comes in aid of the chronologically later incident in Book 6. The first "spot" ends with a memory (actually a looking ahead from the perspective of the young boy) of the time when the poet and his love "roamed in daily presence of this scene" (12.263) of naked pools, border beacons, and bare hills; the "spirit of pleasure and youth's golden gleam" are made all the more sublime "for these remembrances, and for the power / They had left behind" (12.268–69), and yet we do not see the effect of the earlier experience until the structurally later moment in Book 12. The poet's days may be "bound each to each by natural piety" ("My Heart Leaps Up" 9), but there is also a binding by language and narrative in which moments and "far other feelings" years apart are "attached" in a process in which the "immortal spirit grows / Like harmony in music" (1.340–41).

The child stands on a prospect from which he views a scene of "visionary dreariness" (12.256), but one feels that this phrase, surely one of Wordsworth's greatest tropes, is almost a tautology, for what dreariness, what natural matter-of-factness for Wordsworth was *not* visionary? "It was, in truth, / An ordinary sight," he writes (12.253–54), but the effect is quite extraordinary. The separation, the fear, the name carved in the turf—an emblem of the poem itself—combine to impress on Wordsworth

> Profoundest knowledge to what point, and how,
> The mind is lord and master—outward sense
> The obedient servant of her will.
> (12.221–23)

Havens is doubtless right when he says that the terror of the incident both stimulates the boy's imagination and helps the mature poet to remember the experience (*Mind* 49), but the "efficacious spirit" (12.219) or "renovating virtue" (12.210) of the "spot" does not reside in the fear of the moment alone; it resides also in the awe, in the poet's ability to say to his conscious soul: "I recognize thy glory." The visionary quality that invests the dreariness of the actual landscape comes from the child's own heightened imagination; the child, however, does not yet recognize his soul's glory, and it is only through memory—that is, approaching the meaning to restore the experience in a different form—that the speaker is able to see "to what point, and how" his mind was lord and master over the scene. "To what point" implies a reciprocity of mind and scene, an "interchangeable supremacy" (12.84) or "ennobling interchange" (13.375): for Wordsworth the mind's dominion is not absolute. "And how" suggests something mimetic: the text does not explain; it demonstrates.

The second "spot" in Book 12 contains a number of similarities to the first incident, as Jonathan Bishop has noted (145–46). The element of death, present in the first in the details of the murderer's iron chains and the gibbet-mast, is transformed into the death of the speaker's father in the second. A similar moment of arrest is evident; again the episode follows an up-and-down pattern that begins, like the first, with an ascent to a summit (12.297). The speaker is not "faltering and faint" from terror, but "feverish, and tired, and restless" (12.289) from school; he is depressed by "trivial occupations, and the round / Of ordinary intercourse" (12.213–14). The climbing of the crag has its corresponding ascent toward an "anxiety of hope" (12.313), but a downward movement follows in which the speaker descends to the highway and to the grave of his father. A restoration occurs through memory; it is an imaginative recovery of the "kindred spectacles and sounds" (12.324) of

> the wind and sleety rain,
> And all the business of the elements,
> The single sheep, and the one blasted tree,
> And the bleak music of that old stone wall,
> The noise of wood and water, and the mist . . .
> (12.317–21)

—to which, says the poet, "I oft repaired, and thence would drink, / As at a fountain" (12.325–26).

Geoffrey Hartman has detected a double etymological resonance in the word "repair," which can mean "to go" and "to restore." The latter is derived from *reparare*, to repair, but the other sense of the word is derived from *repatriare*, meaning to "return to one's native country"—or more literally, to return to one's fatherland (*patria*, from *pater*, father). Thus the boy's original repairing to the summit, Hartman says, "may already contain proleptically the sense of returning to the father's house" ("Poetics of Prophecy" 26). Wordsworth's phrase "my father's house" (12.307) is perhaps too familiar to warrant comment, yet the biblical echo (John 14:2) persists in its displaced form. Is the repatriation, the return to the father's house, also a repairing to God, "who is our home" ("Intimations" 65)? We recall that the boy "bowed low / To God" (12.315–16) after his father's death. The im-pairing of imagination by an "independent intellect" (11.244) is reversed by a re-pairing to nature, to the "spectacles and sounds" (12.324) from which, "as at a fountain" (12.326), the poet drinks in visionary power.

The rhetorical structure of the "spots of time" gives us a clue as to what Wordsworth means when he says that the experiences demonstrate the power of the mind over nature. That power, I would suggest, is linguistic, an awful power of imagination called rhetoric. The overall passage (from line 208 to the end of Book 12) involves an alternating structure of commentary and narration, beginning with the introductory section "There are in our existence spots of time" (12.208), moving into the first episode, shifting back into commentary with "Oh! mystery of man" (12.272), and concluding with the second narrative episode. Even within each episode there is an alternation from narration to authorial commentary and back to narration, but more specifically to a narrative reiteration of significant elements in the scene. In the first "spot," after the boy has seen the name carved in the turf, he climbs to the top of the "bare common" and sees three striking images": "naked pool . . . beacon . . . girl" (12.249, 250, 251). His commentary follows ("I should need / Colours and words" [12.254–55]), and the three images are repeated in the same order: "naked pool . . . beacon . . . female" (12.258, 259, 260). The poet recalls his later experiences in that same landscape, and these three details are seen for a third time, though with a difference: the "girl" or "female" is displaced by a "loved one" (12.262), so that the imagistic sequence runs: "loved one . . . naked pool . . . beacon" (12.262, 264, 265).

The second "spot" is built on a similar alternating structure. The narrative initially cites three main images, to which others are added. Instead of a "naked pool," Wordsworth lists a "naked wall . . . single sheep . . . blasted hawthorn" (12.299, 300, 301). After the description of the father's death, the poet reiterates these images in a considerably elaborated form:

> And, afterwards, the wind and sleety rain,
> And all the business of the elements,
> The single sheep, and the one blasted tree,
> And the bleak music of that old stone wall,
> The noise of wood and water, and the mist. . . .
> (12.317–21)

And finally, a severely truncated version of the "business of the elements" is repeated in the present tense of the narrative, in the account of "when storm and rain / Beat on my roof" (12.327–28). The repetition of these significant images is complemented by lexical reiteration in less obvious ways, as for example in these fragments: "Thither . . . thither I repaired" (245, 296); "on the grass / I sate . . . I sate" (298–99, 302); "ere we to school . . . ere we had been"

(305, 306); "when I called to mind . . . when from the crag" (311, 312); "thither I repaired . . . to which I oft repaired" (296, 325).

The effect of such syntactic and imagistic repetition is to present a revisioning that is illustrative of the mind, as though the imagination were structured like a language. Sometimes certain rhetorical continuities exist between episodes too: Wordsworth's "visionary dreariness" is to be found in the "dreary crags" (12.264) of the first "spot" as well as in the "dreary time" (12.306) of a father's death in the second. The successive appearances of all these images demonstrate the power of language to re-present experience, to hallow it with rhetorical decoration of ideal grace. What gives man "profoundest knowledge" (12.221) of the mind is language itself.

But what is it that tells the poet that language is lord? Mind and language seem to exist in a "strength / Of usurpation"—interdependent, yet each trying to use the other as its "obedient servant" (12.223). Mind wants to think of language as a tool, a vehicle; language imagines that it can structure mind. As a paraphrase of experience, a periphrasis of life, the "spots of time" suggest that power dwells in the mind. But "visionary power," the poet has told us, lives in language, attending "the motions of the viewless winds" of breath or speech (5.596), or the "turnings intricate of verse" (5.603). Though Wordsworth may complain of "the inadequateness of [his] own powers, or the deficiencies of language," his poetry incorporates such limitations as part of its structure and strategy. The troping of memory and experience as a text, especially one that is able to be revised in the way we have seen, foregrounds an allegory: "Imagination" takes on a linguistic form through the "sensuous incarnation" of signs "embodied in the mystery of words" (5.597).

Epitaph and Abyss

In its earliest form, the structural pattern of the 1799 *Prelude* bears some resemblances to the biblical unit of narrative called the pericope. As Northrop Frye has recently said, the pericope is used in the New Testament as the structuring principle of the biography of Jesus; it involves "a certain context or situation that leads up to a crucial act . . . or to a crucial saying" (*Code* 216). A pericope structure is thus "a sequence of discontinuous epiphanies."[12] The concept is relevant to the discontinuous sequence of the "spots of time" in the 1799 *Prelude*, and to their later version in Book 12 of 1850. The second half of Book 12, we have seen, presents two narrative episodes, separated chronologically by several years and structurally by a frame narrative ("There are in our existence spots of time . . . Oh! mystery of man"). Both episodes contain crucial acts, in the sense of moments that figure importantly in the poet's account of his life, and in the sense of *loci* that involve various figural crossings or intersections: human with divine, mature poet with young child, eternity and infinity with mutability and transience, dreariness with vision. The recurrent "epiphanies" in the "spots of time" reveal those things that are bred whenever man looks into his own mind: "fear and awe" (Prospectus 38) are the characteristic elements of these scenes. But let us pursue their semiological aspects.

In the first incident, the child comes upon a spot exactly where a word, a name, survives to show the trace of a crime. But the carving, if it recalls a past deed, also signifies a present object, writing itself, which survives. A surprising parallel is found in a later poem by Wordsworth, "In the Sound of Mull," where he speaks of the records of tradition,

> stamped by the ancient tongue
> On rock and ruin darkening as we go,—
> Spots where a word, ghost-like, survives to show
> What crimes from hate, or desperate love, have sprung. . . .
> (3–6)

We note, in passing, the metaleptic intersection of speech and writing in the image of records being "stamped," that is, imprinted, by a "tongue." The effect of the boy's meeting with the undecaying name of the murderer is reminiscent of Stephen Dedalus's sight of the word "Foetus" carved in the desk of the anatomy theater:

> On the desk he read the word *Foetus* cut several times in the dark stained wood. The sudden legend startled his blood: he seemed to feel the absent students of the college about him and to shrink from their company. A vision of their life, which his father's words had been powerless to evoke, sprang up before him out of the wood in the desk. (Joyce 90)

Another rising up out of a stain: writing triumphs over speech; the hand-carved "legend" succeeds where the father's voice fails. Like Stephen, Wordsworth is "startled": he flees, "faltering and faint" from the site of the hanging and the sight of the name.

When the boy reaches the top of the hill, he experiences another instance of the sad incompetence of human language. The lines hardly need quoting:

> It was, in truth,
> An ordinary sight; but I should need
> Colours and words that are unknown to man,
> To paint the visionary dreariness. . . .
> (12.253–56)

The "unknown hand" carves, and Wordsworth wishes "to paint" in "unknown" colors and words. He says "in truth" that the landscape was ordinary, yet his language is unable to communicate that "truth." It is not simply that Wordsworth cannot think of the words to describe it; there *are* no words to describe it: they are "unknown to man." The thoughts and feelings that lie too deep for tears are, as Coleridge said, "all too deep for words" ("To William Wordsworth" 11). Again we face the incompetence of language arresting the performance of the poet. The "colours" that he needs "to paint" the visionary landscape are necessary to express the "colouring of imagination," as Wordsworth calls it in his Preface to *Lyrical Ballads* (*Prose* 1:123), that is thrown over the whole scene. But even the combined forces of "colours and words," as two distinct sign-systems, fall short here of a descriptive adequacy. Wordsworth, as the little boy on the hill, stands on that verge where words abandon him.

But of course that is not all that abandons him. The boy, as we have seen, has been "unfathered" by his guide. In our allegory of figure, the abandonment of the child by the guide is the thematized version of the abandonment of the poet by language. The poet is unfathered in the Simplon Pass; he loses his way as language loses its way, becoming error or figure, but he regains his course through a translated voice. The boy in this first "spot" is also lost through language; he eventually finds a word, a name, but one that in its unreadability strains the limits of signification. How is the boy in the second "spot" deserted, and how is his unfathering related to language?

The unfathering in the second episode is a literal one—Wordsworth's father dies—but this primal usurpation is partially and silently restored by a linguistic return to the father through the act of "repairing," which, we noted from Hartman, occurs in two ways, as a "repatriation" in the father and as a return to nature, from which the poet "thence would drink, / As at a fountain" (12.325–26). The troping of natural "spectacles and sounds" (12.324) as a "fountain" recalls similar primal images from the earlier books of *The Prelude*. In Book 2 Wordsworth blesses the "infant Babe" (2.232) who "with his soul / Drinks in the feelings of his Mother's eye!" (2.236–37). What the literal reformulation of this beautiful, multiple metonymic displacement suggests, of course (with additional references at 2.235, 236), is that the babe drinks in the "innocent milk" (5.272) of his mother's breast. Wordsworth describes this experience as "the first / Poetic spirit of our human life" (2.260–61). Why "poetic"? What specifically is poetic about it? We must recognize that the experience of breast-feeding itself is not poetic, *but the troping of it is*: the first poetic spirit of our human life is metonymy, displacement or substitution, making something to be what it is not. The metonymic displacing of the mouth-milk-breast chain by the soul-feelings-eye sequence is but a rehearsal for the larger substitution of a greater mother in nature. The poet projects this first maternal love on nature (perhaps in response to his actual mother's death), and then says, less than a hundred lines after the blessed babe passage, that from nature—specifically from the "ghostly language of the ancient earth" (2.309)—"thence did I drink the visionary power" (2.311). From drinking in feelings from the mother to drinking in power from nature: the two acts are more than analogical; they are rhetorically identical, for the same trope of metonymy is at work in both cases. From feelings to power: the growth has a thematic sanction from the poet, "for feeling has to him imparted power" (2.255). So when the poet in this second "spot" says that he "would drink" from the "kindred spectacles and sounds" of nature (12.324) even as in Book 1 he describes himself as "drinking in a pure / Organic pleasure" (1.563–64) from the landscape, the imagistic and rhetorical continuity with the earlier books is asserted. The unfathering is overcome partly by an intratextual echo in which the boy's repairing is at once a returning to both father and mother.

There is also a turning to Shakespeare in this scene, as de Selincourt once pointed out (615). The "indisputable shapes" of the mist that comes to greet the young Wordsworth at Christmas-time invoke the presence of another dead father, Hamlet Senior. When Hamlet first sees the ghost of his father in Act 1, he says: "Thou com'st in such a questionable shape / That I will speak to thee" (1.4.43–44). "Indisputable shapes," "questionable shape": for

Shakespeare the phrase suggests a ghost that is able to be questioned—"O, answer me!" Hamlet cries (1.4.45); for Wordsworth, ghostly mists that advance in overdetermined forms. Two scenes earlier, in his soliloquy on his mother, Hamlet says:

> ere those shoes were old
> With which she follow'd my poor father's body . . .
> Ere yet the salt of most unrighteous tears
> Had left the flushing in her galled eyes,
> She married.
> (1.2.147–48, 154–56)

"Ere we to school returned," Wordsworth writes (12.305),

> ere we had been ten days
> Sojourners in my father's house, he died,
> And I and my three brothers, orphans then,
> Followed his body to the grave.
> (12.306–09)

The following of the father's body in the context of repeated "ere" constructions makes the echo almost indisputable. "Indisputable," however, is a curious word; this is the only instance of it in Wordsworth's poetry, and neither Milton nor Shakespeare uses it.[13] If there is a reminiscence here of the play that Wordsworth knew so well,[14] it suggests that he may be appropriating the unfathered aspect of Hamlet's character, giving intertextual status to his narrative experience. Here, as elsewhere, the Miltonic intertextuality of the "spots of time" is countered by a Shakespearean underpresence that vies for priority with it.

Viewed in terms of its rhetoric, the second "spot" complements the first through its connection with the epitaph. Whereas in the first episode "monumental letters" are "inscribed" where a grave originally was, in the second the poet creates a memorial enshrining a spirit:

> enshrining,
> Such is my hope, the spirit of the Past
> For future restoration.—Yet another
> Of these memorials. . . .
> (12.284–87)

The image of enshrining a spirit takes us back to Book 5, to the "shrines so frail" (5.49) in which the mind must enclose "her spirit" (5.49). What Wordsworth is troping here is the act of writing, of embodying or giving "substance and life" (12.284) to mind or spirit in language in the same way that a soul is incarnated in a body, or a body memorialized in a tomb. This instance of *The Prelude*'s self-declared awareness of its own rhetoricity, of its status as a piece of language, does not come as a surprise if we understand that the "spots of time" are more concerned with the problems of language—with linguistic adequacy, competence, usurpation—than with the meaning of particular experiences in a referential or historical sense. Thus the second "spot" can be read as one entire epitaph for Wordsworth's dead father, not merely the sudden encounter with a pre-existing memorial text, as in the first "spot," but the actual creation of a monumental writing that enshrines the "efficacious spirit" (12.219) of the past. The restoration that the poet anticipates is figural, referring to a future scene of reading in which language re-presents the experience, rather than to any hoped-for resurrection of the father. The rhetorical similarity between the end of Book 12 and the opening of the poem, especially their shared allusiveness, further determines the text's preoccupation with language as such.

Is the "strength / Of usurpation" that Wordsworth experiences a "counter-spirit" of language, a rhetorical power exercising its "awful dominion" over man (*Prose* 2:84–85)? The poet, "o'ercome" by language, must entrust himself to it before he can proceed. My reading suggests a darkness at the heart of *The Prelude*'s linguistic enterprise: "Shades of the prison-house" of language ("Intimations" 67) descend upon the text, and the poet, having enslaved the sign, remains himself a slave.

The abyss structure of the Simplon Pass, buried deep within the massive rhetorical structure of *The Prelude* as a whole, stands as a critical event in Wordsworth's allegory of reading. The unfathering that Wordsworth undergoes there on the narrative level reflects a de-centering on the linguistic level: the light of sense goes out, and language is suddenly forced to confront itself in an "invisible world" beyond referentiality. With the center, the father, the light of sense, and reference no longer there, figurality is viewed not as deviation but as difference, subordinating the pressure of the outside world to the power of rhetoric. Yet as Roman Jakobson has pointed out, "the supremacy of poetic function over referential function does not obliterate the reference but makes it ambiguous" (371). Such ambiguity is radically apparent in a text that attempts to present the growth of a poet's imagination but that finds itself instead questioning the sufficiency of language to represent mind or, as Wordsworth's note to "The Thorn" puts it, of words "to communicate impassioned feelings" (Brett and Jones 289). Shifting between an imaginative history troped as fiction, figure, and usurpation, and a fiction that purports to be history, autobiography, and epitaph, the text feels obliged to descant on its own deformity.

As "discontinuous epiphanies," the two episodes in Book 12 involve critical events that center on a death. The inscription in the turf stands as the epitaph to an obliterated grave; the "spectacles and sounds" of wall and tree and sheep, which surround the death of the father, are described as "memorials" (12.287) that "enshrin[e]" (12.284) the past. As Wordsworth verges on the boundary of language, the narrative also confronts a bourne, the one from which no traveler returns. The poet would give, as far as words *can* give, a glimpse into that undiscovered country, but language cannot go beyond language, and these epitaphs and memorials remain frail shrines to a linguistic and thematic absence. In its allegory of reading the text repeats its own deficiencies of language.

NOTES

Preface

1. Unless otherwise specified, all book and line references are to the 1850 edition of *The Prelude*, ed. Maxwell. All references to Wordsworth's other poetry are to *Poems*, ed. Hayden, unless otherwise noted.

2. Derrida's fullest demonstration of a deconstructive grammatology may be found in his *Of Grammatology*. I take the formula "the signifier over the signified" from Jacques Lacan, "Insistence" 291, where he derives it from Saussure's *Course in General Linguistics*. For a deconstruction of the concept that "death is a displaced name for a linguistic predicament," see Paul de Man, "De-Facement" 81.

3. Though Derrida articulates this theory throughout his work, I refer here to the succinct explication found in David B. Allison's introduction to *Speech and Phenomena* xxxvii. See also Derrida's *Positions*.

4. See Owen, *Wordsworth as Critic*; Ferguson, *Wordsworth: Language as Counter-Spirit*.

5. W. J. B. Owen's impressive edition of the fourteen-book *Prelude* in The Cornell Wordsworth series unfortunately came into my hands too recently to benefit me. I therefore depend on the *Norton Prelude* and de Selincourt for textual matters pertaining to the 1850 poem.

6. While Geoffrey Hartman uses this phrase in *WP* 99 (see also *WP* 358n13), I am thinking of its more recent use by B. Rajan vii.

7. For a good overview of the major intertextual approaches to literature, see Morgan.

Chapter 1

1. *Prose* 3:6. See also the first sentence of the second paragraph of the Preface: "It may be proper to state whence the poem, of which The Excursion is a part, derives its Title of THE RECLUSE" (*Prose* 3:5).

2. For a comprehensive study of the "design and scope" of *The Recluse* and its historical and interpretive relation to Wordsworth's *oeuvre*, see Johnston. See also Margoliouth 130–31 for his conjecture that the "glad preamble" literally refers to the Prospectus.

3. It has been suggested that the date of the Prospectus could range from 1798 to 1806. Abrams quotes de Selincourt and Darbishire, editors of *PW*, as support for the 1798 dating, but appends a note about Reed's suggestion that the Prospectus possibly dates from 1804 or 1806 (*NS* 470). Hartman says that the Prospectus "may have been written at Alfoxden in 1798" (*WP* 354). Darlington writes in her edition of *Home at Grasmere* that the date of 1798 is unlikely because a reference to the Prospectus that Wordsworth makes in a letter of 6 March 1798 does not echo "On Man, on Nature, and on Human Life" exactly (20). This argument is unconvincing when we recall that even in 1804 and 1805, after the Prospectus must—even by Darlington's estimate—have been begun, Wordsworth still uses inexact echoes of the "Man, Nature, and Human Life" formula. More recent scholarship, however, shifts the date back closer to the original conjecture of 1798 or at least 1800. Jonathan Wordsworth, in "On Man, on Nature, and on Human Life," argues that "there seems to be little doubt that the Prospectus was written c. January 1800" (28). Johnston tends to favor Darlington's dating of 1800–1802 (372). I am inclined to accept a 1798–1800 dating on rhetorical grounds and especially because of certain stylistic similarities between "Tintern Abbey" and the Prospectus.

4. Throughout Wordsworth's career the specific "performances" which were "unfinished" (*The Recluse*) and "unpublished" (*The Prelude*)—not to mention such poems as *Home at Grasmere* and "The Tuft of Primroses"—became the focus of a unique allusiveness in the letters and poems. For a discussion of the self-referential or "fiduciary" nature of Wordsworth's self-echoes, see Larkin; and Hartman, "Words, Wish, Worth."

5. For Derrida's polemical statement that "*il n'y a pas de hors-texte*," see *Grammatology* 158. I refer also to Derrida's extended meditation on "prefacing" in *Dissemination* 3–59.

6. Prospectus 14–23. All line references to the Prospectus are to *Poems* 2:37–40, and will be included parenthetically in the text.

7. All book and line references to *Paradise Lost* (abbreviated *PL*) and to Milton's other poetry are to Milton's *Complete Poems and Major Prose*, and will be given parenthetically in the text.

8. See Abrams' classic essay "The Correspondent Breeze." Close scrutiny of "utterance" sends waves across almost all of Wordsworth's poetry. The word is a trope for an inner/outer structure related to repression and creation. In the "Intimations Ode" the "timely utterance" that gives a "thought relief" (23) is cathartic, while Coleridge's "grief, / Which finds no natural outlet, no relief, / In word . . ." ("Dejection" 22–24) appears reten-

tive by contrast. Giving a thought relief through utterance is associated with what Wordsworth calls "sensuous incarnation" (*Prose* 3:65), with confession, and with the naturalized effect of poetic afflatus. "Utterance" and "expression"—making the internal external—are both part of this figural structure. Derrida pursues some of these issues in his *Grammatology* 32–44, and in his *Speech and Phenomena* 32–37, to show their relation to a metaphysic of presence.

9. For a study of the traditional rhetorical structure of poetic introductions in Virgil and Homer, and their adaptation in Milton, see Condee. My treatment is limited to a description of only two of his five divisions.

10. Hartman has written convincingly on the connection between voice and light in Wordsworth's poetry, relating eye and ear to God's *fiat* in Genesis. I am indebted specifically to "'Timely Utterance' Once More" and "Words, Wish, Worth." In Chapter 3 I go on to explore the relation between voice and writing in Wordsworth.

11. I take the phrase "presence of Milton" from B. Rajan vii. But it also occurs in Hartman, *WP* 99, 358n13.

12. It is interesting, however, that Wordsworth reverts to a slightly modified phrase in a late poem "At Vallombrosa" (*Memorials of a Tour in Italy, 1837*, XVIII): "Vallombrosa! of thee I first heard in the page / Of that holiest of Bards" (25–26).

13. "The meaning, not the Name I call," says Milton of Urania (*PL* 7.5). Would that it were always so in language, but the fact is that Milton calls the name first, not the meaning: "Urania, by that name / If rightly thou art call'd" (7.1–2), he says; the meaning is gradually unfolded over the next forty lines. Like Milton, Wordsworth first calls a name—"Urania"—but then offers to discard the name as inadequate to his meaning.

14. Cf. Ben-Porat 588–90, where she speaks of a metonymical relationship between the alluding and the source texts. I would make a distinction between metonymy and synecdoche on the basis of association versus property, respectively, and thus argue for a synecdochic relationship.

15. See Eliot ("Tradition" 14): "The historical sense involves a perception, not only of the pastness of the past, but of its presence. . . ."

16. For the tradition of the *liber naturae*, see Curtius 308, 319–26.

17. In *Prose* 3:11, Owen gives the source of "heaven of heavens" as *PL* 7.553. It should be clear from my reconstruction of Wordsworth's echo that the proper source is *PL* 7.13.

18. See *PL* 3.345–46: "shout . . . sweet / As from blest voices, uttering joy"; and 7.256, 258: "with joy and shout / . . . and hymning prais'd. . . ."

19. See Blake's marginalia to the Prospectus: "You shall not bring me down to believe such fitting & fitted I know better & Please your Lordship" (656).

20. The revision occurs in MS D, which suggests 1832 or even 1838–39. See de Selincourt 482; and *NP* 507–9.

21. See *Complete Prose Works of John Milton* 6:299–325.

22. See *Mr. William Shakespeares Comedies, Histories, & Tragedies.* 1623 facsimile edition.

Chapter 2

1. "Centripetal" and "centrifugal" are terms which Frye, after Coleridge in the *Biographia Literaria*, Chapter 12, borrows from Newton to describe the "context" of a piece of language, that is, whether it looks inward on itself, or outward to the world of reference, respectively. See *Anatomy* 73–82; *Code* 58–61.

2. See B. Rajan vii; see also Hartman, *WP* 99.

3. See, e.g., Havens, *The Influence of Milton* 177–200, 607–20; Grierson; Wittreich 102–54; Reiger 185–208. Harold Bloom's work on poetic influence has brought Milton and Wordsworth back to the fore; see especially *The Anxiety of Influence* and *Poetry and Repression*.

4. Nearly every commentator has recognized this allusion. See especially Owen, "Annotating" 47–71, and "Literary Echoes" 3–16; Abrams, *NS* 115–16; Hartman, *WP* 255; Onorato 126–34.

5. See Owen, "Annotating" 70; *NP* 28; Onorato 102.

6. See, for clarification, the earlier versions in MS JJ and in 1805 in de Selincourt 4, 642.

7. See *The Poems of William Wordsworth*, ed. with an intro. by Nowell Charles Smith, 3:567.

8. Quintilian 3:388–89. See also *Pro T. Annio Milone Oratio* in *The Speeches of Cicero* 60–61.

9. See Hartman, *WP* 198–202, 239. For a thematic treatment of the imagery of a boundary or border in Wordsworth, see also Jonathan Wordsworth, *The Borders of Vision*, Chapter 1.

10. Later in Book 1 Wordsworth recurs to this very passage in *PL* when he speaks of "immortal verse / Thoughtfully fitted to the Orphean lyre" (1.233). The "Orphean lyre" comes from Milton's "*Orphean Lyre*" (*PL* 3.17), and is the same echo that Coleridge adapts in "To William Wordsworth" to describe *The Prelude*: "An Orphic song indeed..!" (45). The suggestion is that *The Prelude* is the music meant to resurrect Coleridge, as Orpheus attempted to resurrect Eurydice.

11. Behind or within this significant Miltonic echo there is again a Shakespearean underpresence. Wordsworth's language (in 1805) of "messenger" (5), "captive" (6), "immured" (8), and "enfranchised and at large" (9) recalls Don Armado's interview with the messenger Costard in *Love's Labour's Lost* 3.1.112–20:

Armado: Sirrah Costard, I will enfranchise thee.
Costard: O, marry me to one Frances! I smell some l'envoy, some goose, in this.
Armado: By my sweet soul, I mean setting thee at liberty, enfreedoming thy person. Thou wert immured, restrained, captivated, bound.
Costard: True, true, and now you will be my purgation and let me loose.
Armado: I give thee thy liberty, set thee from durance. . . .

12. Wordsworth used the word "memorials" to classify a genre of poems—*Memorials of a Tour in Scotland, 1803*; *Memorials of a Tour on the Continent, 1820*; *Memorials of a Tour in Italy, 1837*, etc. I deal at length with the rhetoric of memorials in my reading of the blind Beggar episode and the first "spot of time."

13. For the definitive treatment of the Romantic quest, see Bloom, "Internalization."

14. See, e.g., McFarland 56–103; Buchan 346–66; Reed 238–53; Margoliouth; Newlyn.

15. For the history of *Lyrical Ballads*, see especially McFarland 56–103; Reed 238–53; and Owen, ed., *Wordsworth and Coleridge: "Lyrical Ballads" 1798* vii-xxxv. While the word "associate" might imply equality (cf. the Latin *socius*), Wordsworth's generous rhetoric here appears to give Coleridge more credit than he deserved.

16. For Wordsworth's perception of the detrimental effect of the "Ancient Mariner" on the success of *Lyrical Ballads*, see *EY* 264. For the cancellation of "Christabel" from the second edition of *Lyrical Ballads*, see *EY* 302–5, and Coleridge's *Collected Letters* 1:631–32.

17. Both Lindenberger 78, and Ogden, "Power of Distance" note that there are four epic similes in the 1805 *Prelude*: 4.247–61; 8.711–51; 9.1–7; 9.9–16. Ogden claims that all four survive in 1850, but strictly speaking, I think that the passage in Book 8 should be read as only a vestigial epic simile.

18. See also *The Prelude* (1805): "the last punctual spot" (10.17). There is also a reminiscence of Gaunt in *Richard II* 2.1: "This other Eden, demi-paradise / This fortress built by Nature for herself / . . . This blessed plot, this earth, this realm, this England . . ." (42–43, 50). Cf. "To M. H.": "The spot was made by Nature for herself . . ." (15). Cf. "The Norman Boy": "Nor kept by Nature for herself" (2).

19. It would be interesting to explore how the echoes of "Lycidas," the reference to Theocritus, and the particular choice of the story of Comates from the Seventh Idyll are all generated by the association of ideas in a state of excitement. After describing his recovery from the effects of the

French Revolution, Wordsworth turns to Coleridge in Sicily. Sicily is conventionally associated with the origin of pastoral poetry, Theocritus having been born there in Syracuse, but the first mention of the island is Etna, followed by Syracuse and Timoleon. The reference to Timoleon throws into relief the degree to which Sicily is "fallen" (11.376) from the democracy established in 343 BC (see "The Life of Timoleon," *Plutarch's Lives* 2:243–84). Etna later generates Empedocles and, through assonance, Enna; Syracuse begets both Archimedes and Theocritus. Coleridge's experience evokes pastoral elegy and thus regenerates the nexus of echoes of Theocritus and "Lycidas." The title of Milton's pastoral elegy is also the name of the character in Theocritus's Seventh Idyll who sings the story of "Divine Comates" (11.444; see *The Idylls of Theocritus* 37–45). The evocation of Enna makes a further connection with the Comates story: Ceres, whose daughter was abducted there, is also the goddess to whose festival Lycidas and his friends are traveling in Idyll Seven (36–38, 45). The Comates story has a more obvious relation, however: if Coleridge is to be compared to the "blessed man" (11.448) who has his "lips / Wet with the Muse's nectar" (11.448–49), he is also, by analogy, a prisoner, but a prisoner who is restored by nature as imaged in the "flat-nosed bees" (*Idylls* 41) that feed the captive in his chest. In a deleted addition to MS A, Wordsworth implores nature to offer "sunny lawns / Of fragrant Hybla" to Coleridge's "lip." "Hybla" points both to the honey ("nectar") on which Comates fed, and to the town of Hybla in Sicily; the Coleridge-Comates connection is thus strengthened (see de Selincourt 424). Though it is not my concern here to speculate on an epistemology of composition, it is worthwhile to trace overdetermined rhetorical connections within the passage and to see the intertextual power of language at work.

20. Compare Wordsworth's echo of the same passage in *The Excursion*, where he describes the Wanderer as one "Who, with an understanding heart, allayed / The perturbation . . ." (2.77). See also Wordsworth's reference to *The Reason of Church Government* in a letter to Poole, 28 April 1814 (*MY* Part 2.146).

21. The most important human agent in the process of Wordsworth's imaginative restoration is his sister, who deserves to be included in the company of "joint labourers" as much as Coleridge and Milton because of her role in *Home at Grasmere* as well as *The Prelude*. Her healing function in *The Prelude*, combined with nature's services, leads the poet back "to those sweet counsels between head and heart" (11.353) that are an attempt to recover something of the "mute dialogues" (2.208) which as an infant he held with his mother. The sister's "voice / Of sudden admonition" (11.336–37), first described in natural terms as "a brook" (11.337), is humanized by being troped as a "companion" (11.340); her voice chastens and subdues the poet, but in a "saving" (11.341) rather than apocalyptic way: her whis-

pering (11.345) contrasts with the "roar of waters, torrents, streams / Innumerable" (14.59–60).

22. See, e.g., Sewell 297, 342; Potts 319; Hartman, *WP* 255.

23. Although Donald Reiman has been arguing for *The Prelude* as a "macro-sonnet" for several years, I first encountered his idea in a paper he read at the Wordsworth Summer Conference at Dove Cottage in 1982, subsequently published as "The Beauty of Buttermere as Fact and Romantic Symbol." Since then, Dr. Reiman has directed me to a note to his essay "Poetry of Familiarity," where he sets out his conviction "that Wordsworth restructured *The Prelude* from thirteen to fourteen books to give it the form of an Italian sonnet, with the books now forming natural groupings of four/four/three/three, with the strongest break occurring between the first eight books and the last six" (176–77). Though I am indebted to Reiman for the interesting (and disarmingly obvious) idea of *The Prelude* as a macro-sonnet, my interests lie in another direction, that of intertextuality and structural allusion, both Miltonic and Shakespearean, which Reiman does not consider. Furthermore, my argument puts in question his claim that Wordsworth *restructured* the poem to give it a fourteen-book form; the fourteen-book version may have been the original form.

24. See de Selincourt xxxii; *NP* 508, 517, 520. Siskin also accepts the idea of an original fourteen-book *Prelude*.

25. I first raised this point of the thirteen-plus-one sonnets at the Wordsworth Summer Conference at Dove Cottage in 1982, in discussion following Seraphia D. Leyda's paper, now published as "Wordsworth's *Sonnets Upon the Punishment of Death*."

26. Consider, e.g., the quotation of "busy hum" (8.680) from "L'Allegro" 118; and the transformed allusion to the balance image in *PL* 4.997–1015 (*Prelude* 8.683–86).

27. The metaphors of "burden" and "embarrassment" are from Bate, *The Burden of the Past*. But see also Bloom, "Keats and the Embarrassments of Poetic Tradition." The metaphor of "anxiety," of course, is central to Bloom's important study *The Anxiety of Influence*, and his subsequent work.

Chapter 3

1. For the concept of linguistic "difference," see Saussure 114–20, and Derrida, *Grammatology* 27–73. For discussion of the writing-speech hierarchy, see Saussure 23–32, and Derrida, *Grammatology* 6–26, 30–44.

2. Chomsky is careful to distinguish competence and performance from *langue* and *parole*. "It is necessary," he writes, "to reject [Saussure's] concept of *langue* as merely a systematic inventory of items and to return rather to the Humboldtian conception of underlying competence as a system of generative processes" (4).

3. The three imperatives come, respectively, from the first essay in *Essays Upon Epitaphs* (*Prose* 2:54); "Lines (Left upon a Seat in a Yew-Tree)," line 1; and "The Solitary Reaper," line 4.

4. While Bernhardt-Kabisch traces "the pervasive monumental element in the canon of Wordsworth's poetry" (511), Hartman is more concerned with defining a genre of "inscription" and relating a number of Wordsworth's poems to this "normal, accepted, even archaic feature of the eighteenth-century literary scene" ("Wordsworth, Inscriptions" 207). Like Bernhardt-Kabisch, Ferguson explores the "virtual omnipresence" of an epitaphic style in Wordsworth's poetry (155–72), and Fry demonstrates "that a . . . widely diffused 'epitaphic moment' prevails in Wordsworth" (413). I differ with Fry's claim that the epitaph represents "the burial of voice" (433), since I attempt to show that the peculiarly Wordsworthian aspect of voice is its persistence beyond death and despite absence. What is baffling in Wordsworth's language is the interpenetration of a voice as enduring as epitaphic inscription with a writing as immediate as the breath of speech. Writing, for Wordsworth, is not the death of voice but the consummation: it is the accomplishment of voice.

5. The "return" to childhood episodes—and hence to tropes of voice—is both structural and chronological. As a variation of the "return poem," *The Prelude* continually doubles back on itself to consider its "progress" (5.12)—not only in Book 8 ("Retrospect") but at the openings of books 5, 7, and 12; the end of Book 14; and, perhaps most explicitly, the beginning of Book 9, where Wordsworth states that he has "turned and returned with intricate delay" (9.8). Book 12 signals a structural "re-troping," or returning, to first considerations through its echoes of the "glad preamble" of Book 1 (12.7–43), including an apostrophe to Nature that reintroduces vocal tropes: "Oh! that I had a music and a voice / Harmonious as your own . . ." (12.29–30). From a chronological perspective Wordsworth is also "returning" to childhood episodes in the sense of reworking earlier passages from the 1799 *Prelude*. For a thorough discussion of the chronology of composition of *The Prelude*, see *NP* 485–526.

6. Compare Wordsworth's "Personal Talk": "Sweetest melodies / Are those that are by distance made more sweet . . ." (25–26).

7. An essay needs to be written on "The Ear and the Object" to supplement Frederick A. Pottle's early study of "The Eye and the Object in the Poetry of Wordsworth" by showing how the "despotic" power of the bodily eye (12.129) is frequently challenged by the "strength / Of usurpation" of the bodily ear. Wordsworth's interest in "the mighty world / Of eye, and ear" ("Tintern Abbey" 105–6) helps to explain how his visual and aural concerns compete or, in other words, how an "image" often quietly becomes an "image of voice."

8. Havens says that Wordsworth uses "silent" or "silence" some 350 times in his poetry (*Mind* 57).

9. De Man, in "Autobiography as De-Facement," has some brief but significant remarks about this episode in relation to his deconstruction of autobiography as genre/figure (80–81).

10. There is undoubtedly an allusion here to the conclusion of Book 4 of *PL*, in which Satan, like the French, is weighed as in a scale to determine his success if he were to fight Gabriel and his fellow angels. Gabriel tells Satan to "look up, / And read thy Lot in yon celestial Sign / Where thou art weigh'd, and shown how light, how weak, / If thou resist" (1010–13).

11. See, e.g., Prospero's apostrophe to "Ye elves of hills, brooks, standing lakes, and groves . . ." (*The Tempest* 5.1.33–57). Jonathan Wordsworth also notes the echo in *NP* 6; *Borders of Vision* 421.

12. For the arbitrariness of the linguistic sign from the seventeenth to the nineteenth century, see Aarsleff 63–64, 363. Saussure, of course, is responsible for the twentieth century's rethinking of the arbitrariness of language.

13. For the "performative" aspect of language, see Austin.

14. See, e.g., Havens, *Mind* 141, 172; Bishop; Ogden, "Structure of Imaginative Experience" 293.

15. The blindness-muteness association has connections with Milton's "blind mouths" in "Lycidas" (119) and with Wordsworth's "Eye among the blind, / That, deaf and silent, readst the eternal deep" ("Intimations" 112–13). Consider also the "eye made quiet by the power / Of harmony" in "Tintern Abbey" 47–48.

16. Cf. Frye, who states that the "dialectic of love"—which includes self-love—"treats whatever it encounters as another form of itself" (*Study of English Romanticism* 122).

17. See also Hertz, "Freud and the Sandman": "There is no term in English for what French critics call a *mise en abîme*—a casting into the abyss—but the effect itself is familiar enough: an illusion of infinite regress can be created by a writer or painter by incorporating within his own work a work that duplicates in miniature the larger structure, setting up an apparently unending metonymic series" (311). For the standard study of the *mise en abyme*, see Dällenbach.

Chapter 4

1. Lacan used the phrase *le stade du miroir* in 1936 to describe what Anthony Wilden terms "the primary alienation of the *infans* from 'himself' and his subsequent discovery of his Self" (xiii, 159–60).

2. Coleridge's term *spectator ab extra* occurs twice in his *Table Talk* (189, 210–11).

3. See, e.g., "Frost at Midnight": "all the numberless goings-on of life" (12). Cf. de Selincourt 532.

4. *OED* sense 20; *Webster's* sense 3. The word was used in this sense in Wordsworth's day. The *OED* gives an example from the restoration comedy *The Rehearsal* to illustrate the theatrical sense of "business." In correspondence with me concerning the gloss of the word, Jonathan Wordsworth concedes the dramatic connotation. Stephen Gill also writes that he finds this reading of "business" "wholly convincing."

5. See Garber 126. In his chapter on "The Theater of Mind," Price explores the spectator/actor paradox from a cosmological rather than rhetorical perspective. "The poet becomes both actor and audience," he writes (343); but the word "both" for Price suggests a fusion rather than a simultaneous alternation expressing difference.

6. The Snowdon passage reworks these elements in a conspicuous way: "A hundred hills their dusky backs upheaved / All over this still ocean" (14.43–44). The Miltonic echo is even clearer in MS D^3 (see de Selincourt 70). Other Miltonic reminiscences occur at 3.57, 184, 203, 286–98.

7. See de Selincourt 526–27, where he corrects Arnold's reading of the line; and Abercrombie 47.

8. Miller, "The Still Heart" 307. See also Ferry 14, where he makes a similar observation about the deathlike stillness of the heart of London.

9. See de Selincourt 563–64, and Reiman, "Beauty of Buttermere," for the historical background to the story of Mary Robinson.

10. E.g., "What Adonais is, why fear we to become?"; "Die, / If thou wouldst be with that which thou dost seek!"; "The fire for which all thirst . . ." (Shelley 405–6).

11. See also Bloom, *Anxiety* 115–36 and *Poetry and Repression* facing 1.

12. See, e.g., Woodman, "Child and Patriot" 88–89; Springer 245.

13. In the "Nativity Ode" Milton writes of "th'enamel'd *Arras* of the Rainbow" (143); here Wordsworth enters Arras in 1790 and walks "through a rainbow-arch that spanned the street" (10.495). Seven lines later he directly invokes Milton in his appropriation of the expression "Atheist crew" (10.502) to describe Robespierre and his followers. The phrase is the one that Milton uses to depict the rebel angels (*PL* 6.370).

14. Wordsworth hears a voice, but it speaks "to the whole city." Macbeth hears a voice that seems to be talking to him, but the voice shifts from what sounds like apostrophe ("Sleep no more") to third-person narrative ("Macbeth does murder sleep"). In both cases there is a transference from the listener to a third party.

Chapter 5

1. Felman 141. This "methodologically unprecedented" type of reading is also found in the work of Derrida, particularly at the end of "Freud and the Scene of Writing," where, with more than a glance at Lacan, he writes that "despite several attempts made by Freud and certain of his successors, a psychoanalysis of literature respectful of the *originality of the literary signifier* has not yet begun. . . . Until now, only the analysis of literary *signifieds*, that is, *nonliterary* signified meanings, has been undertaken" (*Writing and Difference* 230).

2. See also Derrida's extended remarks on Lacan in *Positions* 107n44.

3. See Lacan's *Ecrits*: "*C'est même pourquoi l'inconscient qui le dit, le vrai sur le vrai, est structuré comme un langage . . .*" (868). See also Lacan's essay "Of Structure as an Inmixing," and the discussion following, for extended reflections on the theorem that "the unconscious is structured like a language."

4. For a detailed discussion of this and other *Othello* echoes, and their fortunes in Wordsworth's revisions of the drowned man episode, see Manning. Because his focus is on the drowned man, the discharged soldier, and the later versions of the "spots of time," Manning considers the echo in relation to this version of the first "spot" only in passing (12–13).

5. See also Wordsworth's letter to Scott on 7 November 1805, in which he makes this same allusion to Othello's speech; and *The Prelude* 1.589: "By chance collisions and quaint accidents"—perhaps motivated by "hair-breadth" and "field" ten lines earlier. Cf. *The Borderers* 92–95.

6. Cf. Wordsworth's description in "Guilt and Sorrow" 76–86.

7. For one definition of an index, see Peirce 108–9: "Anything which focusses the attention is an index. Anything which startles us is an index, in so far as it marks the junction of two portions of experience." But also see Barthes, "Proust and Names" on the signifying vs. indicial character of proper names (67).

8. While Wordsworth's "Letter-Phobia" is apparently epistolary rather than graphological, there is no need to limit this strange (and powerful) term to a form of correspondence. Wordsworth elsewhere speaks of his "aversion from writing" (*EY* 407) in terms which would suggest a more general graphophobia. Though Charles Lamb makes fun of Wordsworth's "'aversion from Letter-writing'" in a letter to a friend (15 February 1801 [see Perkins, ed., *English Romantic Writers* 598]), it is nevertheless enticing to seek the etiology of such a Freudian inhibition. Derrida summarizes some relevant speculations by Freud at the end of "Freud and the Scene of Writing" (229).

9. While Daniel 5 certainly stands as a hintertext for this episode, Genesis 40—the story of Joseph and his interpretation of dreams—may also be present here, especially in relation to another hanged man: "And

Joseph answered and said, This is the interpretation thereof: The three baskets are three days: Yet within three days shall Pharaoh lift up thy head from off thee, and shall hang thee on a tree; and the birds shall eat thy flesh from off thee" (Genesis 40:18–19). The Book of Daniel also figures in *The Prelude* 7.369–70, where Wordsworth alludes to the story of Shadrach, Meshach, and Abednego—"those who walked with hair unsinged / Amid the fiery furnace"—of Daniel 3:21–27.

10. See de Selincourt 614. See also *History of Penrith* 99–100 for an account of the murder of Thomas Parker on 18 November 1766 "'on the road from Penrith to Edenhall . . . for which murder, Thomas Nicholson was executed and hung in chains near the same place . . .'" (100). What is of more than incidental interest in this homicide is that both murderer and victim have the same first name.

11. Barthes, "Authors and Writers" 143. See also his essay "The Death of the Author" 142–48.

12. Foucault's question, adapted from Samuel Beckett, is really concerned with speech rather than writing: "What difference does it make who is speaking?" he writes (160). I am modifying Foucault to suit the case of the engraven name. See Foucault 141 for his appropriation of Beckett.

13. For an hypothesis that "literature is the elaboration of a spectral name," see Hartman, *Saving* 111. One should compare Hartman's "spectral name" to Barthes's "semic specter" in "Proust and Names" 61.

14. In her essay "The Economics of the Heart," Theresa M. Kelley has some very perceptive comments about the question of meaning in the engraved name. While Kelley's thesis is largely concerned with Wordsworth's aesthetics in a biographical and historical context, it also addresses his semiotics and the problem of signification. Like Chase, Kelley sees the "monumental letters" as "an emblematic text whose pictorial surface camouflages what we are supposed to understand it to mean" (25). She convincingly shows how the textual movement of revelation and camouflage is intricately related to Wordsworth's "willed suppression . . . and retrieval" (18) of meaning in *The Prelude*'s revisions.

Chapter 6

1. Cf. McGavran, who says that the ineffability of certain moments of experience "is a basic premise of the speaker's existence, and that of *The Prelude* as well, not a sudden, terrible realization by a poet who feels his powers slipping away from him" (45–46).

2. For more extended discussions of Saussure, and of Derrida's reading of him, see Spivak's introduction to *Grammatology*; Norris 24–41; Eagleton 127–34; Culler, *Saussure*, and *On Deconstruction* 89–110, and his essay "Jacques Derrida."

3. See also Hamlin, who argues that the narrative disjunction is symptomatic of self-consciousness (164).

4. Empson's suggestion that "*The light . . . goes out* can mean 'light proceeds from the source' as well as 'the source fails'" (294) is ingenious but unconvincing. But perhaps there is an echo of Spenser, *Faerie Queene* 2.10.30: "But true it is, that when the oyle is spent, / The light goes out, and weeke is throwne away."

5. Cf. Hartman, *WP* 353; Onorato 125–26.

6. Cf. Hartman, *WP* 68; Onorato 141 and 178, where he suggests a satanic association with unfathering in *PL* 5.860.

7. "Fathered" in this context is ambiguous: does Wordsworth mean that to father is to track something to its source rather than to be the source or father in the first place?

8. For another treatment of imagistic "blockage," and its relation to the sublime, see Hertz, "Notion of Blockage."

9. See also James 162, where he corroborates Willey.

10. Havens notes fourteen mysterious moments in *The Prelude* (*Mind* 141–42); Bishop claims that there are perhaps nineteen (134–35); Ogden says that there are over twenty "spots of time" in *The Prelude* ("Imaginative Experience" 293).

11. See Bloom, *Visionary Company* 170; Onorato 369.

12. Frye takes the phrase "discontinuous epiphanies" from Martin Dibelius (*Code* 216, 244).

13. See Ingram and Swaim, eds., *Concordance to Milton's English Poetry*; and Spevack, ed., *Harvard Concordance to Shakespeare.*

14. See the letter to Beaumont (*EY* 587) in which Wordsworth shows considerable familiarity with *Hamlet*, though not as a stage production.

WORKS CITED

Aarsleff, Hans. *From Locke to Saussure: Essays on the Study of Language and Intellectual History*. Minneapolis: U of Minnesota P, 1982.

Abercrombie, Lascelles. *The Art of Wordsworth*. London: Oxford UP, 1952.

Abrams, M. H. "The Correspondent Breeze: A Romantic Metaphor." *English Romantic Poets: Modern Essays in Criticism*. 2nd ed. Ed. M. H. Abrams. New York: Oxford UP, 1975. 37–54.

———. *The Mirror and the Lamp: Romantic Theory and the Critical Tradition*. London: Oxford UP, 1953.

———. *Natural Supernaturalism: Tradition and Revolution in Romantic Literature*. New York: Norton, 1971.

———. "*The Prelude* as a Portrait of the Artist." *Bicentenary Wordsworth Studies in Memory of John Alban Finch*. Ed. Jonathan Wordsworth. Ithaca: Cornell UP, 1970. 180–237.

———. "Structure and Style in the Greater Romantic Lyric." *Romanticism and Consciousness: Essays in Criticism*. Ed. Harold Bloom. New York: Norton, 1970. 201–29.

Altick, Richard D. *The Shows of London*. Cambridge: Belknap, 1978.

Austin, J. L. *How To Do Things With Words*. 2nd ed. Ed. J. O. Urmson and Marina Sbisa. Oxford: Clarendon, 1975.

Baker, Jeffrey. "Prelude and Prejudice." *Wordsworth Circle* 13 (1982):79–86.

Banks, J., trans. *The Idylls of Theocritus, Bion, and Moschus*. London: George Bell & Sons, 1891.

Barker, Arthur E. "Structural Pattern in *Paradise Lost*." *Milton: Modern Essays in Criticism*. Ed. Arthur E. Barker. New York: Oxford UP, 1965. 142–55.

Barthes, Roland. "Authors and Writers." *Critical Essays*. Trans. Richard Howard. Evanston: Northwestern UP, 1972. 143–50.

———. "The Death of the Author." *Image-Music-Text*. Sel. and trans. Stephen Heath. New York: Hill and Wang, 1977. 142–48.

———. "Proust and Names." *New Critical Essays*. Trans. Richard Howard. New York: Hill and Wang, 1980. 55–68.

Bate, W. Jackson. *The Burden of the Past and the English Poet*. New York: Norton, 1972.

Bateson, F. W. *Wordsworth: A Re-Interpretation*. London: Longmans, 1954.

Ben-Porat, Ziva. "The Poetics of Allusion—A Text Linking Device—In Different Media of Communication (Literature Versus Advertising and Journalism)." *A Semiotic Landscape*. Ed. Seymour Chatman, Umberto Eco, and Jean-Marie Klinkenberg. The Hague: Mouton, 1979. 588–93.

Bernhardt-Kabisch, Ernest. "Wordsworth: The Monumental Poet." *Philological Quarterly* 44 (1965):503–18.

Bishop, Jonathan. "Wordsworth and the 'Spots of Time.'" *Wordsworth: The Prelude*. Ed. W. J. Harvey and Richard Gravil. London: Macmillan, 1972. 134–53.

Blake, William. *The Poetry and Prose of William Blake*. Ed. David V. Erdman. Commentary by Harold Bloom. New York: Doubleday, 1965.

Bloom, Harold. *The Anxiety of Influence: A Theory of Poetry*. New York: Oxford UP, 1973.

———. "The Internalization of Quest-Romance." *Romanticism and Consciousness: Essays in Criticism*. Ed. Harold Bloom. New York: Norton, 1970. 3–24.

———. "Keats and the Embarrassments of Poetic Tradition." *The Ringers in the Tower: Studies in Romantic Tradition*. Chicago: U of Chicago P, 1971. 131–42.

———. *A Map of Misreading*. New York: Oxford UP, 1975.

———. *Poetry and Repression*. New Haven: Yale UP, 1976.

———. *The Visionary Company: A Reading of English Romantic Poetry*. New York: Doubleday, 1961.

Bloomfield, Morton W. "The Syncategorematic in Poetry: From Semantics to Syntactics." *To Honour Roman Jakobson*. Vol. I. The Hague: Mouton, 1967. 309–17.

Bostetter, Edward E. *The Romantic Ventriloquists: Wordsworth, Coleridge, Keats, Shelley, Byron*. Seattle: U of Washington P, 1975.

Bowie, Malcolm. "Jacques Lacan." *Structuralism and Since: From Lévi-Strauss to Derrida*. Ed. John Sturrock. Oxford: Oxford UP, 1979. 116–53.

Brett, R. L., and A. R. Jones, eds. "*Lyrical Ballads*": *Wordsworth and Coleridge*. London: Methuen, 1963.

Brinkley, Robert A. "The Incident in the Simplon Pass: A Note on Wordsworth's Revisions." *Wordsworth Circle* 12 (1981):122–25.

Brisman, Leslie. *Romantic Origins*. Ithaca: Cornell UP, 1978.

Brombert, Victor. "The Happy Prison: A Recurring Romantic Metaphor." *Romanticism: Vistas, Instances, Continuities*. Ed. David Thorburn and Geoffrey Hartman. Ithaca: Cornell UP, 1973. 62–79.

Buchan, A. M. "The Influence of Wordsworth on Coleridge (1795–1800)." *University of Toronto Quarterly* 32 (1963):346–66.

Burke, Kenneth. *A Grammar of Motives*. 1945. New York: Meridian, 1962.

Chase, Cynthia. "The Accidents of Disfiguration: Limits to Literal and Rhetorical Reading in Book V of *The Prelude*." *Studies in Romanticism* 18 (1979):547–65.

Chomsky, Noam. *Aspects of the Theory of Syntax*. Cambridge: M.I.T. P, 1965.

Cicero, Marcus Tullius. *The Speeches of Cicero*. Trans. N. H. Watts. London: William Heinemann, 1953.

Clarke, C. C. *Romantic Paradox: An Essay on the Poetry of Wordsworth*. London: Routledge & Kegan Paul, 1962.

Coleridge, Samuel Taylor. *Biographia Literaria*. Ed. George Watson. London: J. M. Dent & Sons, 1975.

———. *Collected Letters of Samuel Taylor Coleridge*. Vol. I. Ed. Earl Leslie Griggs. Oxford: Clarendon, 1956.

———. *Miscellanies, Aesthetic and Literary*. Collected by T. Ashe. London: George Bell & Sons, 1885.

———. *The Poems of Samuel Taylor Coleridge*. Ed. Ernest Hartley Coleridge. London: Oxford UP, 1912.

———. *The Table Talk and Omniana of Samuel Taylor Coleridge*. London: Oxford UP, 1917.

Condee, Ralph Waterbury. "The Formalized Openings of Milton's Epic Poems." *Journal of English and Germanic Philology* 50 (1951):502–8.

Cooper, Lane, ed. *A Concordance to the Poems of William Wordsworth*. New York: Russell and Russell, 1965.

Culler, Jonathan. *Ferdinand de Saussure*. New York: Penguin, 1977.

———. "Jacques Derrida." *Structuralism and Since: From Lévi-Strauss to Derrida*. Ed. John Sturrock. Oxford: Oxford UP, 1979. 154–80.

———. *On Deconstruction: Theory and Criticism After Structuralism*. Ithaca: Cornell UP, 1982.

———. "Presupposition and Intertextuality." *Modern Language Notes* 91 (1976): 1380–96.

Curtius, Ernst Robert. *European Literature and the Latin Middle Ages*. Trans. Willard R. Trask. New York: Pantheon, 1953.

Dällenbach, Lucien. *Le récit spéculaire: Essai sur la mise en abyme*. Paris: Seuil, 1977.

Darlington, Beth, ed. *Home at Grasmere*. By William Wordsworth. Ithaca: Cornell UP, 1977.

de Man, Paul. *Allegories of Reading: Figural Language in Rousseau, Nietzsche, Rilke, and Proust*. New Haven: Yale UP, 1979.

———. "Autobiography as De-Facement." *The Rhetoric of Romanticism*. New York: Columbia UP, 1984. 67–81.

———. "The Epistemology of Metaphor." *On Metaphor*. Ed. Sheldon Sacks. Chicago: U of Chicago P, 1978. 11–28.

———. "Intentional Structure of the Romantic Image." *Romanticism and Consciousness*. Ed. Harold Bloom. New York: Norton, 1970. 65–77.

———. *The Rhetoric of Romanticism*. New York: Columbia UP, 1984.

———. "The Rhetoric of Temporality." *Interpretation: Theory and Practice*. Ed. Charles S. Singleton. Baltimore: Johns Hopkins UP, 1969. 173–209.

———. "Symbolic Landscape in Wordsworth and Yeats." *In Defense of Reading: A Reader's Approach to Literary Criticism*. Ed. Reuben A. Brower and Richard Poirier. New York: E. P. Dutton & Co., 1962. 22–37.

Derrida, Jacques. "Coming Into One's Own." Trans. James Hulbert. *Psychoanalysis and the Question of the Text*. Ed. Geoffrey H. Hartman. Baltimore: Johns Hopkins UP, 1978. 114–48.

———. *Dissemination*. Trans. Barbara Johnson. Chicago: U of Chicago P, 1981.

———."Freud and the Scene of Writing." *Writing and Difference*. Trans. Alan Bass. Chicago: U of Chicago P, 1978. 196–231.

———. *Of Grammatology*. Trans. Gayatri Chakravorty Spivak. Baltimore: Johns Hopkins UP, 1974.

———. *Positions*. Trans. Alan Bass. Chicago: U of Chicago P, 1981.

———. *Speech and Phenomena, and Other Essays on Husserl's Theory of Signs*. Trans. David B. Allison. Pref. Newton Garver. Evanston: Northwestern UP, 1973.

———. "Structure, Sign, and Play in the Discourse of the Human Sciences." *Writing and Difference*. Trans. Alan Bass. Chicago: U of Chicago P, 1978. 278–93.

———. *Writing and Difference*. Trans. Alan Bass. Chicago: U of Chicago P, 1978.

Dryden, John, trans. *Virgil's "Aeneid."* New York: Airmont, 1968.

Eagleton, Terry. *Literary Theory: An Introduction*. Minneapolis: U of Minnesota P, 1983.

Eliot, T. S. *Collected Poems 1909–1962*. London: Faber and Faber, 1963.

———. "Tradition and the Individual Talent." *Selected Essays*. 3rd ed. London: Faber and Faber, 1951.

Empson, William. *The Structure of Complex Words*. 1951. Totowa: Rowman and Littlefield, 1979.

Felman, Shoshana. "On Reading Poetry: Reflections on the Limits and Possibilities of Psychoanalytic Approaches." *The Literary Freud: Mechanisms of Defense and the Poetic Will*. Ed. Joseph H. Smith. New Haven: Yale UP, 1980. 119–48.

Ferguson, Frances. *Wordsworth: Language as Counter-Spirit*. New Haven: Yale UP, 1977.

Ferry, David. *The Limits of Mortality: An Essay on Wordsworth's Major Poems*. Middleton: Wesleyan UP, 1959.

Finch, John Alban. "Wordsworth's Two-Handed Engine." *Bicentenary Wordsworth Studies in Memory of John Alban Finch*. Ed. Jonathan Wordsworth. Ithaca: Cornell UP, 1970. 1–13.

Foucault, Michel. "What Is an Author?" *Textual Strategies: Perspectives in Post-Structuralist Criticism*. Ed. Josué V. Harari. Ithaca: Cornell UP, 1979. 141–60.

Fowler, Alastair. *Conceitful Thought: The Interpretation of English Renaissance Poems*. Edinburgh: Edinburgh UP, 1975.

Fraser, W. G. *Times Literary Supplement* 4 April 1929:276.

Frege, Gottlob. "On Sense and Reference." *Translations from the Philosophical Writings of Gottlob Frege*. Ed. Peter Geach and Max Black. Oxford: Basil Blackwell, 1952. 56–78.

Fry, Paul H. "The Absent Dead: Wordsworth, Byron, and the Epitaph." *Studies in Romanticism* 17 (1978):413–33.

Frye, Northrop. *Anatomy of Criticism: Four Essays*. Princeton: Princeton UP, 1957.

———. *The Great Code: The Bible and Literature*. Toronto: Academic Press Canada, 1981.

———. *A Study of English Romanticism*. New York: Random, 1968.

Garber, Frederick. *Wordsworth and the Poetry of Encounter*. Urbana: U of Illinois P, 1971.

Gill, Stephen, ed. *William Wordsworth*. Oxford Authors. Oxford: Oxford UP, 1984.

Gray, Thomas. *Thomas Gray and William Collins: Poetical Works*. Ed. Roger Lonsdale. Oxford: Oxford UP, 1977.

Grierson, H. J. C. *Milton and Wordsworth*. Cambridge: Cambridge UP, 1937.

Griggs, Earl Leslie, ed. *Collected Letters of Samuel Taylor Coleridge*. Vols. I and II. Oxford: Clarendon, 1956.

Grosart, Alexander B., ed. *The Prose Works of William Wordsworth*. 1876. 3 vols. New York: AMS, 1967.

Hamlin, Cyrus. "The Poetics of Self-Consciousness in European Romanticism: Holderlin's *Hyperion* and Wordsworth's *Prelude*." *Genre* 6 (1973):142–77.

Hartman, Geoffrey H. "The Poetics of Prophecy." *High Romantic Argument: Essays for M. H. Abrams*. Ed. Lawrence Lipking. Ithaca: Cornell UP, 1981. 15–40.

———. *Saving the Text: Literature/Derrida/Philosophy*. Baltimore: Johns Hopkins UP, 1981.

———. "'Timely Utterance' Once More." *Rhetoric and Form: Deconstruction at Yale*. Ed. Robert Con Davis and Ronald Schleifer. Norman: U of Oklahoma P, 1985. 37–49.

———. *The Unmediated Vision*. New Haven: Yale UP, 1954.

———. "Words, Wish, Worth: Wordsworth." *Deconstruction and Criticism*. New York: Seabury, 1979. 177–216.

———. "Wordsworth, Inscriptions, and Romantic Nature Poetry." *Beyond Formalism*. New Haven: Yale UP, 1970. 206–30.

———. *Wordsworth's Poetry 1787–1814*. New Haven: Yale UP, 1964.

The Harvard Concordance to Shakespeare. Ed. Marvin Spevack. Cambridge: Belknap, 1969.

Havens, Raymond Dexter. *The Influence of Milton on English Poetry*. Cambridge: Harvard UP, 1922.

———. *The Mind of a Poet: A Study of Wordsworth's Thought*. Baltimore: Johns Hopkins UP, 1941.

Heath, William, ed. *Major British Poets of the Romantic Period*. New York: Macmillan, 1973.

Hertz, Neil. "Freud and the Sandman." *Textual Strategies: Perspectives in Post-Structuralist Criticism*. Ed. Josué V. Harari. Ithaca: Cornell UP, 1979. 296–321.

———. "The Notion of Blockage in the Literature of the Sublime." *Psychoanalysis and the Question of the Text*. Ed. Geoffrey H. Hartman. Baltimore: Johns Hopkins UP, 1978. 62–85.

History of Penrith. Penrith: n.p., 1858.

Holland, Patrick. "Wordsworth and the Sublime: Some Further Considerations." *Wordsworth Circle* 5 (1974):17–22.

Hollander, John. *The Figure of Echo: A Mode of Allusion in Milton and After*. Berkeley: U of California P, 1981.

Hulbert, James, trans. "Coming into One's Own." By Jacques Derrida. *Psychoanalysis and the Question of the Text*. Ed. Geoffrey H. Hartman. Baltimore: Johns Hopkins UP, 1978. 114–48.

Husserl, Edmund. *Ideas: General Introduction to Pure Phenomenology*. Trans. W. R. Boyce Gibson. 1913. London: George Allen & Unwin, 1931.

Ingram, William, and Kathleen Swaim, eds. *A Concordance to Milton's English Poetry*. Oxford: Clarendon, 1972.

Jakobson, Roman. "Closing Statement: Linguistics and Poetics." *Style in Language*. Ed. Thomas A. Sebeok. Cambridge: M.I.T. P, 1960. 350–77.

James, D. G. *Scepticism and Poetry: An Essay on the Poetic Imagination*. London: George Allen and Unwin, 1937.

Johnson, Lee M. *Wordsworth's Metaphysical Verse: Geometry, Nature, and Form*. Toronto: U of Toronto P, 1982.

Johnston, Kenneth R. *Wordsworth and "The Recluse."* New Haven: Yale UP, 1984.

Jones, John. *The Egotistical Sublime: A History of Wordsworth's Imagination*. London: Chatto, 1954.

Joyce, James. *A Portrait of the Artist as a Young Man*. 1916. Harmondsworth: Penguin, 1960.

Keats, John. *Selected Poems and Letters*. Ed. Douglas Bush. Boston: Riverside, 1959.

Kelley, Theresa M. "The Economics of the Heart: Wordsworth's Sublime and Beautiful." *Romanticism Past and Present* 5 (1981):15–32.

Kneale, J. Douglas. "Wordsworth and Milton." *Approaches to Teaching Wordsworth's Poetry*. Ed. Spencer Hall with Jonathan Ramsey. New York: Modern Language Association, 1986. 119–23.

Kristeva, Julia. *Semiotikè: Recherches pour une sémanalyse*. Paris: Seuil, 1969.

Kroeber, Karl. "'Home at Grasmere': Ecological Holiness." *PMLA* 89 (1974):132–41.

Lacan, Jacques. *Ecrits*. Paris: Seuil, 1966.

———. "The Insistence of the Letter in the Unconscious." *The Structuralists: From Marx to Lévi-Strauss*. Ed. Richard T. de George and Fernande M. de George. New York: Doubleday-Anchor, 1972. 287–323.

———. "The Mirror Stage as formative of the function of the I as revealed in psychoanalytic experience." *Ecrits: A Selection*. Trans. Alan Sheridan. New York: Norton, 1977. 1–7.

———. "Of Structure as an Inmixing of an Otherness Prerequisite to Any Subject Whatever." *The Structuralist Controversy: The Languages of Criticism and the Sciences of Man*. Ed. Richard Macksey and Eugenio Donato. Baltimore: Johns Hopkins UP, 1972. 186–200.

———. *Speech and Language in Psychoanalysis*. Trans. with notes and commentary by Anthony Wilden. Baltimore: Johns Hopkins UP, 1968.

Larkin, Peter. "Wordsworth's After-Sojourn: Revision and Unselfish Rivalry in the Later Poetry." *Studies in Romanticism* 20 (1981):409–36.

Leyda, Seraphia. "Wordsworth's *Sonnets Upon the Punishment of Death*." *Wordsworth Circle* 14 (1983):48–53.

Lindenberger, Herbert. *On Wordsworth's "Prelude."* Princeton: Princeton UP, 1963.

Luther, Susan. "Wordsworth's *Prelude*, VI.592–616 (1850)." *Wordsworth Circle* 12 (1981):253–61.

Manning, Peter J. "Reading Wordsworth's Revisions: Othello and the Drowned Man." *Studies in Romanticism* 22 (1983):3–28.

Margoliouth, H. M. *Wordsworth and Coleridge 1795–1834*. London: Oxford UP, 1953.

Martin, John S. "Wordsworth's Echoes." *English Language Notes* 5 (1968):186–92.

Maxwell, J. C., ed. *"The Prelude": A Parallel Text*. By William Wordsworth. Harmondsworth: Penguin, 1971.

McFarland, Thomas. *Romanticism and the Forms of Ruin: Wordsworth, Coleridge, and Modalities of Fragmentation*. Princeton: Princeton UP, 1981.

McGavran, James Holt. "The 'Creative Soul' of *The Prelude* and the 'Sad Incompetence of Human Speech.'" *Studies in Romanticism* 16 (1977):35–49.

Miller, J. Hillis. "Deconstructing the Deconstructers." *Diacritics* 5 (1975): 24–31.

———. "The Still Heart: Poetic Form in Wordsworth." *New Literary History* 2 (1971):297–310.

———. "The Stone and the Shell: The Problem of Poetic Form in Wordsworth's Dream of the Arab." *Mouvements premiers: Etudes critiques offertes à Georges Poulet*. Paris: Corti, 1972. 125–47.

Milton, John. *Complete Poems and Major Prose*. Ed. Merritt Y. Hughes. New York: Odyssey, 1957.

———. *Complete Prose Works of John Milton*. Vol. VI. Ed. Maurice Kelley. New Haven: Yale UP, 1973.

Morgan, Thaïs E. "Is There an Intertext in This Text? Literary and Interdisciplinary Approaches to Intertextuality." *American Journal of Semiotics* 3 (1985):1–40.

Murray, Roger N. *Wordsworth's Style: Figures and Themes in the "Lyrical Ballads" of 1800*. Lincoln: U of Nebraska P, 1967.

Nadel, Alan. "Translating the Past: Literary Allusions as Covert Criticism." *Georgia Review* 36 (1982):639–51.

Newlyn, Lucy. *Coleridge, Wordsworth, and the Art of Allusion*. Oxford: Clarendon, 1986.

Norris, Christopher. *Deconstruction: Theory and Practice*. London: Methuen, 1982.

Ogden, John T. "The Power of Distance in Wordsworth's *Prelude*." *PMLA* 88 (1973):246–59.

———. "The Structure of Imaginative Experience in Wordsworth's *Prelude.*" *Wordsworth Circle* 6 (1975):290–98.

Onorato, Richard J. *The Character of the Poet: Wordsworth in "The Prelude."* Princeton: Princeton UP, 1971.

Owen, W. J. B. "Annotating Wordsworth." *Editing Texts of the Romantic Period.* Ed. John D. Baird. Toronto: Hakkert, 1972. 47–71.

———, ed. *The Fourteen-Book "Prelude."* By William Wordsworth. Ithaca: Cornell UP, 1985.

———. "Literary Echoes in *The Prelude.*" *Wordsworth Circle* 3 (1972):3–16.

———, ed. *Wordsworth and Coleridge: "Lyrical Ballads" 1798.* 2nd ed. London: Oxford UP, 1969.

———. *Wordsworth as Critic.* Toronto: U of Toronto P, 1969.

Parker, Reeve. *Coleridge's Meditative Art.* Ithaca: Cornell UP, 1975.

Parrish, Stephen Maxfield. *The Art of the "Lyrical Ballads."* Cambridge: Harvard UP, 1973.

Peirce, C. S. *The Philosophy of Peirce: Selected Writings.* Ed. Justus Buchler. London: Kegan Paul, Trench, Truber, 1940.

Perkins, David, ed. *English Romantic Writers.* New York: Harcourt, 1967.

———. *The Quest for Permanence: The Symbolism of Wordsworth, Shelley, and Keats.* Cambridge: Harvard UP, 1965.

———. *Wordsworth and the Poetry of Sincerity.* Cambridge: Belknap, 1964.

Plutarch. *Plutarch's Lives of the Noble Grecians and Romans Englished by Sir Thomas North.* Vol. II. Intro. George Wyndham. London: Nutt, 1895.

Pottle, Frederick A. "The Eye and the Object in the Poetry of Wordsworth." *Wordsworth: Centenary Studies.* Ed. Gilbert T. Dunklin. Princeton: Princeton UP, 1951. 23–42.

Potts, Abbie Findlay. *Wordsworth's "Prelude": A Study of Its Literary Form.* 1953. New York: Octagon, 1966.

Poulet, Georges. *The Interior Distance.* Trans. Elliott Coleman. Baltimore: Johns Hopkins, 1959.

Price, Martin. *To the Palace of Wisdom: Studies in Order and Energy from Dryden to Blake.* Garden City: Doubleday, 1964.

Quintilian. *Institutio Oratoria.* Trans. H. E. Butler. London: William Heinemann, 1955.

Rajan, B. "The Varieties of Presence." *Milton Studies XI: The Presence of Milton.* Ed. B. Rajan. Pittsburgh: U of Pittsburgh P, 1978. vii-xiv.

Rajan, Tilottama. *Dark Interpreter: The Discourse of Romanticism.* Ithaca: Cornell UP, 1980.

Rawnsley, H. D. *Reminiscences of Wordsworth among the Peasantry of Westmoreland.* London: Dillon's, 1968.

Reed, Mark L. "Wordsworth, Coleridge, and the 'Plan' of the *Lyrical Ballads.*" *University of Toronto Quarterly* 34 (1965):238–53.
Reiger, James. "Wordsworth Unalarm'd." *Milton and the Line of Vision.* Ed. Joseph Anthony Wittreich. Madison: U of Wisconsin P, 1975. 185–208.
Reiman, Donald H. "The Beauty of Buttermere as Fact and Romantic Symbol." *Criticism* 26 (1984):139–70.
———. "Poetry of Familiarity: Wordsworth, Dorothy, and Mary Hutchinson." *The Evidence of the Imagination: Studies of Interactions Between Life and Art in English Romantic Literature.* Ed. Donald H. Reiman, Michael C. Jaye, and Betty T. Bennett. New York: New York UP, 1978. 142–77.
Riffaterre, Michael. "Interpretation and Descriptive Poetry: A Reading of Wordsworth's 'Yew-Trees.'" *New Literary History* 4 (1973):229–57.
Robinson, Henry Crabb. *Blake, Coleridge, Wordsworth, Lamb, Etc.* Ed. Edith J. Morley. Manchester: Manchester UP, 1922.
Rollins, Hyder Edward, ed. *A New Variorum Edition of Shakespeare: The Sonnets.* 2 vols. Philadelphia: Lippincott, 1944.
Rosenmeyer, Thomas G. *The Green Cabinet: Theocritus and the European Pastoral Lyric.* Berkeley: U of California P, 1969.
Rousseau, Jean-Jacques. "Essay on the Origin of Language." *On the Origin of Language.* Trans. John H. Moran and Alexander Gode. New York: Ungar, 1966.
Saussure, Ferdinand de. *Course in General Linguistics.* Ed. Charles Bally and Albert Sechehaye in collab. with Albert Riedlinger. Trans. Wade Baskin. New York: McGraw, 1966.
Schneiderman, Stuart. *Jacques Lacan: Death of an Intellectual Hero.* Cambridge: Harvard UP, 1983.
Searle, John R. *Speech-Acts: An Essay in the Philosophy of Language.* Cambridge: Cambridge UP, 1969.
Sewell, Edith. *The Orphic Voice: Poetry and Natural History.* New Haven: Yale UP, 1960.
Shakespeare, William. *The Complete Works.* Ed. Alfred Harbage. Baltimore: Penguin, 1969.
———. *Mr. William Shakespeares Comedies, Histories, & Tragedies.* 1623. Facsimile ed. prep. Helge Kokeritz. Intro. Charles Tyler Prouty. New Haven: Yale UP, 1954.
Shakir, Evelyn. "Books, Death, and Immortality: A Study of Book V of *The Prelude.*" *Studies in Romanticism* 8 (1969):156–67.
Shelley, Percy Bysshe. *Shelley's Poetry and Prose.* Ed. Donald H. Reiman and Sharon B. Powers. New York: Norton, 1977.
Simpson, David. *Irony and Authority in Romantic Poetry.* Totowa: Rowman, 1979.

Siskin, Clifford. "Romantic Genre: Lyric Form and Revisionary Behavior in Wordsworth." *Genre* 16 (1983):137–55.

Spenser, Edmund. *Edmund Spenser's Poetry*. Ed. Hugh Maclean. New York: Norton, 1968.

Spevack, Martin, ed. *The Harvard Concordance to Shakespeare*. Cambridge: Belknap, 1969.

Springer, Carolyn. "Far From the Madding Crowd: Wordsworth and the News of Robespierre's Death." *Wordsworth Circle* 12 (1981):243–45.

Theocritus. *The Idylls of Theocritus, Bion, and Moschus*. Trans. J. Banks. London: George Bell, 1891.

Weiskel, Thomas. *The Romantic Sublime: Studies in the Structure and Psychology of Transcendence*. Baltimore: Johns Hopkins UP, 1976.

Wilden, Anthony, trans. *Speech and Language in Psychoanalysis*. By Jacques Lacan. Baltimore: Johns Hopkins UP, 1968.

Willey, Basil. *The Seventeenth-Century Background*. New York: Columbia UP, 1977.

Wittreich, Joseph Anthony, Jr., ed. *The Romantics on Milton: Formal Essays and Critical Asides*. Cleveland: Press of Case Western Reserve University, 1970.

Woodman, Ross. "Child and Patriot: Shifting Perspectives in *The Prelude*." *Wordsworth Circle* 11 (1980):83–92.

———. "Imagination as the Theme of *The Prelude*." *English Studies in Canada* 4 (1975):406–18.

Woolford, John. "*The Prelude* and Its Echoes." *Times Literary Supplement* 6 June 1975:267.

Wordsworth, Dorothy. *Journals of Dorothy Wordsworth: The Alfoxden Journal 1798. The Grasmere Journals 1800–1803*. 2nd ed. Ed. Mary Moorman. Intro. Helen Darbishire. London: Oxford UP, 1971.

Wordsworth, Jonathan. "On Man, on Nature, and on Human Life." *Review of English Studies* ns 31 (1980):17–29.

———, M. H. Abrams, and Stephen Gill, eds. *The Prelude:1799, 1805, 1850*. By William Wordsworth. New York: Norton, 1979.

———. "Secession at Grasmere." *Times Literary Supplement* 26 March 1976:354–55.

———. *William Wordsworth: The Borders of Vision*. Oxford: Clarendon, 1982.

Wordsworth, William. *Home at Grasmere*. Ed. Beth Darlington. Ithaca: Cornell UP, 1977.

———. *The Letters of William and Dorothy Wordsworth: The Early Years*. Ed. Ernest de Selincourt. 2nd ed. rev. Chester L. Shaver. Oxford: Clarendon, 1967.

———. *The Letters of William and Dorothy Wordsworth: The Middle*

Years. Part I. Ed. Ernest de Selincourt. 2nd ed. rev. Mary Moorman. Oxford: Clarendon, 1969.
———. *The Letters of William and Dorothy Wordsworth: The Middle Years. Part II.* Ed. Ernest de Selincourt. 2nd ed. rev. Mary Moorman and Alan G. Hill. Oxford: Clarendon, 1970.
———. *The Letters of William and Dorothy Wordsworth: The Later Years. Part I.* Ed. Ernest de Selincourt. 2nd ed. rev. Alan G. Hill. Oxford: Clarendon, 1978.
———. *"Lyrical Ballads:" Wordsworth and Coleridge.* Ed. R. L. Brett and A. R. Jones. London: Methuen, 1963.
———. *Poems.* Ed. John O. Hayden. 2 vols. Harmondsworth: Penguin, 1977.
———. *The Poems of William Wordsworth.* Ed. with an intro. by Nowell Charles Smith. 3 vols. London: Methuen, 1908.
———. *The Poetical Works of William Wordsworth.* Ed. Ernest de Selincourt. Rev. Helen Darbishire. 5 vols. Oxford: Clarendon, 1952–63.
———. *"The Prelude": A Parallel Text.* Ed. J. C. Maxwell. Harmondsworth: Penguin, 1971.
———. *The Prelude; or, Growth of a Poet's Mind.* Ed. Ernest de Selincourt. 2nd ed. rev. Helen Darbishire. Oxford: Clarendon, 1959.
———. *The Prelude; or, Growth of a Poet's Mind: An Autobiographical Poem.* London: Edward Moxon, 1850.
———. *The Prelude:1799, 1805, 1850.* Ed. Jonathan Wordsworth, M. H. Abrams, and Stephen Gill. New York: Norton, 1979.
———. *The Prose Works of William Wordsworth.* Ed. Alexander B. Grosart. 1876. 3 vols. New York: AMS, 1967.
———. *The Prose Works of William Wordsworth.* Ed. W. J. B. Owen and Jane Worthington Smyser. 3 vols. Oxford: Clarendon, 1974.
———. *William Wordsworth.* Oxford Authors. Ed. Stephen Gill. Oxford: Oxford UP, 1984.

INDEX